Environmental Criminology

The field of environmental criminology is a staple theoretical framework in contemporary criminological theory. With this book, Martin Andresen presents the first comprehensive and sole-authored textbook on this influential and compelling school of criminological thought. He covers a wide range of topics, including:

- the origins of environmental criminology;
- the primary theoretical frameworks, such as routine activity theory, geometric theory of crime, rational choice theory, and the pattern theory of crime;
- the practical application of environmental criminology;
- an examination of how theories are operationalized and tested; and
- policy implications for the practice of crime prevention.

As well as these "popular topics," Andresen also discusses also a number of topics that are at the leading edge of research within environmental criminology.

This text will be ideal for courses on crime prevention, where students are often encouraged to consider policy problems and apply theory to practice. This book offers up environmental criminology as a theoretical framework for making sense of complex neighbourhood problems, meaning that it will be perfect for modules on geography of crime, crime analysis and indeed, environmental criminology. It would also be a good supplement for courses on criminological theory.

Martin A. Andresen is an Associate Professor in the School of Criminology and Institute for Canadian Urban Research Studies at Simon Fraser University. He is also an Associate Member of the Department of Geography at Simon Fraser University, a Member of the Crime and Place Working Group in the Center for Evidence-Based Crime Policy at George Mason University, and an Editorial Advisory Board Member for the *Canadian Journal of Criminology and Criminal Justice*. He has published over 60 peer-reviewed journal articles and book chapters on environmental criminology, spatial crime analysis, and the geography of crime.

def 29, 30

Environmental Criminology

Evolution, theory, and practice

Martin A. Andresen

Routledge
Taylor & Francis Group

LONDON AND NEW YORK

First published 2014
by Routledge
2 Park Square, Milton Park, Abingdon, Oxon OX14 4RN

and by Routledge
711 Third Avenue, New York, NY 10017

Routledge is an imprint of the Taylor & Francis Group, an informa business

British Library Cataloguing in Publication Data
A catalogue record for this book is available from the British Library

Library of Congress Cataloging-in-Publication Data
Andresen, Martin A.
Environmental criminology : evolution, theory, and practice / Martin
A. Andresen.
pages cm
1. Crime—Environmental aspects. 2. Criminology. I. Title.
HV6150.A63 2014
364.01—dc23
2013032602

ISBN: 978–0–415–85612–6 (hbk)
ISBN: 978–0–415–85613–3 (pbk)
ISBN: 978–0–203–72824–6 (ebk)

Typeset in Baskerville
by RefineCatch Limited, Bungay, Suffolk

For my wife and two children

Contents

Figures

Tables

Preface

The field of environmental criminology is a staple theoretical framework in contemporary criminological theory. The set of theories, and subsequent applications, that we know as environmental criminology today began in the early 1970s. This textbook includes two chapters on the early work in spatial criminology in order to set the stage for environmental criminology—environmental criminology did not emerge from a vacuum. This is followed by a section of chapters covering the seminal theories within environmental criminology: routine activity theory, geometric theory of crime, rational choice theory, and the pattern theory of crime. Each of these chapters is written in the same format that considers the metaphysics of each theory (what is assumed to be true), the theory itself, and some discussion of testing the hypotheses of the theories. This allows the student to explicitly compare the various theoretical frameworks within environmental criminology, noting their differences and their similarities. The last section covers the ways in which environmental criminology has been applied. This includes "popular" topics such as spatial analysis and geographic profiling, but also a number of topics that are at the leading edge of research within environmental criminology. Each chapter also includes a set of review questions that, I believe, capture the "big ideas and concepts" that the student of environmental criminology should be able to explain.

I have purposely written this textbook in an informal manner, only introducing technical jargon as it becomes necessary. Though the discussion looks and reads increasingly like a scientific article or research monograph as it progresses, I have tried to keep the style of the book to be more of a conversation than a scientific article or research monograph. My hope is that this presentation makes the subject matter more readable to the new student of environmental criminology, despite the fact that it may appear a little odd to the established academic. Only time will tell if there is a (good) method to this madness.

I chose to write the book in this manner because this is the way in which I teach my own courses in environmental criminology—I use this method in all of my seminars. Some readers may find this approach a little long-winded, but I have found that the more informal discussion format, as opposed to a terse presentation, keeps the attention of students better than other methods of delivery. The appreciation of this material delivery format has been consistently reported in the student evaluations for my courses in environmental criminology, and elsewhere. However, probably more important than any student evaluation of the course to judge as a guide, I have yet to have a student fall asleep in this class over the past eight years! If that isn't success in teaching, I don't know what is.

Martin A. Andresen
School of Criminology
Institute for Canadian Urban Research Studies
Simon Fraser University
Burnaby, British Columbia
Canada

Acknowledgments

At the School of Criminology, Simon Fraser University I have a fantastic set of colleagues with whom I teach, research, and serve. The Institute for Canadian Urban Research Studies, where almost all of my research data resides, has a brilliant set of scholars with whom I have the pleasure to work. I would specifically like to thank Paul and Patricia Brantingham for welcoming me into their Institute. I have been learning through osmosis from them for over a dozen years now and it is truly a pleasure to be a part of their research team. In addition to the Brantinghams, I work with a phenomenal set of colleagues who are environmental criminologists, despite their varied research areas: Eric Beauregard, Graham Farrell, and Bryan Kinney. Most of all, specifically in the context of this book, I have had the benefit of working with a great set of graduate and undergraduate students. It is because of them that my course notes have been refined to the stage they are at now, and it was this set of notes that were the foundation for the development of this book.

I would also like to take this opportunity to thank Professor D. Kim Rossmo for reading over the early sections of the geographic profiling chapter (Chapter 13) and catching a number of errors on my part in terms of the use of terminology. Professor Rossmo has also graciously supplied the maps (a geoprofile and a jeopardy surface) that aid in the discussion of this technique. However, he cannot be held responsible for any errors or omissions in its present form.

Last, but certainly not least, I would like to thank Thomas Sutton, Nicola Hartley, and Heidi Lee of Routledge. These three individuals not only helped me in the process of writing the original proposal and successfully convinced the publisher to publish this book, but they also proved to be extremely helpful throughout the process.

And, of course, the usual disclaimer regarding any remaining errors in this book applies.

Part I

Early work on the ecology of crime

When studying criminology, one of the things the beginning student will notice is the plethora of theories used to explain criminal behavior. Any textbook on the introduction to criminology or criminological theory will present the Classical School, the Positivist School, differential association, anomie, subculture, labeling, conflict, social control, social learning, and life-course explanations for why *criminals* partake in crime. In many ways, all of these theories are correct, at least for some particular aspect of crime. I would argue that the reason for why particular researchers invoke one theory or another is largely based on where they went to school and, subsequently, path dependence. The influence of particular professors is based on how well material is presented, its elegance, and how it relates to a student's own politics and/or life experience. "Path dependency" is a term used to describe how it becomes increasingly difficult to change the (research or teaching) path you are on the further along that path you have traveled. Think about how increasingly difficult it is to change your major as you take more and more required courses!

My purpose in this book is not to convince you that environmental criminology is *the* theory to understand crime—stay away from professors who tell you something equivalent. Rather, I hope to convince you that environmental criminology is important to understand the spatial and temporal dimensions of crime, as well as how to prevent criminal events—environmental criminology is a very useful and practical set of theories. Why? Because, as I argue throughout this textbook, regardless of *why* crime occurs, it will most often occur in very particular places. We will get into greater detail in later chapters, but think of how few places you spend most of your time in: home, school, work, and a handful of recreational locations. Consider how many different pathways you *can* use to move in between these places, let alone how many you actually use. The nature of our built environment (roads, pathways, buildings, etc.) constrains the ways in which we are able to move through it. Now consider how many people (criminal and non-criminal) also spend their time at the same places and use those same pathways. The point of this discussion is to convince you that the study of environmental criminology complements whichever other theory or set of theories you already use—sometimes people will use the term "spatial criminology," as I will when

I am speaking more generally, but environmental criminology also considers the importance of the temporal dimension of crime.

This first section of the textbook has two chapters: one short and one long. The first, short, chapter has the primary purpose of showing the student of environmental criminology that the study of this phenomenon is far from new. In fact, the earliest known work in spatial criminology dates back almost 200 years and is at a level of sophistication that is most impressive given the statistical tools available to the various authors. The second, long, chapter covers one of the longest-standing theories in spatial criminology: social disorganization theory. As we shall see, social disorganization theory is not as straightforward as many people believe. Social disorganization theory has many nuances and subtleties that make it difficult to understand and test properly. We will go over these nuances and difficulties with the hope that you will be able to see how powerful and insightful this theoretical framework can be.

Chapter 1

The beginnings of the geography of crime

Introduction

The purpose of this introductory chapter is fourfold: 1) to show that spatial criminology is not new, 2) to show that a lot of what we know today is based on research that is almost 200 years old, 3) to provide a transition to the following chapter on social disorganization theory, and 4) to show the trajectory of ever smaller units of analysis in spatial criminology, a topic returned to in Chapter 15.

We will now turn to a brief review of the research in spatial criminology in nineteenth-century France, England, and the United States. As stated above, the general theme of this research is increasingly smaller spatial units of analysis showing heterogeneity in the spatial patterns of crime. We will begin with the work of André-Michel Guerry and Adolphe Quetelet and their analyses of crime in France at the beginning of the nineteenth century. This is followed by a discussion of the research in England during the mid-nineteenth century by authors such as John Glyde. Lastly, the work of Ernest Burgess at the turn of the twentieth century is covered.

France, Guerry, and Quetelet

As with any (criminological) research today, there has been much discussion over who did what first in spatial criminology. The work of Adolphe Quetelet, from Belgium, is cited more frequently than that of André-Michel Guerry, from France. And those who cite André-Michel Guerry tend to point out that his work was published first: Quetelet (1842) and Guerry (1833). However, there is another work by Guerry published in 1832, and Adolphe Quetelet (1842) himself points out that he published another work before Guerry in 1831. But then André-Michel Guerry was the first to publish a crime map in 1829—see Weisburd et al. (2009a) for more details on this history. Needless to say there is a lot of hair-splitting when one debates such issues. The point, however, is that both people contributed significantly to the development of spatial criminology, and Adolphe Quetelet is probably cited more frequently because his work is more readily available in English. In an effort to give both of them credit here, I have used the data from Guerry (1833) and based my discussion on the results presented in Quetelet (1842), because I do not read French! The units of analysis for these data are French departments, approximately equivalent to a United States county.

The property and violent crime rates per 100,000 in France, 1825–1830, are shown in Figures 1.1 and 1.2, respectively. Clearly evident from these maps, and noted by Quetelet (1842), is that southern France has a stronger propensity toward violent crimes and northern France has a stronger propensity toward property crimes—Corsica, the island to the southeast, ranks highly in both cases. Overall, the greatest number of property and violent crimes occur within the departments

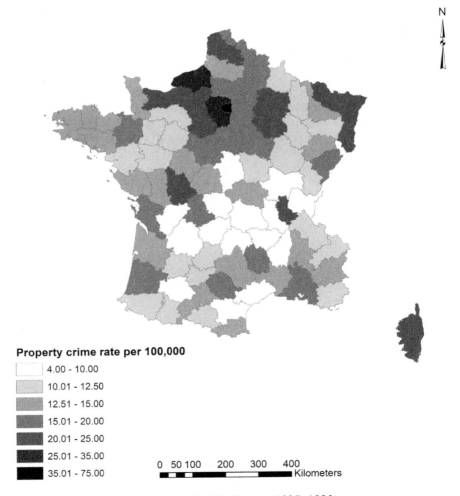

Property crime rate per 100,000

	4.00 - 10.00
	10.01 - 12.50
	12.51 - 15.00
	15.01 - 20.00
	20.01 - 25.00
	25.01 - 35.00
	35.01 - 75.00

0 50 100   200   300   400
                                      Kilometers

Figure 1.1 Property crime per 100,000, France, 1825–1830.
Source: Friendly (n.d.).

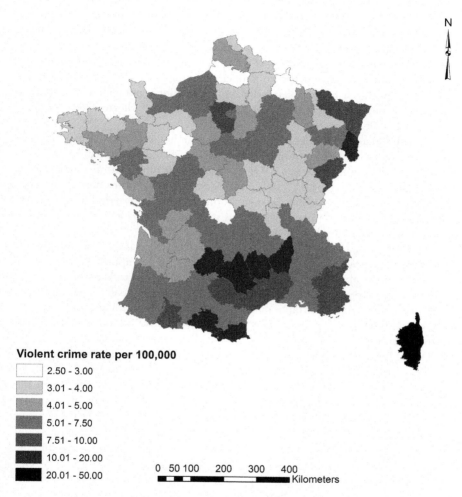

Figure 1.2 Violent crime per 100,000, France, 1825–1830.
Source: Friendly (n.d.).

that are close to or contain a portion of major rivers in France: the Rhone, the Rhine (on France's border), and the Seine. The least number of property and violent crimes occur within the departments that are in the center of France.

Despite these rather obvious patterns of crime in French departments, Quetelet is cautious when making comparisons across the various departments. Quetelet refers to France's population counts as "defective," such that proper comparisons cannot be made, and that there is variation in the degree and severity of punishment in the different courts across the departments. In fact, Quetelet notes that the degree and severity of punishment is known to be greater in the north of France. These are both still issues today in environmental criminology. As discussed in Chapter 8, population at risk measures are still problematic and have significant implications on crime rate calculations. Though not discussed in this textbook, the unequal distribution of the degree and severity of punishment is an important issue that can emerge from differing cultures of policing and the administration of justice: behavior tolerated in one jurisdiction is not tolerated in another and this becomes reflected in crime-related statistics that indicate differences that may not actually be present.

Though Quetelet did not have the statistical methods we have today to investigate the spatial patterns of crime in France, he did use statistical methods to investigate these spatial patterns—he was the first to apply statistical methods to the social sciences, generally, and crime, specifically. One of his findings was the consistency and stability of the above-mentioned spatial patterns in French departments. So, not only were spatial patterns present, but they persisted over time. Today we refer to this phenomenon as ecological stability.

When referring to the causes of crime, Quetelet noted that these causes were so numerous that it was impossible to ascertain their relative importance. This statement is echoed above: all of these theories that are used to explain crime are correct to some degree, but none of them are able to explain all aspects of crime. This again shows the importance of the perspective of environmental criminology: spatial and temporal patterns are present irrespective of which theoretical construct a student or researcher wishes to invoke when studying crime.

Two of the most common arguments one will come across when studying criminology is that we need to reduce poverty and increase education. This will be discussed further in Chapter 2, but in short if we reduce poverty we will reduce the motivation for crime and if we increase education we increase legitimate opportunities for people and, subsequently, reduce crime. However, Quetelet is quick to point out that crime is at its least in the areas of France that are the poorest and the least educated. Quetelet does find, however, that relative deprivation and the rapid movement from being rich to poor leads to greater levels of crime. This subtlety is critical in understanding the relationship between socio-economic status and crime that is missing from current analyses of criminal behavior all too often.

In this brief overview of the spatial aspect of Quetelet's work *A Treatise on Man and the Development of His Faculties*, it should be clear that he and his contemporaries truly set the bar high for subsequent (spatial) analyses of crime. Reading this work is rather humbling, seeing what was learned almost 200 years ago and that in many ways we have not progressed much further aside from a better understanding of *some* of the nuances of crime. Quetelet not only studied the spatial component of crime, but also the impacts of age, gender, climate, poverty, education, and alcohol consumption. All of this work was done without the use of modern computing power! Criminologists today would learn a lot from reading the work of Guerry and Quetelet.

Further work was undertaken by European social scientists after Guerry and Quetelet—see Weisburd et al. (2009a) and Brantingham and Brantingham (1981a) for discussions of these histories—but now our story will jump across the English Channel. As stated above, the trajectory of research in spatial criminology over the past 200 years has been towards increasingly smaller units of analysis. The next stage in this research is the work of John Glyde, studying a county in England. This is a "natural" next step to investigate spatial patterns because larger units of analysis such as states, provinces, counties, and departments most definitely have variations in spatial patterns within them—spatial heterogeneity. In this specific case for Glyde, the county of Suffolk had a population of just under 340,000 whereas the average population in the French departments at the time was just under 380,000; Suffolk is approximately half the geographic size of the average French Department.

Glyde and the English county of Suffolk

Suffolk was a large agricultural county with 80 kilometers of coastline in the Eastern District of England. It was a county composed of seventeen poor law unions in 1851. Crime in Suffolk had been increasing more rapidly than that of its neighboring counties over the previous fifty years.

Glyde (1856) used the ratio of prisoners to population as a measure of criminality. Of course not all crime becomes known to the criminal justice system, and not all of those charged with an offence are sentenced to prison. But even considering the statements made by Quetelet regarding the greater degree and severity of punishment in particular places (this is neither confirmed nor denied in Glyde's work), the variations of this ratio across the seventeen poor law unions is instructive.

The ratios of criminals to population in Suffolk's poor law unions range from 1 in 1344 to 1 in 464—the former ratio indicates lesser levels of criminal behavior. This is quite a variation with prisoners being almost three times as numerous, relatively speaking, in some unions than others. When considering towns, Glyde refers to nine towns in Suffolk, the range is from 1 in 1820 to 1 in 309; this variation with prisoners being almost five times as numerous, relatively speaking, in some towns than others. In a comparison of towns (average population of 5000 persons) and villages (average population of 820 persons), Glyde noted that towns had approximately half of the criminal population, relatively speaking.

In what is probably the most interesting result of Glyde's work, he separates towns from rural country areas and compares eleven of the more serious crime types such as murder, rape, arson, and so on. Glyde found that 83 percent of these more serious crimes were committed by offenders who lived in the rural country— he could not confirm where the actual crimes were committed. Therefore, towns, that comprised 29 percent of the population, only accounted for 17 percent of serious crimes.

This short article by John Glyde very clearly shows the presence of spatial heterogeneity within a county—spatial heterogeneity is defined as smaller units of analysis within larger units of analysis exhibiting significant variation in the phenomenon under study. Though Glyde did not provide any comparisons with the surrounding counties that have not experienced the same increases in crime as Suffolk, it is quite likely that *some* of the poor law unions in Suffolk have higher crime rates than the surrounding counties and others have substantially lower crime rates. As we shall see, this is a common finding in more recent spatial criminology: there is significant spatial heterogeneity within relatively larger spatial units of analysis.

An obvious question to ask now is whether there is spatial heterogeneity *within* areas the size of Suffolk's poor law unions and towns. The answer to that question is, of course, yes.

Burgess and crime within a small city

Ernest Burgess, to the best of my knowledge, performed the first city-wide "neighborhood" analysis of crime in a North American city. Though the city was small, as indicated in the title of his journal article, he was able to find significant variation in the (relatively) few areas he studied—the small city of 12,000 residents under analysis was separated into six Wards. Despite the small size of this city, and the corresponding low number of Wards, Burgess (1916) stated that it was important to study such areas that were often overlooked by researchers because they tended to lack social resources such that crime and deviance problems can often be worse than those in larger cities. Burgess studied juvenile delinquents over a two-year time span, 53 juvenile delinquents brought to the juvenile court.

Ernest Burgess found that the home location of the juvenile delinquents was more important than sex or ethnic group (African-American and Caucasian). One Ward in particular, Ward 4, had one in twelve of its resident juveniles aged 5–16 appear in the juvenile court. Burgess estimated that over time one-half of all the juveniles in this Ward would have appeared in the juvenile court by the time they were 17 years of age. Burgess went further to cite a "low grade home environment" as the cause of the delinquency in this Ward: bad housing conditions, poverty, and poor health. Two interrelated geographical factors stood out: the urban environment and proximity to the business district. Finally, Burgess called for (more) organized recreational activities for juveniles, particularly boys.

This short article by Ernest Burgess, much like the one by John Glyde, very clearly shows the presence of spatial heterogeneity within a small city. Though there are only six spatial units of analysis, this once again shows that one cannot simply assume a spatially aggregate statistic is representative of all the places within the area it represents. Indeed, this is a fundamental finding in the crime and place literature (Weisburd et al., 2012).

Conclusion

In this short introductory chapter I hope to have shown that research in spatial criminology is not new. Rather it dates back to the beginnings of "positivist criminology" almost 200 years ago, with positivist criminology being the application of scientific method, measurement, and quantification to criminal behavior. As stated above, the work these researchers did is quite humbling, especially when considering it was done without the aid of modern computers.

Changing the spatial units of analysis from departments within France to poor law unions within a county to Wards within a small city consistently showed the importance of spatial variation within geographically larger spatial units of analysis, spatial heterogeneity. Though the importance of understanding the implications of your choice of spatial scale is a recurring theme in this textbook, we will revisit the importance of spatial heterogeneity at the end of this textbook in Chapter 15, focusing on some of the most recent cutting-edge research within environmental criminology.

But this short introductory chapter also serves as a transition into the following chapter on social disorganization theory, in a few ways. First, because of the significant role social disorganization theory has played in criminological research, generally speaking, it is often framed as the starting point of research in spatial criminology, whether that framing is intentional or not. We have seen that this is not the case. Second, Ernest Burgess is an important figure in social disorganization theory, particularly its metaphysics. And third, social disorganization theory continues on this trajectory of increasingly smaller units of analysis in spatial criminology, in the large city of Chicago, but necessarily needs a much fuller discussion because of its importance in the history of spatial criminology and in contemporary criminological research.

Review questions

1   What is spatial heterogeneity and why does it matter?
2   Why is it important that Quetelet found stable (and unique) spatial patterns for property crime and violent crime in France?
3   What did Burgess find that was the most important predictor for a juvenile being in juvenile court? Why does this matter for environmental criminology?

References

Brantingham, P. J. and Brantingham, P. L. (1981a). Introduction: The dimensions of crime. In P. J. Brantingham and P. L. Brantingham (eds.), *Environmental criminology* (pp. 7–26). Prospect Heights, IL: Waveland Press.

Burgess, E. W. (1916). Juvenile delinquency in a small city. *Journal of the American Institute of Criminal Law and Criminology*, 6(5), 724–8.

Friendly, M. (n.d.). Map data sets for France, 1830. Data available online at http://www.datavis.ca/gallery/guerry/maps.html [accessed April 10, 2013].

Glyde, J. (1856). Localities of crime in Suffolk. *Journal of the Statistical Society of London*, 19(2), 102–6.

Guerry, A.-M. (1832). Statistique comparée de l'état de l'instruction et du nombre des crimes. *Revue Encyclopédique*, 55, 414–24.

Guerry, A.-M. (1833). *Essai sur la statistique morale de la France*. Paris: Crochard.

Quetelet, L. A. J. ([1831] 1984). *Research on the propensity for crime at different ages* (trans. S. F. Sylvester). Cincinnati, OH: Anderson Publishing.

Quetelet, L. A. J. (1842). *A treatise on man and the development of his faculties*. Edinburgh: W. and R. Chambers.

Weisburd, D., Bruinsma, G. J. N., and Bernasco, W. (2009a). Units of analysis in geographic criminology: Historical development, critical issues, and open questions. In D. Weisburd, W. Bernasco, and G. J. N. Bruinsma (eds.), *Putting crime in its place: Units of analysis in geographic criminology* (pp. 3–31). New York, NY: Springer.

Weisburd, D., Groff, E. R., and Yang, S.-M. (2013). Understanding and controlling hot spots of crime: The importance of formal and informal social controls. *Prevention Science*, in press.

Chapter 2

Social disorganization theory

Introduction

Social disorganization theory is an important theory not only for environmental criminology, and spatial criminology more generally, but for the field of criminology in general. Social disorganization theory dominated criminological thought, albeit within sociology departments, during the 1950s and 1960s, but was also prominent in the 1930s and 1940s—social disorganization theory was still in its infancy and being developed in this time period, however. This is a very long time period for a theory to have such a place in any discipline. In fact, some scholars have stated that few other works in criminology, such as the foundational books for social disorganization theory, have had such an important influence (Sampson and Groves, 1989). Moreover, despite social disorganization theory falling out of favor, to be discussed later in this chapter, it has also had a revival in recent decades. Social disorganization theory is used in many current studies in spatial criminology, not just by environmental criminologists, and many of the other sociological theories of crime are contained within social disorganization theory, some explicitly and others implicitly.

Because social disorganization theory has been around for so long and has such widespread adoption in sociology and criminology it should come as no surprise that, as with most major theories, a lot of people have misunderstood social disorganization theory. As such, I am confident that a lot, but not all, of the criticism of social disorganization theory is a by-product of subsequent theorists, not the theory itself. This situation occurred, I believe, because researchers and students have not read the original works, but accounts of the theory written by others who misread the original works. This situation is most famously present in the statement by the political economy theorist Karl Marx: I am not a Marxist! Karl Marx was referring to those who had taken his work, misunderstood it, and disseminated that misunderstanding. Later in the twentieth century, the Structural Marxists were the dominant school of thought within Marxism. The Structural Marxists were later criticized by the Post-Structural and Post-Modern Marxists. However, the criticisms put forth by the Post-Structural and Post-Modern

Marxists sounded a lot like Karl Marx himself! Consequently, the Post-Structural and Post-Modern Marxists were not criticizing the work of Karl Marx, but the interpretations of the Structural Marxists. Perhaps the most interesting aspect of this situation is that reading the work of the Structural Marxists, Post-Structural Marxists, and Post-Modern Marxists made it clear to me that none of these groups had either read the original Karl Marx or understood it! If they had, the Post-Structural and Post-Modern Marxists would have just called themselves Marxists. Why did this happen? Simple, the works of Karl Marx are difficult to read and you need an understanding of the philosopher Georg Wilhelm Friedrich Hegel. We will not get into the relevant discussions here because it does not matter for the context of environmental criminology, but the point is that it is important to always take other people's accounts with a grain of salt. And that goes for this textbook as well! In order to read the original theoretical works on environmental criminology, I strongly suggest you consider the book I co-edited with Paul J. Brantingham and J. Bryan Kinney, *Classics in Environmental Criminology* (Andresen et al., 2010). Why did this same phenomenon happen with social disorganization theory? My guess is that it is because the original works in this area are not particularly exciting to read; I know, because I have read them! So, researchers and students "trust" those who appear to have read these works and summarized them in their own books. I only hope history will deem my account of social disorganization as being correct.

The misrepresentation in social disorganization theory that I have come across is primarily related to the relationship between the economic conditions of an area and its crime rate: as economic conditions get better, crime rates fall. However, Clifford Shaw and Henry McKay, the primary developers of social disorganization theory, never stated that there was a direct causal relationship between economic conditions and crime rates; we will return to this issue in the context of testing social disorganization theory. Rather, poor economic conditions led to high rates of population turnover, because people wished to leave the area as soon as they could in search of better economic conditions. Because of the high rate of population turnover, housing was relatively cheap for both purchase and renting. Consequently, immigrants who initially had little money moved into these areas. These two factors led to great difficulties in establishing community cohesion: those who planned to leave the area would not be willing to invest time to develop the community they wished to leave, and immigration led to language and cultural barriers that also made it more difficult to establish a community.

The end result, in its most basic sense, is that socially disorganized places are areas that are not able to establish a common set of values and a sense of community because of population turnover and ethnic heterogeneity. This hinders any solutions to common problems, such as crime. If no one cares about the area, or people have difficulty communicating with their neighbors, few people will even look outside and no one will know who you (or any offenders) are. This is an area ripe for criminal activity.

Metaphysics: social ecology and the concentric zone model

Before we turn to social disorganization theory itself, we must first cover the material that the developers of social disorganization theory considered to be true. Specifically, it is important to understand their view on city growth, with their specific focus in Chicago, Illinois. However, it should be noted that most North American cities followed this model of city growth, at least up until recently— many cities have undergone urban transformations such as gentrification (Lees et al., 2007). It is important to understand this model of city growth, because it is the foundation from which they seek to understand the differences (in crime) between and across urban areas.

Generally speaking, most areas within cities are dominated by a particular land use. There has been an increase in "mixed land use" areas in which people may live, shop, get entertained, and work, but these areas tend to be relatively small compared to those areas dominated by one land use classification. Some areas of the city are for business, some for industry, and others for residential dwellings. These residential areas, in particular, are further divided into areas occupied by those who have low socio-economic status, areas with people who are very wealthy, and everything in between. If you think for a moment of the city in which you grew up, you should be able to identify these areas rather quickly. This is a model of the city put forth by the sociologist Ernest W. Burgess in 1925, and is called concentric zone theory. Assuming there are not any natural barriers such as mountains and/or bodies of water, the city is expected to have a radial expansion of city growth. If a city borders a large body of water, such as Chicago and Lake Michigan, and can only expand over 180 degrees, then the concentric zones will simply be semicircular.

Figure 2.1 depicts a theoretical concentric zone model for a city. At its core, Zone 1 represents the central zone, that of the Central Business District and Industrial District. Zone 2 is often referred to as the Zone in Transition (ZIT). This name works well for its acronym because it is often viewed as the zit on a city's complexion. This area is most often considered skid road/row or a slum area. Zone 3 is the Working Class Residential Zone. And Zone 4 is the Professional Class Residential Zone. Ernest Burgess included a fifth zone that he called the commuter zone. This may include suburban areas and/or satellite cities, but this is not necessary to understand the foundations of the concentric zone model.

The concentric zone model has a number of interesting static properties. Zone 1 is relatively straightforward to understand. Being the Central Business District (or downtown), this is the center of business activity and, at a time when transportation was not as cheap, in terms of time and money, at the turn of the twentieth century, it was important for the business owners to have their factories and warehouses close to their head office in the central business district; this was important for the monitoring of factories and warehouses but also because central business districts tend to be well connected to transportation networks. In the case of

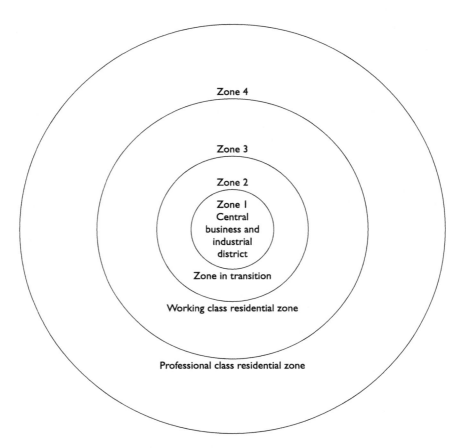

Figure 2.1 Concentric zone model.
Source: Adapted from Burgess (1925).

Chicago, the central business district is on the shores of Lake Michigan with its industrial area (historically) beside the central business district and along the banks of the north and south arms of the Chicago River.

Zone 2, skid road/row or the slums is such an area for very clear reasons back at the turn of the twentieth century. If one were to "think back" to the early twentieth century using history books or documentary films, would the industries of the time be considered clean? What about the industries of today? Definitely not, for both cases. Contemporary industry tends to have the appearance of being cleaner today, at least in the Western world, because we do not see factories pumping smoke and soot into the air. These factories tended to be noisy, smelly, dirty, and unattractive. Though many factories in the developing world must have the cleanest conditions (high-technology factories, for example), one does not have to look very hard on the internet for pictures and stories about noisy, smelly, dirty, and unattractive factories and accompanying areas in the developing world. The point of this discussion is: who would *want* to live in or close to such an area? The wealthy would definitely not want to live in such an area because they can afford to live in much nicer areas without the noise, the smell, and the dirt. More likely, the unemployed, the underemployed, the poor, and the destitute will live in these areas. In fact, the less money one has, the more likely that one will have to live in these areas, because the rent is cheaper.

As you move away from the industrial district, places will become cleaner because of a process of distance decay. This simply states that, as you move away from the source of a phenomenon (pollution, sound, heat), the effect of that phenomenon lessens. Consequently the zone that borders the Zone in Transition, the Working Class Residential Zone, will be more expensive than the slums but not too much more expensive. As you get further into Zone 3, and away from Zone 2, the prices of homes (for both purchase and rent) will increase proportionately. This is typically what the working classes can afford.

The professional classes, however, have the means to purchase and/or build in many other areas of the city. As such, they had a tendency to live far away from the noisy, smelly, dirty, and unattractive factories/warehouses, skid road/row, and (perhaps most importantly) their employees. Compared to today, these were times of very poor working conditions for most of the working class and you would not want to bump into your employees while out shopping or in some other social situation.

Overall, this model does well to describe Chicago, and should not be a surprise given this was the location where the model was developed! Land use, demolitions (old property), population change, families on relief (welfare or social assistance), rent, and ethnic populations all correspond well to the concentric zone model in Chicago. I suspect that if you grew up in a North American city you would be able to identify these zones, particularly when considering that city before the 1980s.

Though both interesting and instructive, this static view is not a very realistic one for understanding the nature of our cities. Rather, cities grow and are incredibly dynamic. And as a city grows, so does the Central Business District and its corresponding Industrial District (this has changed since the 1980s with deindustrialization in North America, however). Consequently, Zone 1 encroaches, or invades to use an ecological term, into Zone 2. This subsequently forces the Zone in Transition to invade into Zone 3. It is this invasion that, in part, generates even more population turnover because people will not want to remain in the neighborhood anymore. They withdraw from the community and it becomes socially disorganized, ripe for criminal activity.

Taken together, this is the social ecology of social disorganization theory. Our cities are understood from a spatial perspective such that they are divided into a number of zones. We compete over space. And that competition is resolved through economic means.

Shaw, McKay, and social disorganization theory

At this point, you may ask: So what? That is a very simple model that happens to correspond well to some of Chicago's social-demographic, socioeconomic, and physical characteristics. What about crime? Clifford Shaw and Henry McKay (in collaboration with some colleagues) undertook an enormous research initiative in the City of Chicago to test this model of the city in the context of criminal activity, juvenile criminal activity to be specific. Their first book, *Delinquency Areas*, was published in 1929, a government report, *Social Factors in Juvenile Delinquency*, was published in 1931, and their magnum opus, *Juvenile Delinquency and Urban Areas*, was published in 1942 with a revised edition published in 1969 after the death of Clifford Shaw (Shaw et al., 1929; Shaw and McKay, 1931, 1942, 1969). The subtitle of their 1942 book is of particular interest for the discussion here: "a study of rates of delinquency in relation to differential characteristics of local communities in American cities." This title is of interest for two reasons. First, they sought to understand the relationship between (juvenile) delinquency and the characteristics of neighborhoods. As such, they were not interested in individual characteristics, but the sociological/societal influences on (juvenile) delinquency; this becomes an important factor for social disorganization theory falling out of favor in later years. Second, Shaw and McKay, though focusing on Chicago, wanted to make their case across a number of different cities in the interests of generalizability. In fact, in the 1969 edition of *Juvenile Delinquency and Urban Areas*, Shaw and McKay analyzed six cities: Chicago, IL; Philadelphia, PA; Boston, MA; Cincinnati, OH; Cleveland, OH; and Richmond, VA.

In the beginning of *Juvenile Delinquency and Urban Areas*, Shaw and McKay outline eight questions they hope to address, at least in part. Most notably, they ask:

1   Are delinquency rates correlated with neighborhood characteristics?
2   How strong is the correlation between delinquency rates and neighborhood characteristics such as those related to economic, social, and cultural factors?
3   Are these patterns, if they exist, stable over time?
4   Are these relationships, if present, related to the people or the places they live in?

In their analyses, Shaw and McKay investigate three aspects of neighborhoods that they posit will relate to crime: the physical status of a neighborhood, the economic status of a neighborhood, and the population characteristics of a neighborhood. Each is discussed, in turn.

Shaw and McKay measured the physical status of a neighborhood using variables that represented industrial areas, commercial areas, the distribution of condemned buildings, and, as a proxy for other physical status conditions, population change. The most interesting result they found from these variables relates to population change: Shaw and McKay found that population change was not linearly related to juvenile delinquency rates. What does this mean?

Small changes in population led to large changes in juvenile delinquency rates, whereas large changes in population led to very small changes in juvenile delinquency rates.

As shown in Figure 2.2, initial changes in population (let us ignore whether or not population is going up or down, there is just turnover) that are small in magnitude lead to changes in juvenile delinquency that are large in magnitude. However, as the percentage change in population (population turnover) increases the corresponding change in juvenile delinquency lessens, eventually reaching its maximum at c*. After c*, though the impact on juvenile delinquency is still positive, subsequent increases in population turnover have a lesser impact on juvenile delinquency. Theoretically, after some point, further changes in population turnover will no longer impact the juvenile delinquency rate.

So I must return to my question: What does this mean? Only individual (micro-level) data can truly answer this question, but I have the following hypothesis. It seems that initial changes in population (potentially from the invasion of populations from the Zone in Transition to the Working Class Residential Zone) lead to relatively large magnitude changes in juvenile delinquency. This is followed by people who are paying close attention to neighborhood conditions, recognizing what is happening, and leaving immediately. This leads to further population turnover and a subsequent increase in juvenile delinquency. This phenomenon continues from the invasion of Zone 2 populations and the exodus of Zone 3

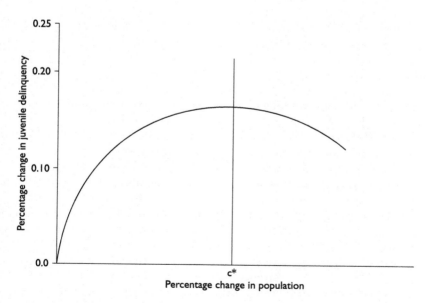

Figure 2.2 Nonlinear relationship between population change and juvenile delinquency.

Note: Hypothetical relationship drawn by the author.

populations, and eventually the impact diminishes. After all, a neighborhood can only decline so far.

Though instructive in the context of social disorganization theory, this non-linearity is also instructive more generally when it comes to testing theoretical constructs. In Figure 2.2, the overall relationship is positive, so a linear relationship may be assumed that may not impose bias on other statistical results—but this is no guarantee. However, if a researcher were to assume a linear relationship here, as is the case with a simple correlation, the nuances of the relationship between population turnover and juvenile delinquency would be lost. This shows the need to inspect and graph data when testing any relationship and that theoretical development and theoretical testing are interrelated processes involving both deduction and induction.

Turning to the economic status of a neighborhood, Shaw and McKay analyzed the percentage of families on relief (welfare), median rental cost, and home ownership. The percentage of families on relief had a very strong and positive relationship with juvenile delinquency rates: $r = 0.89$. This is much higher than the correlation for population change that ranged from 0.50 to 0.70. The correlation between juvenile delinquency and median rental cost was $r = -0.61$, and the correlation between juvenile delinquency and home ownership was $r = -0.49$. Consequently, Shaw and McKay found that juvenile delinquency was related to the variables that they measured and in the ways that they expected. However, Shaw and McKay were also very clear to point out that, although they had found strong relationships between juvenile delinquency and the economic status of a neighborhood, they did not necessarily find causal relationships. If they had, policy makers would simply have to decrease the number of families on relief (through policies to improve opportunities, not simply take people off welfare), increase median rent, and increase home ownership.

To make this point, Shaw and McKay pointed to a natural experiment that occurred in the period from 1929 to 1934. This time period was the beginning of the Great Depression, a severe economic downturn that was worldwide and resulted in official unemployment rates as high as 25 percent in the industrialized world. Families on relief in Chicago during these years increased tenfold. But there was no change in the juvenile delinquency rates for the same time period. If there were truly a causal relationship between the number of families on relief and juvenile delinquency, it would have emerged here. Shaw and McKay state that their found relationship between the number of families on relief and juvenile delinquency was in regard to the relative status of a neighborhood: the neighborhoods with the most families on relief will have the most juvenile delinquency *relative* to the other neighborhoods in the city. Consequently, it is critical that we are careful how we analyze juvenile delinquency (or any crime) rates. If we analyze the "wrong" dimension of juvenile delinquency, we may not find a relationship at all (the number of families on relief and juvenile delinquency rates at the city level), or we may find the most significant relationship in our analysis that has a very particular interpretation.

With regard to population characteristics, Shaw and McKay found that the percentage of foreign-born and African-American households was strongly and positively related to juvenile delinquency rates, $r = 0.60$. Shaw and McKay were very quick to point out, however, that it was not ethnicity, per se, that was related to juvenile delinquency. Rather, in a given area or neighborhood over time, the juvenile delinquency rates remained the same while the ethnic composition of that area of neighborhood had changed. Therefore, it was not that a particular ethnic group was associated with juvenile delinquency; it was the place that was associated with that juvenile delinquency. This is a problem in inference that tends to emerge in the absence of critical thought. However, there is a reason why some people believe that particular ethnic groups are related to the juvenile delinquency (or delinquency, in general) in a given area.

Historically speaking, ethnic groups tend to cluster in particular areas, a phenomenon that is present in many larger cities. In Vancouver, Canada, for example, there is a Chinatown and a Punjabi Market, there was Little Italy (now an area just referred to as Commercial Drive), another area is still known for its Greek restaurants but does not have an ethnically based name, and still another area has much Korean-based shopping and restaurants. The reasons for this are simple. If someone immigrates into a new cultural area and there is an established ethnic cluster tied to the immigrants' heritage, it is likely that that person will move close to or into that area and spend time there; this may be done because it eases the transition into the new cultural area: familiar foods, language, and customs. And, by becoming part of this ethnic cluster, the cluster itself is maintained and, perhaps, expands. If the ethnic cluster happens to be in a relatively high crime area, it is common for that ethnic group to become associated with the corresponding criminal activity.

However, over time the ethnic composition of a neighborhood will change. A new and different immigrant population may move in and old immigrant populations move out. If the neighborhood was a high crime neighborhood, the immigrant population would want to move to another neighborhood if they could, as would anyone who had the means to do so. Or, perhaps, the children of the immigrants move elsewhere for any one of a number of reasons (work, property prices, etc.) and the original ethnic population passes on. The point is that the ethnic composition of neighborhoods does change, albeit slowly.

Shaw and McKay had data on this phenomenon and noted that, regardless of ethnic background, juveniles had very similar ranges of delinquency rates. Also, once a particular ethnic group moved out of one neighborhood and into another, the behavior of that ethnic group changed: they adapted to the new environment in which they lived. This led Shaw and McKay to state it was the neighborhood that led to juvenile delinquency, not the individuals, because over time the different neighborhoods retained their relative rates of juvenile delinquency while their ethnic compositions changed. So, what social disorganization theory is really referring to is probability: you are more likely to be a (juvenile) delinquent if you are in a social situation that is more conducive to that delinquent activity.

The spurious relationship between ethnicity and crime is probably no more apparent in the United States than with the African-American population. One does not have to look very hard to find stories about ethnic profiling and the overrepresentation of the African-American population in the criminal justice system. There are many socio-historical factors behind this relationship, but the claim that any one group of people can be defined by which shade of brown their skin is makes little sense to me. In a very interesting article by John Worrall and Travis Pratt, published in 2004, these authors were able to find that as the percentage of African-Americans increased, so did crime. Worrall and Pratt did this using one very common statistical method that happens to be inappropriate for an attempt to ascertain such a relationship. However, when Worrall and Pratt used a more appropriate statistical method, they found that the relationship between crime and the percentage of African-Americans was *negative* and statistically insignificant. Of course this is just one study, but it goes to show that using the inappropriate statistical method may lead one to false inference.

There is more to social disorganization theory than has been covered here, but the foundational ideas have been covered, as well as some of what I believe to be important misrepresentations of the theory. As stated above, I am confident that some of the criticisms of social disorganization theory are because of these misrepresentations.

An obvious question to ask at this point is: If social disorganization theory was so great, why did it fall out of favor? There are many reasons why a theory may fall out of favor in academia: it may no longer have empirical support, those who supported the theory ended their career with no one to follow in their footsteps, no new developments were forthcoming so researchers looked for something different, and so on. In 1988, John Bursik published an article that outlined some of the reasons why social disorganization theory fell out of favor. The subsequent revival of social disorganization theory, which was occurring at the time Bursik published this article, addressed some but not all of these reasons.

Bursik outlined five criticisms of social disorganization theory, but they should not all be considered criticisms, per se. The first criticism was that a disciplinary shift in emphasis occurred. Rather than being interested in neighborhoods, or areas of some sort, researchers became interested in individuals. Consequently, an individual would not come from a poor neighborhood, but from a low-income family. Whenever I teach environmental criminology I am almost certainly told by a student about a poor neighborhood that they grew up in or knew that was quite socially organized and low-crime. But finding exceptions to the rule does not disprove a theory. What matters here is the possibility of the ecological fallacy: what is true of the whole is not necessarily true of all its parts. So, someone may be from a neighborhood with many juvenile delinquents, but that does not mean that all juveniles in that neighborhood are delinquent. Using a finer scale of resolution in the analysis (the person, not the neighborhood) allows for more of the nuances in understanding criminal behavior to become manifest.

Second, social disorganization theory, almost by definition, must assume stable ecological structures. This criticism relates to the discussion above regarding ethnic compositions within neighborhoods and their corresponding juvenile delinquency rates: Shaw and McKay found that neighborhoods maintained their relative standings in juvenile delinquency (ecological stability) despite changes in the ethnic compositions of neighborhoods. In order to be able to make such a claim, the researcher must have data over a relatively long timespan, preferably decades. Shaw and McKay had such data and were, therefore, able to make the claims that they did. However, much of the research that followed Shaw and McKay employed cross-sectional data: neighborhood level data for an entire city, but only for one year. In order to make any claims regarding such a study, the researcher must assume that the spatial distribution of crime and the relevant socio-demographic and socio-economic variables are stable over time and represented in their particular year of data.

This assumption of ecological stability is important because, if the variables you are measuring are not stable (i.e., not in equilibrium), then any relationship found in a statistical analysis may simply be a result of the particular year of data that the researcher has at their disposal. In fact, when using common statistical methods to analyze one year of neighborhood data, an ecological cross-section, it is implicitly assumed that the data are in equilibrium and the results of the statistical analysis represent long-run relationships.

But there is more to ecological stability than the various variables being assumed to be in equilibrium. The concentric zone model of city growth, the metaphysical foundation of social disorganization theory, does not work well in many contemporary cities, a phenomenon that began to take place shortly after the end of the Second World War. Dirty industries left Zone 1 to be in the suburbs, or even other (developing) countries. Downtown living became a luxury, and former working class neighborhoods have been invaded by professionals in the process of gentrification (Lees et al., 2007). This has completely altered the underlying structure of cities and, therefore, causes the metaphysics of social disorganization theory to be called into question. Does this mean that social disorganization theory can no longer be applied to such cities? Not necessarily, but it does mean that social disorganization theory, and its corresponding metaphysics, must be re-evaluated. In my own work on spatial crime patterns in Vancouver, Canada, a city that has undergone the gentrification described above, social disorganization theory still proves to be instructive because the geography of crime is rather persistent.

The third criticism relates to how social disorganization is measured. Measurement, as we will discuss in Chapter 8, is a very important aspect of environmental criminology, or any other theory for that matter: in order to test any theory, variables that matter to that theory must be operationalized such that the phenomenon of interest is actually being measured. For example, in order to truly get at the underlying dimensions of social disorganization, methods such as interviews, surveys, and fieldwork are all necessary much like the original work done by Shaw and McKay. Though many of the variables that Shaw and McKay discussed are available through most censuses, these variables are rather crude, not truly capturing the necessary aspects of the theory. For example, as discussed above, poverty does not cause crime; poverty leads to different social situations that are more conducive to crime. The difference is paramount, yet poverty is quite often used as an explanatory variable in statistical analyses—I am guilty of this practice myself.

The fourth criticism is related to the third, the measurement of crime and delinquency, covered in depth in Chapter 8. One of the primary concerns here relates to the reporting of crime. Is it reasonable to believe that all crimes are reported to the criminal justice system? Of course not. In Canada, the percentage of crimes being reported to the police has been decreasing in recent years: 37 percent in 1999, 34 percent in 2004, and 31 percent in 2009 (Perreault and Brennan, 2010). These crimes that are unknown to the police, and the criminal justice system more generally, are known as the dark figure of crime, a concern in quantitative-based studies of crime dating at least back to the early nineteenth century (Bulwer, 1836). Perhaps most importantly is the spatial distribution of crime known to the police. We know that we are only investigating a fraction of actual crime, but if the spatial distribution of actual crime and reported crime are the same, then much of the inference garnered from statistical analyses will still be instructive. I am only aware of one study that compares police crime data to self-reported victimization data, but the spatial distributions are different (Ceccato and Lukyte, 2011). This research was conducted on the non-Western country of Lithuania and used geographically large districts to compare the different crime data sources, but it is very instructive. More research is needed here, because the implications extend far beyond that of testing social disorganization theory.

Lastly, the fifth criticism refers to the normative assumptions of social disorganization theory. Within social disorganization theory, socially disorganized places are not conforming to some "norm" or standard of behavior. However, once you move away from the more serious violent and property crimes, you will have difficulty obtaining a consensus regarding what is and what is not deviant behavior; culture, previous and current socio-economic status, and age will all impact what may be viewed as deviant, and labeling a neighborhood as socially organized or social disorganized.

But it must be remembered that Clifford Shaw and Henry McKay were not trying to devise a theory of everything delinquent. They were trying to understand and explain patterns of juvenile delinquency in Chicago, IL. Their theory stood the test of time despite inappropriate empirical applications and inferences, no doubt a testament to the strength of social disorganization theory. It still performs rather well and is often used in spatial criminology to this day.

Testing social disorganization theory

There are many tests of social disorganization theory, including the original empirical validations performed by Clifford Shaw and Henry McKay. However, for our purposes we are going to focus on two tests of social disorganization theory because of their methodological prowess—the first, published in 1989 by Robert Sampson and Byron Groves, and the second, published in 2003 by Christopher Lowenkamp, Francis Cullen, and Travis Pratt, that is a replication of the article published by Sampson and Groves.

Sampson and Groves began their article stating the importance of social disorganization theory, but then stated that it had never been tested directly. If we were to consider *Juvenile Delinquency and Urban Areas* (Shaw and McKay, 1942) as the starting point of social disorganization theory, then almost fifty years had passed and no proper test of the theory had taken place; if we consider their 1931 government report (Shaw and McKay, 1931) or their first book (Shaw et al., 1929), as many as sixty years had passed and a proper test had not been performed. This is not to say that no tests of social disorganization theory had been performed. Rather, the tests of social disorganization theory that had been undertaken relied primarily on census data. Census data, though instructive, could not be used as a direct test of social disorganization theory because such data could only measure the community structure (housing value, single-parent households, income, low income, etc.) and not the variables that mediated the relationship between community structure and crime. Remember, as discussed above, poverty does not cause crime, but it impacts other factors that do impact crime. Also, though I consider this to be a lesser point, previous attempts to test social disorganization theory relied on official crime data. These limitations were discussed above, but I am confident that this data issue is of lesser importance than being able to properly measure social disorganization when testing social disorganization theory!

Sampson and Groves addressed both of these issues in their 1989 journal article using the British Crime Surveys from 1982 and 1984—238 localities and 10,905 residents in 1982, 300 localities and 11,030 residents in 1984. The British Crime Survey allowed Sampson and Groves to be able to use self-report crime data instead of official crime data, and construct measures of both community structure and the mediating factors of social disorganization theory. As such, this work of Sampson and Groves was the first direct test of social disorganization theory. Because of this importance, it should come as no surprise that this journal article has been cited more than 2,000 times.

We will not go into all the details of the data and methodology of Sampson and Groves here, but it is important to understand how they operationalized social disorganization with the British Crime Survey. As shown in Figure 2.3, Sampson and Groves have their causal model with community structure variables impacting the mediating factors of social disorganization that impact crime and delinquency. Note that they allow the community structure variables to have a direct impact on crime and delinquency, but the mediating factors of social disorganization also play a role, unlike previous research/testing on social disorganization theory. The mediating factors of social disorganization theory were measured directly from questions within the British Crime Survey.

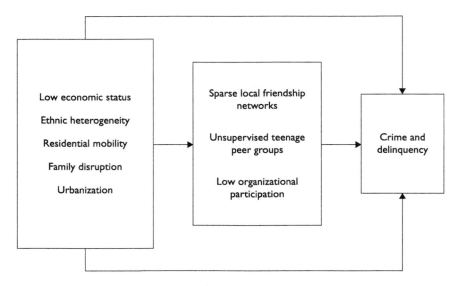

Figure 2.3 The causal model of Sampson and Groves (1989).
Source: Adapted from Sampson and Groves (1989).

In the results for the analysis of the 1982 British Crime Survey, Sampson and Groves found, as expected, that low economic status, ethnic heterogeneity, residential mobility (population turnover), family disruption, and urbanization all related to aspects of the mediating factors of social disorganization. Sparse local friendship networks were positively associated with residential stability and negatively associated with urbanization. Unsupervised teenage peer groups were negatively associated with socio-economic status, but positively related with ethnic heterogeneity, residential stability, family disruption, and urbanization. Lastly, organizational participation was positively associated with socioeconomic status. Overall, when the statistical relationships were statistically significant, the relationship was positive or negative, as would be expected.

When Sampson and Groves investigated the relationships of all these variables with mugging/street robbery, stranger violence, and total victimization, all the statistically significant results they found were as expected. In the context of mugging/street violence, ethnic heterogeneity, urbanization, and unsupervised peer groups were statistically significant and positive, whereas local friendship networks and organizational participation were statistically significant and negative. For stranger violence, the only statistically significant community structure variable was family disruption, with unsupervised peer groups and organizational participation also being statistically significant, positive and negative, respectively. And total victimization had statistically significant and positive results for family disruption, urbanization, and unsupervised peer groups, with negative and statistically significant results for local friendship networks and organizational participation.

In the context of property offences, burglary, automotive theft, and vandalism had more statistically significant results, but the explanatory power of these results was not as strong as for violent and total victimization. For burglary, there were positive and statistically significant results for socio-economic status, ethnic heterogeneity, family disruption, urbanization, and unsupervised peer groups, with negative and statistically significant results for local friendship networks and organizational participation. The only result here that may be considered "unexpected" related to the positive and statistically significant relationship between socio-economic status and burglary. However, higher levels of socio-economic status implies, on average, more expensive and greater numbers of goods to steal—target-rich environments. Automotive theft had positive and statistically significant results for family disruption, urbanization, and unsupervised peer groups, with negative and statistically significant results for socio-economic status, residential stability, and organizational participation. Lastly, vandalism only had a positive and statistically significant result for unsupervised peer groups, with negative and statistically significant results for socio-economic status and residential stability. The results for the 1984 British Crime Survey are quite similar and not worthy of separate discussion here.

The main point in the discussion here is that the community structure variables, as expected, had statistically significant relationships with the mediating factors of social disorganization and the various forms of criminal victimization. As such, the important take-away message here is that excluding variables representing the mediating factors of social disorganization necessarily imposes bias on statistical results. So, not only did Sampson and Groves include the relevant variables to properly and directly test social disorganization theory, they showed that these variables mattered.

Despite the fact that Sampson and Groves published an article properly and directly testing social disorganization theory, one of the most important aspects of (social) science is the ability to replicate the results of other researchers. Lowenkamp, Cullen, and Pratt noted that it was possible that the work of Sampson and Groves was an artifact of the particular set of data they used. As such, Lowenkamp, Cullen, and Pratt sought to replicate the study of Sampson and Groves using data from the 1994 British Crime Survey.

In terms of the community structure variables impacting the mediating factors of social disorganization theory, the results of Lowenkamp, Cullen, and Pratt were very similar to those of Sampson and Groves. When statistical results were statistically significant for both 1982 and 1994, they were the same sign and most often similar in magnitude; however, there were some differences in the results, but not worthy of discussion here. Similarly for both sets of variables representing the community structure and mediating factors of social disorganization with total victimization: when statistical results were statistically significant for both 1982 and 1994, they were the same sign and most often similar in magnitude.

Overall, the work of Lowenkamp, Cullen, and Pratt produced a lot of support for social disorganization theory, completely independent of its comparison with Sampson and Groves. It is quite simply an excellent piece of work that should be read by all scholars in the field. Moreover, Lowenkamp, Cullen, and Pratt were able to generate results that were generally consistent with those of Sampson and Groves. This is important for the testing of social disorganization theory, because there is a level of consistency that allows us to feel confident in the empirical validation of the predictions of social disorganization theory, albeit within one country. Additionally, the fact that Lowenkamp, Cullen, and Pratt found support for social disorganization theory using 1994 British Crime Survey data suggests that social disorganization theory may still prove to be instructive in studying the spatial patterns of crime. It would prove to be interesting for further research to use the more recent British Crime Survey data for another replication.

This, of course, is not the end of social disorganization theory. As stated above, researchers continue to use social disorganization theory to inform their empirical analyses of criminal activity. But much, if not all, of this research does not incorporate direct measures of the mediating factors of social disorganization theory. Regardless, it is an instructive theoretical framework that is sometimes used alone, but often in conjunction with routine activity theory.

Review questions

1   Why is it important that the test of social disorganization theory by Christopher Lowenkamp and colleagues was able to support the research of Sampson and Groves?
2   According to Shaw and McKay, what were the two primary factors that led to high crime rates, and why?
3   What theoretical model did Shaw and McKay use as the foundation for their explanation of crime in Chicago? Briefly describe this model. What are the implications of using this theoretical model in today's context?
4   How do Shaw and McKay explain the relationship between ethnicity and crime?
5   Sampson and Groves (1989) was the first paper to actually test social disorganization theory. True or false? Explain your answer.
6   Is a poor neighborhood necessarily socially disorganized? How do Shaw and McKay refute a direct link between poverty and social disorganization in the context of the 1930s?

References

Andresen, M. A., Brantingham, P. J., and Kinney, J. B. (eds.) (2010). *Classics in environmental criminology*. Burnaby, BC: SFU Publications/Boca Raton, FL: CRC Press.
Bulwer, H.L. (1836). *France, social, literary, political*, vol. I, book I, *Crime*. London, UK: Richard Bentley.

Burgess, E. W. (1925). The growth of the city: an introduction to a research project. In R. E. Park and E. W. Burgess (eds.), *The city: Suggestions for investigation of human behavior in the urban environment* (pp. 47–62). Chicago, IL: University of Chicago Press.

Bursik, R. J. Jr. (1988). Social disorganization and theories of crime and delinquency: Problems and prospects. *Criminology*, 26(4), 519–51.

Ceccato, V. and Lukyte, N. (2011) Safety and sustainability in a city in transition: The case of Vilnius, Lithuania. *Cities*, 28(1), 83–94.

Lees, L., Slater, T., and Wyly, E. K. (2007). *Gentrification*. New York, NY: Routledge.

Lowenkamp, C. T., Cullen, F. T., and Pratt, T. C. (2003). Replicating Sampson and Groves's test of social disorganization theory: revisiting a criminological classic. *Journal of Research in Crime and Delinquency*, 40(4), 351–73.

Perreault, S. and Brennan, S. (2010). *Criminal victimization in Canada, 2009*. Ottawa, ON: Statistics Canada.

Sampson, R. J. and Groves, W. B. (1989). Community structure and crime: Testing social-disorganization theory. *American Journal of Sociology*, 94(4), 774–802.

Shaw, C. R. and McKay, H. D. (1931). *Social factors in juvenile delinquency*. Washington, DC: U.S. Government Printing Office.

Shaw, C. R. and McKay, H. D. (1942). *Juvenile delinquency and urban areas: A study of rates of delinquency in relation to differential characteristics of local communities in American cities*. Chicago, IL: University of Chicago Press.

Shaw, C. R. and McKay, H. D. (1969). *Juvenile delinquency and urban areas: A study of rates of delinquency in relation to differential characteristics of local communities in American cities*, revised edition. Chicago, IL: University of Chicago Press.

Shaw, C. R., Zorbaugh, F., McKay, H. D., and Cottrell, L. S. (1929). *Delinquency areas: A study of the geographic distribution of school truants, juvenile delinquents, and adult offenders in Chicago*. Chicago, IL: University of Chicago Press.

Worrall, J. L. and Pratt, T. C. (2004). On the consequences of ignoring unobserved heterogeneity when estimating macro-level models of crime. *Social Science Research*, 33(1), 79–105.

Part II

Theories within environmental criminology

In this second section of the textbook, we move into the theories of environmental criminology proper. One of the first aspects of environmental criminology to notice is its change in focus. As should be clear from the early work in spatial criminology, its focus was the area, or neighborhood. This is what dominates the sociological approach to spatial criminology. However, there is much more to understanding crime than the areas in which it occurs. This is what led Brantingham and Brantingham (1981a) to refer to environmental criminology as a shift from a sociological imagination to a geographical imagination.

Brantingham and Brantingham (1981a) also put forth the four basic dimensions for understanding the varied phenomena of crime: the legal dimension, the offender dimension, the victim dimension, and the place (or situational) dimension. The legal dimension is concerned with the creation, formation, and interpretation of laws; the offender dimension, the subfield of criminology that was dominant at the time, is concerned with the motivation of the offender and how that motivation changes over time; the victim dimension is concerned with why particular people and/or places are the victims of crime; and the place or situational dimension is concerned with the spatial and/or temporal aspects of crime. The research within the fourth dimension of space–time before 1969 was primarily concerned with only the spatial component, and the primary spatial unit of analysis was the area or neighborhood. Environmental criminology, however, is primarily focused on individuals and discrete points in space–time. Though analyses may be undertaken using areal data at some scale (street segments, neighborhoods, municipalities, and even states/provinces), the underlying theoretical framework is still based on the individual making choices, not neighborhoods that generate crime. Consequently, the geographical imagination allows environmental criminologists to consider how an individual moves through the environment rather than how the individual is impacted by the sociological conditions of the neighborhood.

The term "environmental criminology" is an umbrella term that is used to describe a number of theoretical frameworks: routine activity theory, geometric theory of crime, rational choice theory, and pattern theory—pattern theory is itself a metatheory of the other three theoretical approaches. The roots of

environmental criminology, however, are in crime prevention. In fact, C. Ray Jeffery coined the term "environmental criminology" on the last page of his seminal book *Crime Prevention Through Environmental Design* (Jeffery, 1971, p. 279). At that time, C. Ray Jeffery called for the establishment of a new school of thought within the field of criminology. The primary focus of this new school of thought was to prevent crime before it occurred and do so through an understanding of the environment within which crime occurs.

Despite the importance of Jeffery's *Crime Prevention Through Environmental Design*, discussed further in Chapter 7, his published ideas regarding the impact of the environment on crime date back two more years. In 1969, C. Ray Jeffery published an article titled "Crime prevention and control through environmental engineering," in which he began to outline his theory of crime prevention through the modification of the environment. The evolution of the subsequent theories in environmental criminology is shown in Figure PII.1.

What you should notice immediately is that there are two "streams" that lead to environmental criminology: the one on the left originating with C. Ray Jeffery, and the one on the right originating with Oscar Newman's work published in 1972, *Defensible Space: Crime Prevention Through Urban Design*. The similarities and

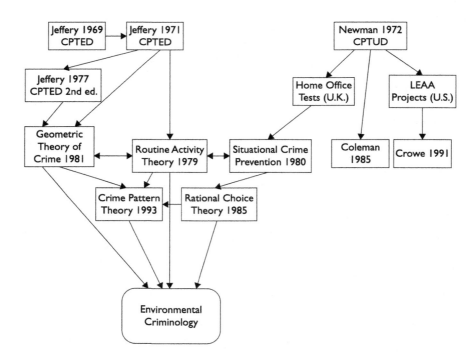

Figure PII.1 The evolution of environmental criminology.

differences between these two approaches will be discussed in Chapter 7, but it is important to note here that both C. Ray Jeffery and Oscar Newman were working on very similar ideas at essentially the same time. This tells me that the time was ripe for the field of environmental criminology to enter into criminological debates.

Figure PII.1 provides a reference for the connections between the various theories within environmental criminology. In Part II of this textbook we will cover routine activity theory, geometric theory of crime, rational choice theory, and crime pattern theory—crime prevention, and situational crime prevention, will be discussed in Chapter 7.

Chapter 3

Routine activity theory

Introduction

In this first chapter on an environmental criminology theory, there is a change in focus. To some, this change will appear to be subtle, but others may notice a sharp change in the ways in which we will look at criminal activity. Within social disorganization theory, the unit of analysis was the neighborhood. As stated in Chapter 2, this meant that the theory did not focus on individuals. Therefore, you may think of social disorganization theory as a theory explaining the criminality of place. Recall that Clifford Shaw and Henry McKay found that neighborhoods retained their relative ranking with regard to juvenile delinquency rates despite changes in the ethnic composition of the neighborhood and the changing economic circumstances. This meant that people were not intrinsically criminal, but were products of their environments.

The focus in environmental criminology, generally speaking, is on the criminal events themselves. Rather than considering the social characteristics of the neighborhoods, that may impact the probability of a criminal event occurring, environmental criminologists will focus on the specific location of the criminal event, the specific time of the criminal event, the specific day of the criminal event, and so on—the social characteristics are part of the equation, but only a part. This difference, as I hope to show, is significant when it comes to understanding criminal events.

With this focus on the criminal event, and with routine activity theory specifically, we will consider the simultaneous interaction between the offender, the victim (whether the victim be a person or a person's property), and whether or not there is the presence of someone or something capable of preventing the criminal event from occurring. This interaction necessarily takes place at a discrete location, much more specific than a "neighborhood," but it also takes place at a specific time. As such, routine activity theory, and environmental criminological theories more generally, are spatial-temporal theories. This addition of the temporal dimension is the critical difference between the theories within environmental criminology theories and other theories. More on this when we discuss the metaphysics of routine activity theory.

In their article published in 1979, Lawrence Cohen and Marcus Felson begin by stating a sociological paradox. This paradox was that despite the economic improvements in society since the beginning of the post-Second World War era, crime rates continued to rise. Considering that variables such as educational achievement and income levels were rising, while unemployment and the number of people living in legally defined poverty were falling, this was a time of prosperity. In fact, the 1950s and 1960s have been referred to as the Golden Age of Capitalism. Though there are critics of this Golden Age of Capitalism, referring to this as the Golden Age Illusion (Rigby and Webber, 1996), the advancement of wealth cannot be denied; one may, however, ask the question of increased wealth for whom, but that subject matter is covered in a different course.

Gross domestic product per capita, a measure of average income in a society, increased steadily from the 1950s up to current times in all Western nation-states. Of course, there have been a few blips along the way (some of them rather significant for particular groups of people), such as the recessions in the early 1980s, the early 1990s, and of course more recently in 2008–2009. But the trend is clear: we are getting richer, on average. The Golden Age of Capitalism also encompassed the Civil Rights Movement and Second Wave feminism, both great social strides forward in the Western World. Of course, these are processes that are still developing, but the point is that the 1950s and 1960s were a time of economic and social growth.

The sociological paradox emerges because in these times of increased standard of living, both economically and socially, crime rates increased substantially. From a sociological perspective, though not necessarily social disorganization theory, the alleviation of poverty and other social ills should have led to a decrease in crime rates. Figures 3.1a and 3.1b show the increases in crime from 1960 up to the 1990s, with subsequent decreases—we will discuss the decreases in crime in Chapter 12. In these thirty years, property crime rates increased 300 percent in both Canada and the United States. In these same years, violent crime rates increased by 500 percent in Canada and by 400 percent in the United States. Lawrence Cohen and Marcus Felson were considering data from 1947 to 1974, so these magnitude increases were not present in their data, but the trend was the same—they refer to increases in the order of 150–250 percent. In fact, when considering the correlation between gross domestic product per capita (average income) and violent crime, the correlation is $r = 0.95$ using Canadian data; the same general pattern holds for property crime in Canada but with a slightly weaker correlation, $r = 0.80$. Of course, correlation does not mean causation, but the strength of the relationship between property and violent crime rates with average income is positive and large in magnitude. Moreover, this was a general pattern in industrialized nations, not simply a phenomenon occurring in Canada and the United States.

This discussion should set off alarm bells with regard to our sociological explanations for crime. The more material goods the average person has, the less likely that average person will steal material goods from other people. This clearly was not going on in the so-called Golden Age of Capitalism. But recall that Shaw and

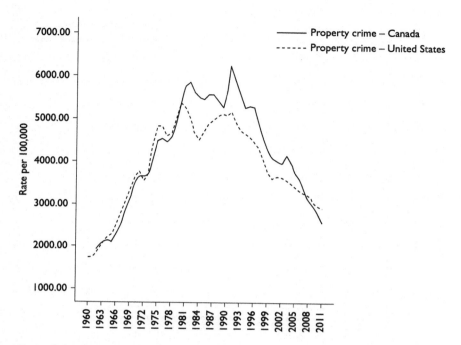

Figure 3.1a Property and violent crime rates for Canada and the United States, 1960–2011, property crime.

Source: Brennan (2012) and Federal Bureau of Investigation (2013).

McKay warned about making such simple inferences with regard to the relationship between the state of the economy and criminal activity. Remember their example of the Great Depression: families on relief (welfare) increased ten times, while city-level crime rates remained unchanged. In their analysis, it was the relative economic standing of neighborhoods that mattered for crime, not their absolute economic standing.

Of course, there are other theories that may be invoked to explain this apparent paradox. Anomie theory comes to mind here: legitimate and illegitimate means of achieving the same societal goals. Such a situation may arise in the context of massive increases in average wealth during the Golden Age of Capitalism because not all people were the beneficiaries of the increased income—this is one of the points made by David Rigby and Michael Webber. But we are not going to walk down this path. Rather we will think about the positive relationship between average income and (property and violent) crime rates from a different perspective, a perspective that is actually simpler to explain than invoking anomie.

When Lawrence Cohen and Marcus Felson were discussing the sociological paradox, they stated that the relationship between economic variables and crime

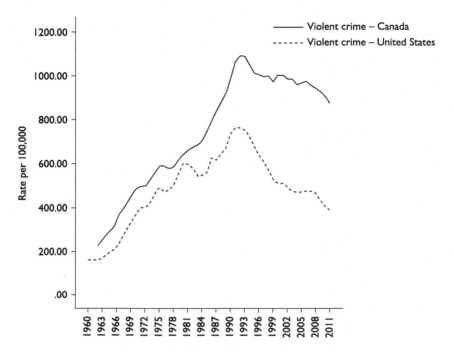

Figure 3.1b Property and violent crime rates for Canada and the United States, 1960–2011, violent crime.

Source: Brennan (2012) and Federal Bureau of Investigation (2013).

had inconsistent empirical evidence. Cohen and Felson sought to explain this apparent paradox by proposing a new theory that focused on the routine activities of daily life. But before we discuss their theory, we must first discuss their metaphysics.

Metaphysics: human ecology

The metaphysical stance of routine activity theory is human ecology—see Hawley (1944, 1950, 1981, 1986). Human ecology is similar to the social ecology invoked by Shaw and McKay through the emphasis of the importance of space, but human ecology also considers the importance of time. This is the spatial-temporal component of routine activity theory discussed above.

When considering a spatial-temporal approach with human ecology, space is critical to understanding human behavior, but space is only one aspect of human behavior. Equally important is the temporal component of human behavior. Therefore, knowing when we go to work, school, and recreation activities is just as important as knowing where we go to work, school, and recreation activities.

Consider skid row/road in your local city: you will feel very different in that environment during the day than you will at night. Even if you are uncomfortable in skid row/road, no matter what time it is, you will most likely feel more uncomfortable at night, when it is dark.

Generally speaking, human ecologists define (human) ecology as understanding how a population survives in an ever-changing environment. Consequently, space is clearly an important aspect of that survival, but it is only one of the important dimensions; if we focus on only one of the important aspects of survival, much information is either lost or ignored. Moreover, "ever-changing" has multiple implications. First, of course, this may refer to changes in the spatial environment. Second, "ever-changing" in the temporal dimension may refer to changes within a day such as the skid row/road example mentioned above, or it may refer to changes across long periods of time. This proves to be critical for routine activity theory because the temporal rhythms of society change over long periods of time such as decades, but are also different for different individuals at the same time.

The focus of social ecology on space is not the only criticism put on social ecology. Another criticism of social ecology is its focus on competitive behavior. Particularly in the context of social disorganization theory, this competition manifests itself as spatial competition: where people are able to live. This competition is resolved using financial resources such that the poor people live in the cheapest, and least desirable, neighborhoods.

Of course, only focusing on a couple of aspects of ecology does not make social ecology inherently wrong. This may simply have been done because of data availability or the operationalization of research—making things happen. At times, operationalizing variables may be very difficult. But the simple point to make here is that there is much more to our societal relations than the competitive behaviors of people. And again, just as with only focusing on space, much information may be lost without considering non-competitive behaviors.

Human ecology provides us with two concepts that can help us think about how we humans adapt to our ever-changing environment in a non-competitive way: symbiosis and commensalism. Symbiosis refers to the mutual dependence of organisms that have functional differences. Think of the cleaner shrimp that eats various parasites on larger fish; or, on land, the red-billed oxpecker that eats ticks embedded in large mammals such as the impala, rhinoceros, and domesticated cattle. This relationship may also be thought of in the context, or relationship, between predator and prey. The predator feeds on the prey, but the gene pool of the prey benefits because the "weaker" members of the prey tend to be eaten. Of course, "weaker" is a relative term that refers to the particular circumstances the prey is in; change the circumstances and "weak" may become "strong." Incidentally, a symbiotic relationship does not need to be positive for all involved, despite its common usage, though this relationship may be considered advantageous for the species in the long run. In a human context, think of different people undertaking different jobs within a company. Each of the jobs is functionally different, but they are all important to the functioning of the company.

Commensalism refers to the relationships among organisms that are based on their functional similarity. An example of this phenomenon would be two or more people performing the same job in a company. In this case, the relationship does not cause harm to either of the organisms. A second, or third, person may be hired to do the same job simply because there is too much work for the first person to complete on their own.

From these two concepts of human adaptation, human ecology then discusses a community. A community is defined as the structure of all the relationships through which a population provides its needs; and a community is based on both symbiotic and communalistic relationships as they occur over time and space. As such, a community is not defined on the competition between individuals as it is in social ecology, but on two forms of non-competitive or cooperative behavior. This shows that a social environment does not need to be based on competition. So, you can think of the Burgess (1925) concentric zone model as a restrictive type of ecology that only focuses on space and resolves the issue of limited space in a society by invoking competition.

In human ecology, there are three temporal components of community structure: rhythm, tempo, and timing. Rhythm is the regular periodicity in which events occur. The rhythm of work activity, for example: every day at 10 a.m. you have your coffee break or at 12 p.m. every day you have your lunch break. Tempo is the number of events per unit of time. Think of the number of criminal events per day in a given area. This is clearly related to rhythm, but it is a different measurement of our actions. And timing is the coordination of interdependent activities, such as the coordination of one person's work rhythm with another. One way to think of these three temporal components is a production line in a factory. The event is the turning of a bolt on the production line. There is a rhythm to that activity as it happens, hopefully, at regular time intervals. The number of bolts turned in an hour can be measured at each workstation such that we have the tempo. And because of the next person's event, potentially turning the bolt again(!), timing is important, because the next person's task is dependent on the previous event being completed by a particular time.

An obvious question to ask at this point is: Why do these concepts matter for crime? This is simply because it is all background for understanding what Lawrence Cohen and Marcus Felson called "routine activities" and how they changed over time. Their thoughts did not drop from the sky. Rather, as they state, these ideas had been around for some time in other fields of research but had not yet been incorporated into criminological research.

Routine activity theory

Lawrence Cohen and Marcus Felson defined routine activities as "any recurrent and prevalent activities which provide for basic population and individual needs, whatever their biological or cultural origins" (1979, p. 593)—basically, all those things we all do throughout the day to maintain ourselves: work, school, shopping, recreation activities, provided they are "routine" and not out-of-the-ordinary activities. These routine activities are most often based on symbiosis and commensalism. Routine activities most often occur at the same or similar times each day (rhythm), we can measure their frequency rate (tempo), and these activities involve the coordination of multiple persons moving through societal space (timing). And, by and large, these routine activities do not revolve around competition. They are regular activities that are legal and very commonplace. Cohen and Felson use this concept of routine activities, specifically the changes in routine activities, to explain the changing crime rate trends of the time.

At this point, the general thrust of the Cohen and Felson article, as well as their subsequent work (Felson and Cohen, 1980, 1981) and some of the subsequent work by Marcus Felson (Felson, 1994, 1998, 2002; Felson and Boba, 2010), was that social ecology and social disorganization theory had not progressed much since the work of Shaw and McKay and social ecology ignores important aspects of human ecology (the temporal dimension and non-competitive behavior). Addressing these issues through routine activities, or what Marcus Felson referred to later as "everyday life," can help us understand crime. History shows that routine activity theory has proven to be a formidable force in criminological theory; routine activity theory used an approach that was similar to that of social disorganization theory, but sought to explain more criminal behavior—and it did. This is the hallmark of a good (new) theory: it is able to explain the facts explained by previous theories, as well as being able to explain new facts.

The next step in understanding routine activity theory is to know which crimes Cohen and Felson were trying to explain. Though Marcus Felson had expanded the realm of routine activities since the original work published in 1979, Cohen and Felson did not put forth a general theory of crime. Consequently, routine activity theory is not in the same classification as theories such as social control theory or the general theory of crime (Gottfredson and Hirschi, 1990; Hirschi, 1969). Rather, Cohen and Felson sought to explain criminal events that they referred to as direct-contact predatory violations. Direct-contact predatory violations involve at least one offender, one personal or property target, and the absence of a guardian who could prevent such a violation. So, the lack of any one of these conditions will prevent criminal events and, therefore, you can predict the number of criminal events in a given neighborhood by measuring the frequency with which these factors converge in time and space with space being the neighborhood of interest (Felson, 1986).

An important aspect of the analysis and use of direct-contact predatory violations is that Cohen and Felson were not concerned with the motivations for "crime." Environmental criminologists often consider criminal motivation important, and the traditional theories of crime apply here, but they are "held constant" in most analyses involving environmental criminology. It is simply believed that focusing on the criminal event, and not criminal motivations, adds to the understanding of crime and does not in any way reduce the importance of traditional theories.

It is also important to note that, with the direct-contact component of these criminal events, the offender and the victim or object must both be tangible. As such, in its original formulation, routine activity theory was not a theory of white collar crime—as mentioned above, Marcus Felson had expanded the scope of routine activity theory in his subsequent work. Because of this limitation, routine activity theory considers crimes such as: robbery, various assaults, homicide, break and enter (burglary), and various forms of theft.

These direct-contact predatory violations are also considered to be rational acts such that the people (offenders and victims) involved clearly gained or lost. Cohen and Felson did not deny that irrational criminal events existed, merely that the majority of crimes were the result of (a set of) rational choices. As discussed in Chapters 4, 5, 6, and 7, routine activity theory, geometric theory of crime, rational choice theory, pattern theory of crime, and crime prevention are all related approaches to the study of the criminal event, partially because of the commonality of rationality in their approaches. Additionally, direct-contact predatory violations are assumed to occur most often outside of the home. Cohen and Felson supported this assumption with empirical data and did not deny the existence of crimes within the home and by family members. Rather, they simply found that the vast majority of direct-contact predatory violations were committed away from the home and by strangers. The key aspect here for routine activity theory, however, is that the direct-contact predatory violations most often occur away from the home of the victim—residential burglary is clearly an exception here.

Lastly, there is a qualifier for targets in routine activity theory. Cohen and Felson always referred to "suitable" targets. Therefore, if some item is to be stolen, for example, that item must be desirable to the offender. Desirability is defined in four ways: value, visibility, access, and inertia.

Value is a straightforward concept in the context of a criminal event. Is the item actually worth stealing? An offender is not likely to go through a lot of time and resources to steal something that cannot be sold for a lot of money. For example, a residential burglary is hardly worth the trouble to steal only a DVD player nowadays; many of these once high-valued items may be purchased *new* for as little as $20. Visibility relates to potential offenders knowing about the presence of a target. Consider the difference between having your recently purchased items in the cab of your automobile versus the trunk. Assuming you were not spotted by a potential offender placing items into your trunk, those items are much safer in the trunk than in the cab of your automobile. Access simply refers to the ability of the offender being able to break into (or simply enter) an area to obtain a target. Lastly, and very important for Cohen and Felson, is the inertia of a target. Inertia refers to the mass of a target (if it can actually be lifted/removed), whether or not it is locked down or has some other security device, or (in the context of a personal assault) if the person is able to defend themself.

Based on the minimal elements of a direct-contact predatory violation (motivated offender, suitable target, lack of a capable guardian), Cohen and Felson identified two primary ways in which the increasing crime rate trends of the 1950s and 1960s can be explained in spite of the alleged sociological paradox. These are changes in the routine activities of people and changes in target suitability.

Changes in the routine activities of individuals, in the context of the sociological paradox, are best understood when considering the general rise in average incomes and the standard of living in the post-Second World War period. If the income of a person increases and that person has more disposable income— disposable in terms of both after taxes *and* after the rent or mortgage is paid— there is more money available to go out shopping, go out to eat, and go to other activities that involve recreation: movies, bowling, sporting activities, and so on.

In addition to these changes in income in the post-Second World War period, there were also changes in the social and cultural dimensions of Western society. More young people were able to leave home early for a post-secondary education—this is particularly true for young women, an historically important fact to note. There was also an increase in the number of women in the workforce. And these changes in routine activities could not have occurred in an earlier time period, because home ownership and the increased quality of life for the working class, in general, only occurred after the end of the Second World War. As mentioned above, this time period has been referred to as the Golden Age of Capitalism.

The primary point here is that this change in income and the corresponding changes in social and cultural dimensions of society drew ever more people outside of the relatively protective environment of the home. This placed them at greater risk of criminal victimization (property and personal victimization), because when an individual is at home, s/he is better able to protect person and property through barriers such as locked doors and windows. With routine activities more often away from the home and people at a greater risk of criminal victimization, crime rates rose. As Cohen and Felson noted, economic conditions do matter for understanding crime, but not necessarily in the standard sociological explanation that states the more an individual has, the less that individual is inclined to steal from others. Economic conditions matter in a more particular and indirect way for crime: changes in income impact the routine activities of individuals, that then impacts the frequency with which they are outside the relatively protective environment of the home.

The second minimal element of direct-contact predatory violations that matters for changing crime rate trends is target suitability. This brings us back to value, visibility, accessibility, and inertia. Of course, value and visibility are important aspects here, but we will focus on accessibility and inertia. As stated above, accessibility generally refers to the ability of a potential offender to break into (or enter) an area and remove an item of interest. But accessibility may also be thought of in terms of the number of items available. Because the greater the number of goods out there, the greater the probability of one of those goods being accessible to a potential offender. Consider the presence of mobile telephones in contemporary society. It was not too long ago when mobile telephones were few and far between. These phones were rather large, very expensive, and tended only to be used by business people, the wealthy, and drug dealers. But now almost everyone has a mobile telephone, with mobile telephone theft accounting for an increasing presence in crime statistics (Mailley et al., 2008; Whitehead and Farrell, 2008). But this phenomenon is not restricted to mobile telephones. As noted by Cohen and Felson, both spending and shipments of consumer electronic goods increased substantially between 1960 and 1970. The more people who bought these consumer electronic goods, the less expensive (and more widespread) they became because of production conditions that made more people purchase consumer electronic goods during this time period.

Perhaps more importantly, the inertia of these and other goods changed radically. Because the mass of goods decreased dramatically, as well as their size, they were much easier to steal. For example, computers used to take up whole rooms, but now we have the same computing power (maybe more!) as NASA had in the 1950s on our smart phones. Another example is televisions. Televisions were commonly encased in wooden cabinets that would almost certainly lead to a hernia if one tried to move them. These televisions were made of solid wood and glass rather than plastic and were extremely heavy. This is all part of a general trend discussed by Cohen and Felson. Since the 1960s, consumer goods, particularly consumer electronic goods, have become increasingly smaller, lighter, and more widespread. This makes these goods much easier to steal, and more of them.

Testing routine activity theory

That is the theoretical aspect of routine activity theory, with some concrete examples of how the theory *may* explain changes in crime rate trends. But how does routine activity theory stand up empirically? This is, I would argue, one of the hallmarks of the original article published by Cohen and Felson in 1979. Not only did they put forth a theoretical explanation for a phenomenon with concrete examples of why it may explain that phenomenon, but they also provided empirical support for their theory using what I consider to be an ingenious use of data. Their empirical analysis was performed at the national level in the United States.

Cohen and Felson used some official sources of criminological data, such as victimization surveys and the Uniform Crime Report that comes from the Federal Bureau of Investigation (2013), both in the United States. But they also used resources such as the Sears Catalog, *Consumer Reports* magazine, and other readily available industry publications in order to obtain information on the mass, size, and volume of deliveries of items such as consumer electronics. This goes to show that as a researcher you do not have to have access to special data or information. You need to have a good idea that you can investigate somehow and it does not have to be anything particularly fancy. And the fact that this theory has made it into the mainstream of criminology, not just environmental criminology, shows how far a great idea can take you.

In the statistical portion of their article, Cohen and Felson outlined a number of their expectations. They expected that people living in single-adult households and those who worked outside the home were more likely to spend time away from the relative protective environment of the home and have higher rates of direct-contact predatory criminal victimization. They also expected that adolescents, young adults, and non-married persons would have higher rates of direct-contact predatory criminal victimization. Generally speaking, Cohen and Felson were able to confirm their expectations in the empirical evaluation of routine activity theory, but there were some notable exceptions in their analysis. For example, unemployed persons had very high rates of direct-contact predatory criminal victimization. Cohen and Felson argued that this was consistent with routine activity theory, because unemployed persons may tend to live in close proximity to high concentrations of the offender population, in search of cheap rent.

When Cohen and Felson considered change in the activity patterns of those living in 1960 versus 1971, they found a substantial increase in the percentage of households left unattended by anyone over the age of 13 years for almost all times of the day. They also found substantial increases in the rate of out-of-town travel and the number of vacations taken by Americans that created more opportunities for residential burglary—no capable guardians.

The last analysis performed by Cohen and Felson that we will discuss here involved the relationship between household activity patterns (the movement towards more activities away from the family and the home) and five official index crime rates, 1947–1974: nonnegligent homicide, forcible rape, aggravated assault, robbery, and burglary. Cohen and Felson found that no matter how they performed their statistical analysis, changes in household activity (increases in the time spent away from the relatively protective environment of the home) was positively associated with all crime types.

Though this original empirical assessment by Cohen and Felson was instructive and supportive of their theoretical perspective, it was a very aggregate analysis using national level data. Such an analysis was the appropriate way to test long-term changes in the routine activities of the population. However, changes in routine activities, as mentioned above, may occur across much shorter time frames, but also across space in one time period. For example, it was well established, particularly by Cohen and Felson, that individuals who were young and single spent more time away from the relatively protective environment of the home. If different places have different concentrations of such populations that are more prone to direct-contact predatory criminal victimization, those places should have higher crime rates. There are many studies that analyze routine activity theory at scales finer than the nation—too many to list; that includes a lot of my own research. Generally speaking, this research also confirms the expectations in routine activity theory and, as I have found, is better able to explain crime patterns than social disorganization theory. There are also a number of studies that have evaluated routine activity theory using individual level data. Probably the most well known, and considered a "classic" by Andresen et al. (2010), is the journal article published by Leslie Kennedy and David Forde in 1990.

Kennedy and Forde evaluated routine activity theory using the Canadian Urban Victimization Survey that contained more detail on the routine activities of individuals than previous research on the topic. These data were from the calendar year 1981 and contained the seven major urban centers in Canada: Vancouver, Edmonton, Winnipeg, Toronto, Montreal, Halifax-Dartmouth, and St. John's. The sample sizes per urban center ranged from approximately 7,000 to approximately 10,000, with a total sample size of almost 75,000 individuals. Individuals were coded as either being a victim of crime or not for the following crime types: breaking and entering (residential burglary), automobile theft, robbery, and assault. Kennedy and Forde included a number of routine activity variables in their analyses, as well as control variables for the potential victim characteristics (family income, sex, married, and age) and structural variables representing the areas they lived within (single-parent families, one-person households, detached household, unemployment, divorces, and low-income families).

The one routine activity theory variable that consistently emerged as statistically significant and positive was whether or not the individual spent time at a bar or pub; this was the case for all four crime types. In the context of break and entering, having sports activities, working or going to school, spending time walking or driving, and having a full-time occupation were all statistically significant and positively related to victimization. This is consistent with routine activity theory because these individuals would be spending a lot of time away from the relatively protective environment of the home and, therefore, would not be protecting the home itself. For automobile theft, working or going to school significantly increased the probability of victimization. Not only is this result consistent with routine activity theory because these individuals do not guard their automobiles at home, but it is also consistent with subsequent research on the risk of automotive theft based on where an automobile is parked. Based on data from the 1994 British Crime Survey that considered the time spent at various locations, Mayhew and Braun (2004) found that automobiles parked in public car lots were four times more vulnerable than when parked outside of the home or work location of the victim, and 200 times more vulnerable than when parked in the garage of the owner. The probability of assault was positively and significantly related to working or going to school as well as spending time driving or walking. And the probability of robbery was positively and significantly associated with spending time walking and driving. In the context of these two violent crimes, this result is consistent with routine activity theory because, by definition, these activities mean that the individuals were outside of the relatively protective environment of the home, placing the individuals at a greater risk of direct-contact predatory criminal victimization.

Needless to say, routine activity theory has support for its relevance at multiple scales of analysis. As such, routine activity theory is quite fungible in its applications and should (must!) be considered in the analysis of criminal events at any scale. The original work of Cohen and Felson, published in 1979, is one of the most highly cited journal articles related to criminological research. Suffice it to say, the incorporation of the temporal aspect of human activities has proven to be most instructive in understanding criminal behavior.

Review questions

1   According to routine activity theory, what must happen for a crime to occur?
2   What is the sociological paradox that Cohen and Felson (1979) use to motivate their paper? Be sure to state the paradox.
3   Cohen and Felson (1979), using the human ecology approach, criticize social disorganization theory's use of social ecology from two standpoints. What are those standpoints and why do they matter?
4   Cohen and Felson (1979) state that the economic conditions of society do matter for crime rate trends since the Second World War, but in a particular way. What is that particular way?
5   What is another way to explain the sociological paradox that Cohen and Felson (1979) use to motivate their theory?

References

Andresen, M. A., Brantingham, P. J., and Kinney, J. B. (eds.) (2010). *Classics in environmental criminology*. Burnaby, BC: SFU Publications/Boca Raton, FL: CRC Press.

Brantingham, P. J. and Brantingham, P. L. (1981a). Introduction: The dimensions of crime. In P. J. Brantingham and P. L. Brantingham (eds.), *Environmental criminology* (pp. 7–26). Prospect Heights, IL: Waveland Press.

Brennan, S. (2012). *Police-reported crime statistics in Canada, 2011*. Ottawa, ON: Statistics Canada.

Burgess, E. W. (1925). The growth of the city: an introduction to a research project. In R. E. Park and E. W. Burgess (eds.), *The city: Suggestions for investigation of human behavior in the urban environment* (pp. 47–62). Chicago, IL: University of Chicago Press.

Cohen, L. E. and Felson, M. (1979). Social change and crime rate trends: A routine activity approach. *American Sociological Review*, 44(4), 588–608.

Coleman, A.M. (1985). *Utopia on trial: Vision and reality in planned housing*. London, UK: Hilary Shipman.

Crowe, T.D. (1991). *Crime prevention through enviornmental design*. Stonehan, MA: Butterworth-Heisemann.

Federal Bureau of Investigation. (2013). Uniform Crime Reporting Statistics. Available online at http://bjs.gov/ucrdata/ [accessed May 8, 2013].

Felson, M. (1986). Predicting crime potential at any point on the city map. In R. M. Figlio, S. Hakim and G. F. Rengert (eds.), *Metropolitan crime patterns* (pp. 127–36). Monsey, NY: Criminal Justice Press.

Felson, M. (1994). *Crime and everyday life: Insight and implications for society*. Thousand Oaks, CA: Pine Forge Press.

Felson, M. (1998). *Crime and everyday life*, 2nd edition. Thousand Oaks, CA: Pine Forge Press.

Felson, M. (2002). *Crime and everyday life*, 3rd edition. Thousand Oaks, CA: Sage Publications.

Felson, M. and Boba, R. (2010). *Crime and everyday life*, 4th edition. Los Angeles, CA: Sage Publications.

Felson, M. and Cohen, L. E. (1980). Human ecology and crime: A routine activity approach. *Human Ecology*, 8(4), 398–405.

Felson, M. and Cohen, L. E. (1981). Modeling crime trends: A cumulative opportunity perspective. *Journal of Research in Crime and Delinquency*, 18(1), 138–64.

Gottfredson, M. R. and Hirschi, T. (1990). *A general theory of crime*. Stanford, CA: Stanford University Press.

Hawley, A. H. (1944). Ecology and human ecology. *Social Forces*, 22(4), 398–405.

Hawley, A. H. (1950). *Human ecology: A theory of community structure*. New York, NY: Ronald Press Company.

Hawley, A. H. (1981). Human ecology: Persistence and change. *American Behavioral Scientist*, 24(3), 423–44.

Hawley, A. H. (1986). *Human ecology: A theoretical essay*. Chicago, IL: University of Chicago Press.

Hirschi, T. (1969). *Causes of delinquency*. Berkeley, CA: University of California Press.

Jeffery, C. R. (1969). Crime prevention and control through environmental engineering. *Criminologica*, 7(3), 35–58.

Jeffery, C. R. (1971). *Crime prevention through environmental design*. Beverly Hills, CA: Sage Publications.

Kennedy, L. W. and Forde, D. R. (1990). Routine activities and crime: an analysis of victimization in Canada. *Criminology*, 28(1), 137–52.

Mailley, J., Garciab, R., Whitehead, S., and Farrell, G. (2008). Phone theft index. *Security Journal*, 21(3), 212–27.

Mayhew, P. and Braun, G. (2004). Parking lot security. *Crime Prevention Studies*, 17, 121–45.

Newman, O. (1972). *Defensible space: Crime prevention through urban design*. New York, NY: Macmillan.

Rigby, D. L. and Webber, M. J. (1996). *The Golden Age Illusion: Rethinking postwar capitalism*. New York, NY: Guilford Press.

Whitehead, S. and Farrell, G. (2008). Anticipating mobile phone "smart wallet" crime: Policing and corporate social responsibility. *Policing: a Journal of Policy and Practice*, 2(2), 210–17.

Chapter 4

Geometric theory of crime

Introduction

As discussed above, crime is a complex event. In order for a criminal event to occur, four things must be in concurrence: a law, an offender, a target, and a place/time. Without the law, there is literally no criminal event. There may be social norms violated at times, but such violations are not considered criminal events unless a law is broken. Without an offender, the person who commits the criminal event, there is no criminal event. And without some target or victim there is no criminal event. Of course these statements are tautological, but the point is that these aspects of criminal events are necessary. These first three dimensions of a criminal event have been studied quite extensively throughout the history of criminology (Brantingham and Brantingham, 1981b). The fourth dimension is spatial-temporal and this is the focus within the geometric theory of crime, particularly the spatial. It is important to note here again that those who follow the theories within environmental criminology, including the geometric theory of crime, consider the first three dimensions to be important. It is just that much of pre-1970 criminology did not address the fourth dimension. One may argue that social disorganization theory did address this dimension, and it did, but from a sociological rather than a geographical imagination.

Two important concepts to discuss at this point are space and place. Though some authors will use these concepts interchangeably or in the opposite way I will here, it is important now to define how I will be using these terms. Space is generally used as the short form of cartographic space. These are objective geographical dimensions such as distance and direction. Place is more of a subjective concept that I will use to describe particular coordinates within cartographic space. In other words, I will use place to describe the context of some set of coordinates.

Understanding the differences between these two concepts is critical because when considering the geometric theory of crime, the study of crime begins by asking: Where and when did the criminal event occur? What types of built environment (roads, buildings, etc.) are at and near the criminal event site? What are the social characteristics of the area? What is it about the routine activities of the offender and the target that allowed them to intersect at this particular place? And lastly, how does the location of this criminal event relate to the spatial distribution of offenders and victims?

Generally speaking, the geometric theory of crime investigates how the spatial-temporal dimension of a criminal event interacts with the other three dimensions of crime to produce a criminal event. Consequently, any criminal event is a dynamic, social, and patterned phenomenon. A criminal event is dynamic because it involves at least one component moving through space and time. A criminal event is social, because it involves an interaction between an offender and a victim, either directly (violent crime) or indirectly (property crime); however, the victim does not wish to be a part of this social event! And a criminal event is patterned because, as we shall see here and as discussed in the context of *routine* activity theory, our general behavior is quite patterned and, therefore, predictable.

Metaphysics: environmental backcloth, place, pathways, activity nodes, and edges

In order to understand a criminal event, we must consider the interaction of people, both offenders and victims/targets within a complex environment. One of the reasons why this environment is complex is because most criminals are, generally speaking, law-abiding citizens most of the time. It would be a lot of work (and rather risky) to always be committing some form of a criminal offence. Therefore, a criminal event may be understood as a by-product of normal, non-criminal activity patterns. Why? Because even the most prolific offender who engages in deliberate searches for victims is still constrained by physical, social, and cognitive environmental barriers.

These physical, social, and cognitive environmental barriers can be summarized using the terms "environmental backcloth," "place," "pathways," and "activity nodes." Influenced by the work of Kevin Lynch (1960), who was trying to understand the role and impact of planning on the city, Paul and Patricia Brantingham pushed our understanding of crime further through an explicit incorporation of the spatial dimension.

The environmental backcloth is used in the same way as context is used, but the term "environmental backcloth" is invoked by Patricia and Paul Brantingham (1981b, 1993a) to emphasize movement and change. A metaphor used by Paul and Patricia Brantingham is that of a flag: the context of the flag consists of the emblems, colors, and designs of the flag in two dimensions, but the environmental backcloth comes into play with a third dimension as the flag begins to wave in the wind. Consider an intersection in skid row/road in your local municipality. Would you feel safe walking around in that area, say in a five-block radius, at noon? Would you feel safe walking around in that same area at two o'clock in the morning? At the very least, anyone walking through such an area at two o'clock in the morning will have a heightened sense of awareness compared to the same activity at noon. This reflects that third dimension. The static context is the same: the road network, the buildings, the street signs are all the same; the third, dynamic, dimension modifies our perceptions when we alter the temporal component of that same place.

The environmental backcloth does not have to change so quickly. In the example above, the environmental backcloth changed over a matter of hours and it may change in a matter of minutes or even seconds—a "tough bar" may close, sending all its patrons into the street. In other situations, the environmental backcloth may change so slowly that it appears static. Gentrification is a process—described in Chapter 2, "Social disorganization theory"—that represents such a slow moving change. And so does the transformation of old industrial areas into residential developments. In both cases, little, if any, change will be noticeable. Professionals begin to move into an old working-class neighborhood, factories and warehouses cease to be in operation and get sold. More and more people move into the same neighborhood and more factories and warehouses shut down. In the former case of gentrification, the professionals begin to bid up property prices through demand and renovations, making it more attractive for the incumbents to sell, and over a period of years, maybe a decade or longer, the neighborhood has completely changed. In the latter case of the industrial area, construction starts to take place and because these areas are typically close to, or adjacent to, the central business district, it is common for high-rise condominiums to be built and sold. The end result is that an old industrial area that may have had a high crime rate becomes some of the most expensive real estate (per square foot) in the city. Again this process takes years to materialize. But the end result is the same: the *place* has completely transformed.

The concept to consider is place. We carry out our daily activities in discrete locations and travel discrete pathways between these locations. We can think of these discrete locations and pathways as our action or activity spaces. Our action spaces change over time because we will move, change our employment, recreate in different locations, but generally speaking these action spaces are fixed for relatively long periods of time. And because of this fixed nature of our action or activity spaces we develop an awareness of the areas around our activity spaces. These broader areas can be referred to as our awareness spaces. The term "awareness space" is used because over time we develop knowledge and attachments to different locations and, perhaps, the pathways between them. This knowledge and attachment leads to a sense of place. We end up identifying with certain areas, feeling comfortable or uneasy in certain areas. At times, both motivated offenders and potential targets feel comfortable in these places generating a lot of crime—more on this later in the chapter. It should be noted that a sense of place might also be negative: a fear of place. This sense of various places may arise because of what we have seen in the areas, what we have heard (stories from friends, family, and the media), or from direct experience. Regardless, we develop an "understanding" of the area such that it is no longer just a set of coordinates on a map.

Pathways, as just discussed, are the locations through which we make our movements throughout the day. These pathways may be a road network that we use to get to work, school, or recreation activities. Pathways may be the road network for cars, trucks, and buses, but also mass transit systems such as a monorail or a train system. But these paths may also be footpaths not accessible by any form of automobile: trails, walking pathways around campus, or a route moving from classroom to classroom and office to office. Pathways are part of our planned physical environment such that we are most often channeled through particular areas. Think of the freeways, major arterial roadways, and transit lines in your own municipality.

A sense of place develops along pathways. Suppose your routine pathway has a traffic congestion issue. This may force you through detours or have you trying an alternative route that is close to your routine pathway allowing you to get a better understanding of the area around the routine pathway. We are creatures of habit, so we will not often change our routines unless we are forced to do so. This is why the spatial and temporal dimensions of crime are so important to understand: patterns emerge very quickly once you start to look for them.

"Activity node" is the term used to describe those places/locations where we spend most of our time. And because of the planned physical structures of modern environments most of these activity nodes are designated as mass activity nodes. These are most obvious on the context of: business districts, entertainment districts, shopping districts, industrial districts, and bedroom communities (suburban areas). Most areas within most municipalities have one dominant land use. There are areas with mixed land use (residential housing being in close proximity to restaurants, shopping, and retail, for example) but these areas tend to be relatively small and are scattered in a few places even in relatively large municipalities.

An edge is a fascinating aspect about our environment. And as it turns out, our environment is full of edges. These edges may be physical such as a body of water, a major arterial road, or crossing the railroad tracks. But edges may also be perceptual in the sense that as you move from one area to the next you are able to notice that something has changed despite the fact that you have not crossed any physical boundary. Most often a boundary has been crossed, a social boundary. Another obvious edge is when land use classifications change, such as from moving from residential land use to commercial or industrial land use. Such a transition should sound familiar: the Zone in Transition from the concentric zone model presented in Chapter 2. In this particular case, the whole zone is an edge.

The interesting factor about an edge is that many different people have legitimate access to an edge such that there are very few "outsiders." Consider the neighborhood park, for example. A neighborhood park will have residents from the neighborhood itself playing there, or having their children play there. But there will also be people present who are from a relatively far distance away. This, of course, will depend on the nature of the park. If it has a soccer or baseball field, people from far and wide may spend time at the park. The point here is that at an edge (a park in this example) people will have anonymity because they are not necessarily locals.

An interesting fact regarding edges is that they are not always present at any given location. For example, if you are at a music or sporting event an edge emerges around this function. Most large municipalities have large "city parks" that are used for these functions, sometimes referred to as festivals. Most of the year, these parks may be occupied by particular social groups (parents with young children or senior citizens, for example) but during these festivals individuals from far more walks of life tend to be present; these people have legitimate access to the area for the time frame of the festival and would not be considered outsiders.

A consequence of the planned physical structure of our environments is that crime tends to cluster in or near major pathways and activity nodes. The geometric theory of crime brings these concepts together to develop an explicitly spatial theory for understanding crime. Because our movements through our environment are rather complex, so is an understanding of the geometry of crime, but considering these simple concepts proves to be very instructive for that understanding.

Geometric theory of crime

The concentration of criminal events along major pathways and activity nodes should come as no surprise, particularly if you consider routine activities. This is because the volume of criminal events is most often associated with the volume of people who occupy the same pathway or activity node (residential burglary is an obvious exception here). This is one of the reasons why the volume of criminal events varies from place to place and time to time. For example, there will not be many robberies in the central business district at night when everything is closed; there may be more commercial burglaries, but that is a different crime type— understanding the importance of detailed crime types becomes especially important for crime prevention in Chapter 7. In an analysis of residential and commercial burglary, Greg Jenion (2003) found that residential burglary peaked from 10 a.m. to 2 p.m., whereas commercial burglary peaked from 10 p.m. to 2 a.m.—completely reversed temporal patterns. Of course, however, this makes perfect sense: if you wish to burgle a residence or a commercial outlet and wish to minimize the probability of getting caught, you commit the crime when no one is there. Many residences are empty between 10 a.m. and 2 p.m. because the occupants are either at work or at school, and many commercial outlets are empty between 10 p.m. and 2 a.m. because they are closed for business.

We will now move into the application of these concepts to some examples of criminal activity. But before that is to occur, the basic model of criminal behavior in the geometric theory of crime needs to be discussed. First, as with routine activity theory, there exist individuals who have the motivation to commit criminal events. The purpose of this assumption, as with routine activity theory, is to move beyond the confounding impact of changed motivations for crime. Yes, motivation may increase or decrease impacting criminal event volumes and rates, but we can explain a lot about criminal events without concerning ourselves with the motivation factor—it simply exists. Given that motivated offenders exist, the process of a criminal event is multi-staged. First, the environment emits signals about its various characteristics. This is where our awareness space comes into play. Because we have a sense of place, we are able to "read" our environment. Motivated offenders use the same process to identify suitable targets. Through time, the motivated offender learns which environmental cues are good and which environmental cues are bad, subsequently constructing a template that is used for target selection. And once the crime template is established, it becomes relatively fixed, influencing future criminal behavior.

This crime template may be thought of as a checklist of items or circumstances that must be present or absent. If enough of the items or circumstances are satisfied, then the motivated offender will commit the criminal event. In the context of residential burglary, for example, this checklist may include the following: no guard dog, no burglar alarm, no one home, relatively affluent area, well-kept home, absence of neighbors, and so on. In fact, it can be argued that all people have a crime template, even those who do not commit any criminal events. The difference between the crime templates of an individual who commits criminal events versus another who does not is that the individual who does not commit any crimes has an extremely strict crime template. Such a crime template has too many items and/or circumstances to be satisfied, making it "impossible" for a criminal event to be committed, or all of the items and/or circumstances must be met with one or more of them "impossible" to be satisfied, such as a zero probability of being caught. The important aspect of the crime template to remember is that it is based on the motivated offender making (rational) choices given a set of information about the potential criminal event, including the environmental cues—more on rationality in the following chapter.

The simplest case to discuss the geometric theory of crime has with a basic search area for a motivated offender with a uniform distribution of potential and suitable targets with the offender having only one activity node, home. Of course this is an extreme simplification regarding both the uniform distribution of targets and that motivated offenders only have one activity node, but this very simple representation of reality proves to be rather powerful for understanding the criminal event. For example, empirical work has consistently shown that offenders commit their crimes close to home. The research studies vary in their average distance, but the journey to crime is short, particularly for violent crimes—see White (1932), van Koppen and de Keijser (1997), Rengert, Piquero, and Jones (1999), Wiles and Costello (2000), Costello and Wiles (2001), and Townsley and Sidebottom (2010) for examples of this empirical research and discussions of its limitations.

This short journey to crime, sometimes referred to as the distance to crime (Rengert, 2004) because the "journey" is a more comprehensive phenomenon, is a very common spatial behavior for all types of activities. The general term for this spatial behavior is "distance decay." In the context of criminal events, a motivated offender has a lower probability of committing an offence as s/he moves further away from the home. The rationale for this is rather simple: it takes time, money, and effort to overcome distance. Why travel further than you have to in order to complete any task? This is represented in Figure 4.1, showing that the greatest intensities for criminal opportunity search are close to home, but not too close, to prevent recognition.

This phenomenon of distance decay is also represented in Figure 4.2. This figure is essentially a cross-section of Figure 4.1, showing the probability of target selection on the vertical axis and the distance away from the home on the horizontal axis. Much more visible in this particular figure is the lower probability of target selection close to the home, a "buffer zone." This buffer zone is present because if a motivated offender were to commit a criminal event too close to home s/he would be more likely to be recognized in the criminal event. The probability is not zero, however, indicating that if the suitable target is attractive enough it may be worth this increased risk of detection and identification from being close to home.

Though this view of the criminal event from a motivated offender's perspective is instructive, it is also rather limited. As stated above, one aspect about criminals is that most of them behave like ordinary law-abiding people most of the time. And because of that fact, offenders are not tied to their home base all the time, but move around in their environment. In fact, many criminals will even have regular jobs. These people also look for or respond to offending opportunities when other people would not. So, like everyone else, offenders have action/activity spaces,

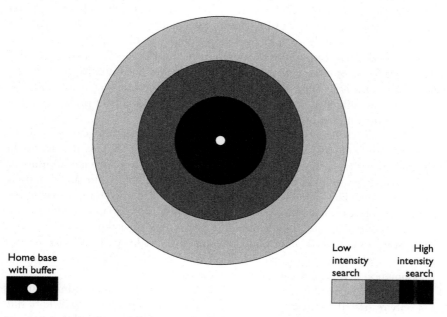

Figure 4.1 A simple search by an offender.
Source: Adapted from Brantingham and Brantingham (1981b).

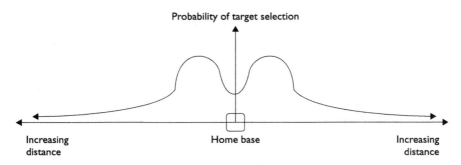

Figure 4.2 Distance decay and search intensity.
Source: Adapted from Brantingham and Brantingham (1981b).

awareness spaces, pathways, and activity nodes. Some offenders work, go to school, shop, recreate, and travel along well-established pathways to move from activity node to activity node. And now, because we are considering multiple activity nodes and pathways, the spatial pattern of crime becomes much more complex but much more realistic.

This scenario is depicted in Figure 4.3 with four activity nodes (home, work, shopping, and entertainment) and pathways between all of the activity nodes. Immediately obvious is that the search area for the motivated offender is much more distant from home, but still follows the same basic format as represented in Figure 4.1. The search for targets is more intense at the activity nodes of the offender and along the pathways between them. And as you move away from the direct proximity of those activity nodes and pathways, the intensity of the search decreases. This is because the awareness space of the offender is most reliable (informing the offender's crime template more reliably) in direct proximity to the activity nodes and pathways of the offender.

It should be clear from Figure 4.3 that the area where an offender will commit crimes is not random, but constrained to the places in the environment s/he spends most of his or her time. This is also going to be true for victimization: an individual will most likely be victimized in those places where s/he spends most of his or her time. This is one reason why some people suffer from repeat victimization. If the places where you spend a lot of your time are also places where many motivated offenders spend their time, the probability of victimization is greater. Moreover, it is not always easy to modify our activity nodes, pathways, and routine activities without the significant disruption of our lives. We will discuss the phenomenon of repeat victimization in Chapter 14.

The constraint of places in which a motivated offender may commit crimes is not only restricted by their own awareness and activity spaces, but by where suitable targets are located. Consequently, a motivated offender will likely concentrate his or her search for suitable targets in those places rich in suitable targets

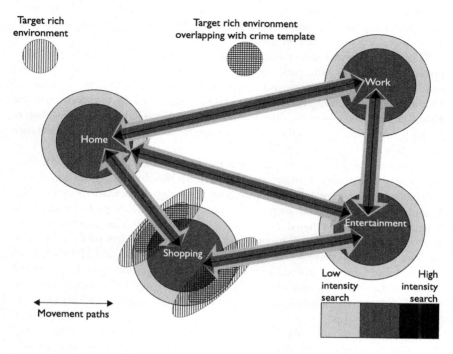

Figure 4.3 A complex search by an offender.
Source: Adapted from Brantingham and Brantingham (1981b).

rather than searching for the proverbial needle in a haystack. These suitable target rich areas may be close to or part of an activity node or along a portion of the pathway, depending on the crime type of interest to the motivated offender. For example, if the crime type of interest to the motivated offender is theft from a vehicle, an area that contains a parking lot would be of interest. But we can also further restrict the area of likely offences by recalling that motivated offenders develop and follow a crime template. Consequently, just because many targets overlap with any particular motivated offender's awareness space does not mean that the motivated offender will commit a criminal event at that place—this is only shown for the shopping activity node in Figure 4.3, but is likely to be present for all activity nodes for an offender.

The process of target selection described above helps explain why particular criminal events can be so highly concentrated in particular places. Because of the planned nature of our environment and that we have many districts across our environment (business, commercial, entertainment, etc.), suitable target rich environments will be common for many motivated offenders. If there are similarities in the crime templates of the motivated offenders, this will further concentrate criminal activities. Of course, there will be offender specific aspects of their respective crime templates, but there will be obvious commonalities such as those listed above regarding residential burglary.

Though Paul and Patricia Brantingham (1981b) consider a number of other possibilities, we will only consider one more, particularly because of its recent activity in criminological research: co-offending—see, for example, the work of Carrington (2002, 2009), van Mastrigt and Farrington (2009), and Andresen and Felson (2010). The geometric theory of crime considers the dynamic interaction of multiple offenders and, I believe, is instructive for understanding the importance of co-offending in criminological research.

During any activity that we take part in, we have the potential to learn from others who do the same activity: learning to ride a bicycle, ride a skateboard, play baseball, compete in martial arts, and so on. These are all activities that we likely learn from our friends and/or parental units. We typically learn from watching, listening, thinking, and then doing. Crime is no different. Research on co-offending has found that those who are involved with co-offenders early tend to be involved in more crimes and more serious crimes later in life (Conway and McCord, 2002; McCord and Conway, 2002; Zimring, 1981). There is some argument over this issue, but the reasoning should be clear: the more offenders you spend your time with, the more types of crimes and/or methods of committing criminal events you will learn.

Part of the reason why co-offending will aid in the expansion of criminal activities is directly related to the geometric theory of crime. When a motivated offender spends time with other motivated offenders, there will very likely be an expansion of activity and, therefore, awareness spaces. This is no different than if you started spending time with a new friend in legitimate activities. When multiple individuals (offenders) start to spend their time together they will go to new places. The different individuals may live far enough away from one another such that awareness spaces expand only by a lesser degree, or by a greater degree if entirely new and distant locations become incorporated into the activity and awareness spaces of the others. Because of this expansion in awareness spaces, criminal events begin to move into these new areas as well. This is because the motivated offenders will not only learn new things, but new ways to recognize suitable targets for crime.

The general picture here is that crime is neither randomly nor uniformly distributed across space. Rather, it occurs in particular places and, most often, at particular times. Consequently, in order to obtain a good understanding of the criminal event, one must consider the fourth dimension (spatial-temporal). To summarize, the spatial patterns of crime in any (urban) area depend on the following: the spatial distribution of motivated offenders, the spatial distribution of suitable targets, the general awareness spaces of motivated offenders, whether or not these awareness spaces include potentially "good" targets that are found in "good" crime areas (i.e., correspondence with crime templates), and that the dynamic interchange of information between motivated offenders modifies awareness spaces.

Following from these properties of the geometric theory of crime, Paul and Patricia Brantingham (1981b) outlined a number of consequences, or implications, of the theory. First, older cities that follow the concentric zone model discussed in Chapter 2 will tend to have a spatial crime pattern that clusters criminal events in the central business district and they decrease quickly as one moves away from that central business district. The reason for this is because there is *one* activity node that is shared by vast numbers of people in the population.

Second, more recently developed cities will have a more dispersed spatial crime pattern. Such a dispersed spatial crime pattern will emerge because the populations are more dispersed, as are the primary activity nodes within the municipality. Entertainment districts and central business districts are separated by greater distance than concentric zone model cities from their residential areas. Consequently, most individuals, including motivated offenders, will have awareness spaces that cover a greater area that leads to a target search area that is also greater.

Third, municipalities with shopping districts that are rather dispersed (including significant portions of strip commercial development) have a greater potential for property crime. In such a planned environment, motivated offenders will not have to travel far to commercial-based areas that are ripe for property crime.

Fourth, as discussed above in the context of shared routine activities, the development of arterial transportation networks necessarily leads to a concentration of criminal events along these arterial transportation networks. The logic here is based on overlapping awareness spaces, much like the concentric zone model. In the concentric zone model, there is a commonly shared activity node, the central business district; in this particular case, there are commonly shared pathways. Yes, criminal events will be more dispersed than with the concentric zone model, but the degree of concentration within relatively small areas will be great.

Fifth, municipalities, or neighborhoods within them, that have a grid-based street network, often referred to as a Manhattan Grid, have a greater potential for criminal events than areas with convoluted street networks. This is simply because it is easier for individuals, motivated offenders and others alike, to find their way around and, therefore, obtain an awareness of the area. Cul-de-sacs, winding roads, and dead-ends are frustrating to infrequent visitors and have a tendency to deter certain types of crime. Research investigating the relationship between the permeability of a neighborhood (street network complexity leads to a decrease in permeability) and crime, quite commonly residential burglary, has found that increases in the permeability of a neighborhood lead to increases in criminal event risk (Beavon et al., 1994; Bevis and Nutter, 1977; White, 1990). The most definitive research in this area is that performed by Shane Johnson and Kate Bowers in 2010, supporting the hypothesis that greater permeability leads to greater (residential burglary) criminal event risk.

Sixth, older municipalities that have dispersed low-income housing and public transit will have concentrations in the spatial pattern of crime around these areas as well as the central business district. This is quite simply because these social groups lack the opportunities for legitimate employment, most often providing them with greater levels of economic incentives to commit property crime.

Seventh, just as newer municipalities will have a more dispersed spatial crime pattern because there are more activity nodes separated by greater distances than in concentric zone model municipalities, so will older municipalities that modify their built environment to move employment centers out of the core of the municipality to suburban areas. Again, the same underlying theme is present here for understanding the changing spatial pattern of criminal events: changes in the number of activity nodes in which people (motivated offenders and others) spend their time and the spatial pattern of crime will adapt to these changed environmental circumstances.

Eighth, major entertainment districts and entertainment complexes (sports arenas, cinemas, shopping areas, etc.) are likely to generate criminal events. These areas tend to attract a lot of youth, who are the most criminogenic subpopulation (Boyd, 2000; Hirschi and Gottfredson, 1983) and, again, are the activity nodes for many individuals, law-abiding citizens and motivated offenders alike.

Ninth, municipalities that have a "red light district" (prostitution, gambling, drinking establishments, etc.) are likely to have greater levels of crime in those areas. As with major entertainment districts, these areas attract youth, particularly male youth, in large numbers, bringing together a high concentration of motivated offenders and potential targets/victims.

Though these are the consequences/implications outlined from Patricia and Paul Brantingham in their original work on the geometric theory of crime, a number of these consequences can be generalized using two concepts they developed in subsequent work that happen to manifest themselves at edges: crime generators and crime attractors (Brantingham and Brantingham, 1995a). Crime generators and crime attractors, as we shall see, are necessarily activity nodes and/or major hubs in the transportation network (pathways). Crime generators are places that generate a lot of criminal events simply because of the volume of people present. This volume of people is simply large numbers of motivated offenders and large numbers of suitable targets converging in time and space. Crime attractors, on the other hand, actually attract motivated offenders to the area because of (well-)known criminal opportunities. Most often, it is discussed that crime generators become crime attractors over time because the word is spread regarding the volume of suitable targets in the area. However, work recently published by James LeBeau in 2012 has shown that crime attractors may also revert to crime generators, at least in the context of hotels and motels. These two concepts embody the consequences itemized above that are based on overlapping awareness spaces of large numbers of people. This is precisely what is occurring in the context of crime generators and crime attractors. Of course, these two concepts are more general than the specific consequences listed above, but they are instructive for this general phenomenon that can be made more or less specific in terms of which crime type is of interest.

Testing the geometric theory of crime

It should be clear from the discussion above that testing the geometric theory of crime is a difficult task. But some of the consequences of the theory can be tested. In fact, a number of them have been, as discussed above. However, in order to truly test the geometric theory of crime, one must obtain information regarding the awareness spaces of offenders and compare those awareness spaces to actual criminal events. Such research is incredibly data intensive, requiring interviews with numerous offenders in order to identify their activity nodes and pathways, their known criminal activity, and their unknown (to the police) criminal activity. We are not there yet, but some research over the past few decades has proven to be instructive, with some very recent research coming very close to testing the geometric theory of crime.

One dimension of this research has been investigating the directionality preferences of offenders. It should be clear from Figure 4.3 that offenders (all individuals) only use a relatively small portion of the potential areas within any municipality; think of your own routine activities and how few activity nodes and pathways you actually have. A consequence of this relatively small use of urban space is that we tend to travel within a relatively small number of possible directions. This phenomenon is depicted in Figure 4.4, representing the awareness spaces of two individuals only showing their movement paths and activity nodes for simplicity. Figure 4.4 shows two possible cases: a) strong directionality and b) weak directionality. For the individual with a strong directionality bias, the vast majority of this individual's activities are constrained within a 45-degree angle. Consequently, if the criminal event activity of this individual follows the predictions outlined above, his or her criminal event activities will also be contained within this 45-degree angle. However, in the case of a weak directionality, this individual's activities are effectively in all directions such that no directional bias can be expected, *a priori*. A consequence of considering these two forms of activity space is that the strength of directionality, in general, is going to depend on the relative frequency of strong and weak directionality activity spaces in the general population. However, it should be noted that if the majority of people's activities

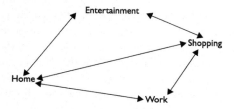

Figure 4.4a Strong versus weak directionality.

a) Strong directionality

Source: Adapted from Frank et al. (2012).

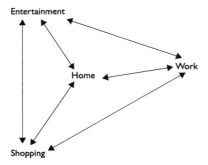

Figure 4.4b Strong versus weak directionality.
b) Weak directionality
Source: Adapted from Frank et al. (2012).

were concentrated along one particular vector (work or recreation, for example), directionality would be present. Given the fact that most people work every weekday and go to recreational activities on few days, if we weighted the movement paths based on how frequently they are traveled, a strong directionality bias would likely emerge for the individual who appears to exhibit weak directionality.

There are a number of direct and indirect empirical tests of the directionality preference of offenders, but we will focus on two: the first, undertaken by George Rengert and John Wasilchick, used a novel method for investigating the presence of directional bias in offending; and the second, undertaken by Richard Frank, Martin Andresen, and Patricia Brantingham, compared actual offending behavior data to computer simulation data in order to definitively identify a directional bias using a very large sample of offenders.

In two editions of a book, published in 1985 and 2000, Rengert and Wasilchick investigated the presence of directionality in criminal behavior through the development of what has been called the protractor method. In this method all of the offenders' home locations are "normalized" by "dragging" them to the origin on a protractor. Once this is done, all of the criminal event locations are plotted on the protractor according to their location relative to the home of the offender. When this is done for a number of offenders, it can be seen if offenders have a tendency to travel within a relatively narrow range of directions to their respective criminal events, measured using degrees. An example of this (not using real data) is shown in Figure 4.5. Immediately obvious from Figure 4.5 is that the majority of offenders depicted here commit their offences within a 45-degree angle of home. It is important to note that not all offenders travel in the *same* direction when they are in this "zone" of the protractor; they are simply restricted in their directional movements, measured in degrees, in the same way. In the research undertaken by Rengert and Wasilchick, they found that 78 percent of criminal event locations (residential burglary) were within a 45-degree angle of the

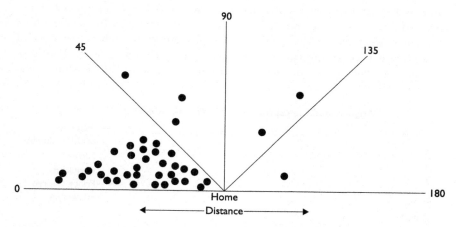

Figure 4.5 Directionality and the protractor method.
Source: Adapted from Rengert and Wasilchick (1985).

movement path from home to work. Moreover, there were a few more criminal event locations that were in the next zone (45–90 degrees) but very close to home; if those were included, then 85 percent of criminal event locations would follow that same directional bias. Important to note here is that a 45-degree angle only represents 12.5 percent of the possible search area available to any given offender, assuming no natural boundaries such as bodies of water and mountains are in the way. Therefore, according to the research of Rengert and Wasilchick, criminal event locations are highly clustered along the movement path that is arguably the most important part of most people's awareness space.

Though extremely intuitive and instructive, Rengert and Wasilchick did not have a very large sample—40 residential burglaries and 14 burglars. An obvious criticism of this work, despite its support of the geometric theory of crime, is that the results are not representative of the general offending population. Some research I have been working on with Richard Frank and Patricia Brantingham has investigated the directional bias of offenders using a data set that consisted of 2,622 offenders who committed at least two residential burglaries, a total of 8,126 residential burglaries in the province of British Columbia (Frank et al., 2012, 2013)—more work is planned for other crime types, but we used residential burglary to be consistent with Rengert and Wasilchick. We compared these 8,126 residential burglaries with a random directionality data set. This random data set was generated from a computer simulation that randomized data for each offender's home location and the criminal event locations. This randomized data set consisted of 100,000 offenders, who each committed 4 to 21 criminal events, that totaled 1,000,000 for the entire data set.

The results of the analyses are shown in Figure 4.6. In this figure, the angles necessary to capture 50, 75, and 100 percent of all crimes are plotted for the random data set, the province of British Columbia and three of its municipalities. In a comparison of the randomized data set and the province of British Columbia as a whole, when considering 50 percent of the offender population, an angle of 20 degrees is necessary to capture 50 percent of their criminal event locations, whereas an angle of 40 degrees is necessary to capture 50 percent of the

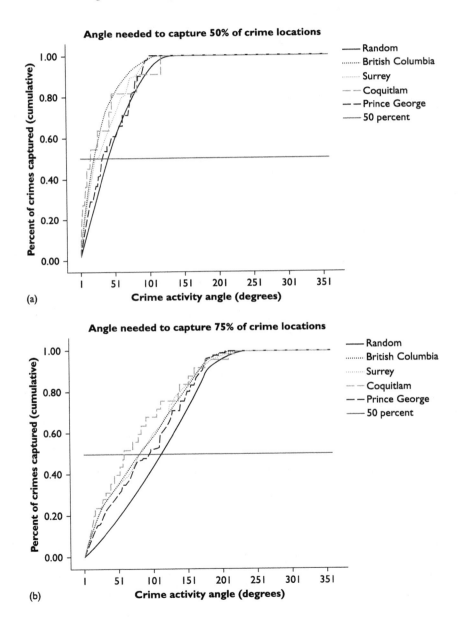

(a)

(b)

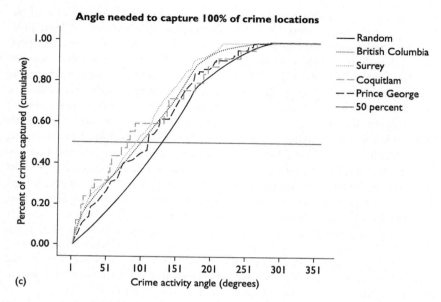

Figure 4.6 Directionality bias versus random paths.
Source: Adapted from Frank et al. (2012).

randomized criminal event locations. For a more direct comparison to the previous work of Rengert and Wasilchick, 55 percent of the randomized population would have an angle of 45 degrees or less, whereas the offender population satisfying this constraint is 78 percent. This clearly indicates a significant difference between the expected directionality preference for individuals using the randomized data set and what is seen in actual offender activity. Moreover, only 5.5 percent of the potential directions available to offenders are used by the offenders when committing their criminal events.

When considering 75 percent of the criminal event locations, there is a difference of 31 degrees between the randomized data set and the actual offender population. Within the results from the randomized data set, only 16 percent of the population is expected to have a 45-degree angle to capture 75 percent of their criminal event locations, but in the offender population, it is approximately 34 percent. When considering 100 percent of the offenders' criminal event locations and 50 percent of both populations, there is a difference of 30 degrees between the randomized and offender population results. And the randomized data predict that 15 percent of the population will need a 45-degree angle to capture 100 percent of their criminal event locations, but in the offender population it is approximately 29 percent.

The results from the three individual municipalities (Coquitlam, Surrey, and Prince George) are of particular interest. Surrey, the largest of the three municipalities, follows the same general pattern as British Columbia as a whole. Prince George exhibits a lesser, though significantly different from random, directionality preference. And Coquitlam exhibits a much stronger directionality preference than Surrey, Prince George, and British Columbia, generally speaking. The specific details of the differences are not important here, but it is interesting to note that different municipalities exhibit different degrees of directionality bias, one of the predictions of the geometric theory of crime—a directionality bias is always apparent, however. Overall, Coquitlam has the strongest directionality bias and has a land use pattern that explains why: there is a single large shopping district in the City of Coquitlam that services Coquitlam as well as at least two more moderately sized municipalities. This area is a large commercial district with mass transit systems, a high school, community center, community college, and aquatic center. Surrey, on the other hand, has more of these facilities but they are spread across the entire municipality. Consequently, the take-home message here is that the strength of any directionality bias is going to be dependent upon the underlying nature of the environment within which criminal events occur. This, of course, is the underlying theme of this whole textbook and spatial criminology, more generally: criminal events vary from place to place and time to time, criminal events vary by the nature of the environmental backcloth.

Lastly, some of the recent work by Kim Rossmo, Yongmei Lu, and Bernie Fang published in 2012 is worth discussion here. Rossmo and colleagues analyzed the spatial and temporal patterns of a group of reoffending parolees. The offenders were being electronically monitored by global positioning systems that allowed these researchers to obtain accurate depictions of the activity spaces of these offenders. Rossmo and his colleagues were able to analyze the spatial patterns of these offenders before, during, and after the offence on parole. This information could then be used to identify whether their spatial patterns of offending could be distinguished from their spatial patterns of noncriminal activities.

Though their sample size was small (14 parolees) Rossmo and colleagues had substantial detail on the spatial and temporal movement patterns of these individuals. Though a few of the offenders whom they studied appeared to have particular movement patterns before their offences that may have proven useful for predicting their criminal events, there were no peculiarities for many of the offenders. This is a strong indication that, aside from two cases (drug crime and sexual assault), the movement patterns of offenders are not different whether they are offending or not.

Overall, though the geometric theory of crime has not had a "complete" testing because of the intensive data needs for such testing, its individual predictions have stood the test of time. With the increasing presence of large criminal justice data sets, it may be possible in the future to combine such data with qualitative data on the awareness spaces of offenders in order to perform a more comprehensive test of the geometric theory of crime. Such a form of testing would prove to be most instructive because piecemeal testing of a theory is not proper testing as it assumes the other aspects of the theory are "held constant." Most often this is not the case.

Review questions

1   Why is it that the poor commonly rob the poor? Provide an example of a situation that has a "poor" person that commits crime in a "rich" area.
2   Why do environmental criminologists believe that crime is to some extent a by-product of normal, non-criminal activity patterns?
3   What is the significance of the environmental backcloth? Does it change?
4   What is a pathway and why is it significant for crime?
5   What is an activity node and why is it significant for crime?
6   Why is distance a factor in selecting criminal targets?
7   What does it mean to shift from a sociological imagination to a geographical imagination?
8   What is a crime template?
9   What is an edge and how does it relate to crime? Provide an example.
10 What is the difference between a crime generator and a crime attractor?

References

Andresen, M. A. and Felson, M. (2010). The impact of co-offending. *British Journal of Criminology*, 50(1), 66–81.

Beavon, D. J. K., Brantingham P. L., and Brantingham, P. J. (1994). The influence of street networks on the patterning of property offences. *Crime Prevention Studies*, 2, 115–48.

Bevis, C. and Nutter, J. B. (1977). *Changing street layouts to reduce residential burglary.* Paper presented to the American Society of Criminology annual meeting in Atlanta, GA.

Boyd, N. (2000). *The beast within: Why men are violent.* Vancouver, BC: Greystone Books.

Brantingham, P. L. and Brantingham, P. J. (1981b). Notes on the geometry of crime. In P. J. Brantingham and P. L. Brantingham (eds.), *Environmental criminology* (pp. 27–54). Prospect Heights, IL: Waveland Press.

Brantingham, P. L., and Brantingham, P. J. (1993a). Nodes, paths and edges: Considerations on the complexity of crime and the physical environment. *Journal of Environmental Psychology*, 13(1), 3–28.

Brantingham, P. L. and Brantingham, P. J. (1995a). The criminality of place: Crime generators and crime attractors. *European Journal on Criminal Policy and Research*, 3(3), 5–26.

Carrington, P. J. (2002). Group crime in Canada. *Canadian Journal of Criminology*, 44(3), 277–315.

Carrington, P. J. (2009). Co-offending and the development of the delinquent career. *Criminology*, 47(4), 301–35.

Conway, K. P. and McCord, J. (2002). A longitudinal examination of the relation between co-offending with violent accomplices and violent crime. *Aggressive Behavior*, 28(2), 97–108.

Costello, A., and Wiles, P. (2001). GIS and the journey to crime: An analysis of patterns in South Yorkshire. In A. Hirschfield and K. Bowers (eds.), *Mapping and analysing crime data: Lessons from research and practice* (pp. 27–60). London, UK: Taylor and Francis.

Frank, R., Andresen, M. A., and Brantingham, P. L. (2012). Criminal directionality and the structure of urban form. *Journal of Environmental Psychology*, 32(1), 37–42.

Frank, R., Andresen, M. A., and Brantingham, P. L. (2013). Visualizing the directional bias in property crime incidents for five Canadian municipalities. *Canadian Geographer*, 57(1), 31–42.

Hirschi, T. and Gottfredson, M. (1983). Age and the explanation of crime. *American Journal of Sociology*, 89(3), 552–84.

Jenion, G. W. (2003). *Analysis of the burglary phenomena: Problem solving unspecified temporal break and enters in the City of Burnaby*. Unpublished MA Thesis, School of Criminology, Simon Fraser University. Available online at http://summit.sfu.ca/item/8513 [accessed May 23, 2013].

Johnson, S. D. and Bowers, K. J. (2010) Permeability and burglary risk: Are cul-de-sacs safer? *Journal of Quantitative Criminology*, 26(1), 89–111.

LeBeau, J. L. (2012). Sleeping with strangers: Hotels and motels as crime attractors and crime generators. In M. A. Andresen and J. B. Kinney (eds.), *Patterns, prevention, and geometry of crime* (pp. 77–102). New York, NY: Routledge.

Lynch, K. (1960). *The image of the city*. Cambridge, MA: MIT Press.

McCord, J. and Conway, K. P. (2002). Patterns of juvenile delinquency and co-offending. In E. Waring and D. Weisburd (eds.), *Advances in criminological theory*, vol. 10 (pp. 15–30). New Brunswick, NJ: Transaction Publishers.

Rengert, G. F. (2004). The journey to crime. In G. J. N. Bruinsma, H. Elffers, and J. de Keijser (eds.), *Punishment, places and perpetrators: Developments in criminology and criminal justice research* (pp. 169–81). Devon, UK: Willan.

Rengert, G. F., Piquero, A., and Jones, P. (1999). Distance decay re-examined. *Criminology*, 37(2), 427–45.

Rengert, G. F. and Wasilchick, J. (1985). *Suburban burglary: A time and place for everything*. Springfield, IL: Charles C. Thomas.

Rengert, G. F. and Wasilchick, J. (2000). *Suburban burglary: A tale of two suburbs*, 2nd edition. Springfield, IL: Charles C. Thomas.

Rossmo, D. K., Lu, Y., and Fang, T. B. (2012). Spatial-temporal crime paths. In M. A. Andresen and J. B. Kinney (eds.), *Patterns, prevention, and geometry of crime* (pp. 16–42). New York, NY: Routledge.

Townsley, M. and Sidebottom, A. (2010). All offenders are equal, but some are more equal than others: Variation in journeys to crime between offenders. *Criminology*, 48(3), 897–917.

van Koppen, P. J. and de Keijser, J. W. (1997). Desisting distance decay: On the aggregation of individual crime trips. *Criminology*, 35(3), 505–15.

van Mastrigt, S. B. and Farrington, D. P. (2009). Co-offending, age, gender and crime type: Implications for criminal justice policy. *British Journal of Criminology*, 49(4), 552–73.

White, G. F. (1990). Neighbourhood permeability and burglary rates. *Justice Quarterly*, 7(1), 57–67.

White, R. C. (1932). The relation of felonies to environmental factors in Indianapolis. *Social Forces*, 10(4), 498–509.

Wiles, P. and Costello, A. (2000). *The "road to nowhere": The evidence for traveling criminals*. Home Office Research Study 207. London, UK: Research, Development and Statistics Directorate.

Zimring, F. E. (1981). Kids, groups and crime: Some implications of a well-known secret. *Journal of Criminal Law and Criminology*, 72(3), 867–85.

Chapter 5

Rational choice theory

Introduction

We are now going to turn to the realm of explicit rationality. Rationality is always operating in the background within environmental criminology, but there is also a theoretical framework for rational choice: rational choice theory.

When considering/discussing rationality and crime together, it is quite often the case that individuals will get emotional. This occurs because of one simple reason: most people have no trouble accepting that some criminal events are rational acts, but not all. Most often, the topic of rationality and property crimes does little to get people's emotions active. We all need money, and a means to get it, and for some individuals it may be easier and/or faster to steal something. One does not like to be a victim of a property crime, but at least one does understand the decision process. But in the context of violent crime, people tend to have more difficulty accepting the fact that these crimes are, in fact, rational. We have to remember that just because we may have a desire or urge to do something does not mean that we automatically do it. On the contrary, we must make a conscious choice to act on that desire or urge. Moreover, just because an action is not rational for you does not mean that it is not rational for someone else. The same principles must be followed for rational choices to take place, but different individuals do not have to make the same choices. This should be evident with a quick scan of your environment: different people doing different things, taking different courses, wearing different clothes, all acting rational. Crime is just another choice.

Some time ago, someone I knew interviewed someone named Norman Parker. Norman Parker was a person who lived in the London underworld. He was notorious for armed robbery and eventually killed someone in the process. He was a violent criminal who, ironically, now does research on violent and dangerous people. A number of this person's students were able to interact with Norman Parker and they were quite surprised when they did. Norman Parker was articulate, well educated, intelligent, and had a stable and caring childhood. Both of his parents had good jobs, a stable relationship, and a top-tier education. This was not what the students expected, particularly for a convicted murderer, because he was not anything like what they had learned about a "criminal" in their other criminology courses. Now, of course, you can always find an exception to the theoretical rule. I am not making any claim here that all theories that make predictions based on socio-economic status are wrong, far from it. What I found most interesting about Norman Parker and his history was that he said crime was a choice.

In a study first published in 1962, Victor and Mildred Goertzel studied the childhoods of more than 700 famous men and women (Goertzel et al., 2004). They studied people like Albert Einstein, Winston Churchill, Sigmund Freud, Helen Keller, and Mahatma Gandhi. They are all remarkable people who made incredible achievements, not only within their own time, but also from a historical perspective. Basically, Victor and Mildred Goertzel found that these people were generally not born of privilege, class, and status. Rather, they had many disadvantages placed before them on the path of life. Victor and Mildred Goertzel eventually concluded that their success was partially because of a desire to compensate for their disadvantages. They succeeded *in spite of* numerous negative factors in their childhood such as poverty, broken homes, and physical ailments. This is a very different story than what you will hear from most sociological perspectives.

The important point here is that these all too common sociological causes of crime are neither necessary nor sufficient for crime to occur. Good sociological theorists know that factors such as poverty, education, and family stability impact the *probability* that an individual will engage in criminal events, but again this must mean that choice is involved for all individuals who engage in crime. Sometimes, that choice is just harder than at other times.

Metaphysics: rationality

Before we move into rational choice theory with regard to criminal behavior, we are going to cover rational choice theory generally. This is critically important because before we talk about rational choice and crime, we should know what makes a rational choice rational.

The four panels in Figure 5.1 depict the primary elements of rational choice theory. Figure 5.1a represents the choice set: we choose combinations of x_1 and x_2, with the quantities of each increasing as we move away from the origin of the graph where the lines for x_1 and x_2 intersect. P_1 and P_2 represent the prices for x_1 and x_2, respectively. B represents our budget. If this were a textbook for microeconomics, x_1 and x_2 would be goods that we buy, P_1 and P_2 would represent the monetary prices for these two goods, B would represent how much money we have, and B/P_1 and B/P_2 would represent the maximum number of items of each good we could purchase if we spent all of our budget on one item.

However, an alternative view may be taken here that is constructive for our purposes. We may think of x_1 and x_2 as "quantities" of legitimate and illegitimate activities—we will use "illegitimate" here instead of "illegal" or "criminal"

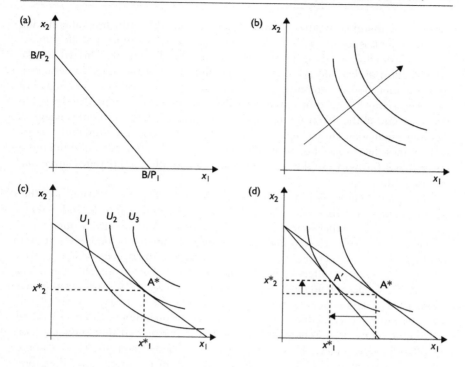

Figure 5.1 Making the rational choice.

to be more general. Our budget, B, is our time budget and P_1 and P_2 would represent the amount of time necessary to partake in one unit (whatever that unit is) of legitimate and illegitimate activities. Just as we are constrained by how much money we have, we are constrained by time—this becomes important in another way in Chapter 11. The line in Figure 5.1a represents the outermost possibilities of our spending and/or activities: spending all of our money or using all of our time. It is always assumed that we live our lives on this budget line. This is for two reasons. First, it makes solving the model much easier. And second, we have to do something with our time and money: even sitting on the couch or saving our money for a later time period is doing *something* with it.

Figure 5.1b represents what economists call utility. Each of the curves in Figure 5.1b is called an indifference curve—the set of indifference curves is called an indifference map. On an indifference curve, an individual is, guess what, indifferent to the different combinations on the curve: each gives the individual the same amount of utility, or happiness. These indifference curves are shaped the way they are to represent our desire for diversity in consumption. We would prefer to have equal numbers of apples and oranges, for example, so if I must give up one apple you will have to compensate me with more than one orange. This is called diminishing marginal utility: the more I have of something, the less value having one more item is to me. This works in the context of legitimate and illegitimate activities as well. Everything a person does cannot be illegitimate. This would take a lot of effort and would not be worth the effort most of the time. Sometimes it may be easier to steal something than it is to work for it, but other times it may just be easier to buy it with your money, possibly obtained from criminal activity. On the other end of the spectrum, it becomes increasingly difficult to only engage in legitimate activities. Do you always drive within the speed limit? And lastly, utility or happiness increases with more of all goods: more is better. So, an indifference curve that is further from the origin is better than another indifference curve that is close to the origin.

The optimal choice is represented in Figure 5.1c. This figure brings together Figures 5.1a and 5.1b to show how the budget constraint and the indifference curves are used together to make the rational choice. Additionally, as mentioned above, we can see why the rational choice is always made on the budget constraint. U_1, U_2, and U_3 are a set of indifference curves that show increasing utility: $U_3 > U_2 > U_1$. U_1 crosses the budget constraint in two places. This means that the utility level at U_1 is achievable to the person making a choice here. U_3, however, does not cross or touch the budget constraint anywhere. This means that, even though it is a greater utility level and this person would rather be on indifference curve U_3 than indifference curve U_1, it is not achievable with this person's current budget. U_2, on the other hand, is achievable because it touches the budget constraint at one point, A*. U_2 is preferable to U_1 because it is further from the origin and, therefore, means a greater level of utility or happiness. Because U_2 just touches the budget constraint, any indifference curve that is any further out is not achievable. As such, U_2 represents the greatest level of utility and A*, representing (X^*_1, X^*_2), is the optimal choice in this scenario. Any other combination of x_1 and x_2 would lead to a lower level of utility. Experiment with a set of indifference curves, an indifference map, and other points on the budget constraint and prove this to yourself.

Figure 5.1d is a representation of how the optimal choice changes when you change one of the parameters in the rational choice model. Recall from Figure 5.1a that B/P_1 represents our budget divided by the price of x_1 to see how many of x_1 we could purchase if we only purchased that particular good. Consequently, if the price of x_1 increases, the number of x_1s that may be purchased decreases and the budget constraint shifts inward, keeping B/P_2 in the same place, as shown in Figure 5.1d. Because the budget constraint has shifted in this manner, A* is no longer achievable and the optimal choice must necessarily change. In fact, even if A* were still achievable, the optimal choice would necessarily change because x_1 is now relatively more expensive—an individual is predicted to decrease spending on that product because it is relatively more expensive than x_2. As shown in Figure 5.1d, the optimal choice for this individual now includes a lesser number of x_1 and a greater number of x_2, A'.

In this model of (rational) individual choice, the individual responds to changes in the price of one good: decreasing the quantity of the good that has increased its price and increasing the quantity of the good that has not changed its price. The application is obvious when thinking about consumer choice: you buy apples and bananas and the price of bananas goes up, so you buy fewer bananas and more apples. But if we think of the budget constraint as representing the time we can spend on activities and the prices as how much time it takes to undertake those activities, this model can be applied to criminal choices. If you increase the "price" of a criminal activity, rationally motivated offenders will substitute out of that relatively more expensive activity into another activity, hopefully non-criminal. How do we increase the "price" of a crime? We will go into this topic more in the following two sections of this chapter, but think of the following: a security guard, target hardening (better locks, burglar alarms, etc.), and electronic immobilizers. These activities make crime more expensive for shoplifting, residential burglary, and automotive theft, respectively, because they will likely increase the time necessary to complete a criminal event.

It should be clear that this "pure" form of rational choice is not only complex, but rather unrealistic in the real world, where we do not have perfect and complete information to make such choices. This formal view of the economics-based rational choice model of crime is criticized by criminologists, as briefly discussed below. Generally speaking, the criticisms of using "pure" rationality (and the corresponding optimization of utility, or happiness) revolve around the following: the limitations of the human mind, especially when a split-second decision must be made in a criminal context; gathering and processing information is costly, particularly in terms of time constraints present in criminal events; and that decision-makers are supposed to know what they are trying to optimize. The economist Herbert Simon (1957, 1982) hypothesized that we do not act rationally in the traditional sense put forth in microeconomics, but heuristically. This heuristic process has been shown to be important in many contexts, including offenders' decision-making processes in target selection (Cromwell et al., 1991; Klein, 1999, 2004, 2009). In this approach, we act heuristically in all of our decision-making processes, legitimate and illegitimate, seeking pleasure and avoiding pain. We go through this process because most situations are complex and it is very difficult to process and compute every available option or action for every potential choice. This heuristic decision-making process is referred to as limited or bounded rationality. In the end, we behave in a manner that is as optimal as possible given the information we can process. Or, in other words, we make the best decisions we can with the information available to us; when we know better, we do (optimize) better. Limited and bounded rationality has the additional property of allowing "rational decision-making" to be subjective, or at least individual-specific. Rationality is an individual specific phenomenon, not what "makes sense" to the rest of us because we all have different preferences that manifest themselves in different indifference maps. Of course, the more rigid models of rational choice do not force one person's rational choice to be the same as another person's rational choice, but the use of bounded rationality makes this distinction very clear to the student of rational choice theory, especially in a criminological context.

Rational choice theory

Now that we have a general understanding of a rational choice—if you want to learn more, take a microeconomics course—we can move into how this theory is applied in the criminological literature. As discussed at the beginning of this section of the textbook, rational choice theory in criminology officially began in 1985 with the work of Ronald Clarke and Derek Cornish. However, this approach had its true beginning five to ten years earlier in Ronald Clarke's work on situational crime prevention. We will discuss some of this work below and in Chapter 7.

As outlined by Ronald Clarke and Derek Cornish in 1985, there were a few existing approaches studying the rationality of offending in sociology, criminology, economics, and cognitive psychology. Though instructive for the understanding of criminal events along certain dimensions, the theoretical frameworks of these disciplines were considered limited for the modeling of offenders' decisions. These frameworks were considered problematic along the lines of generalizability (sociology of deviance), lacking a coherent theoretical perspective (criminology), being too abstract and mathematical (economics), and being too general within the context of criminological decision-making (cognitive psychology). Ronald Clarke and Derek Cornish recognized the common use of rational choice theory applied to criminological issues in these varied fields and their goal was to generate a general approach that dealt with criminal events as a sequence of rational choices that was not burdened by the theoretical baggage and modeling methods of these disciplines. Therefore, what Clarke and Cornish sought to do was bring together the common elements of these different approaches without the focus on mathematical methods. Consequently, their model of criminal choice was more of a heuristic approach.

Specifically, Clarke and Cornish wished to stay away from a purely economic perspective:

1   The rewards of crime are only monetary.
2   Crime is not differentiated between its various types.
3   Punishment may be difficult to impose and criminals can easily avoid detection.
4   Crime may take place at work or by working people, such that a criminal career is not chosen in lieu of legitimate employment.
5   Many offenders are too young to use employment choice models anyway.
6   There may be a supply of victims, but there is no demand to be victimized.
7   The formal mathematical modeling approach used in economics-based rational choice has data availability issues and/or unrealistic assumptions.
8   The optimization behavior assumed by economists does not always fit the (at times) reckless behavior of offenders.

However, I would argue here that these criticisms of the economics-based rational choice model is not as restrictive as posed in this early work undertaken by Clarke and Cornish. As such, I would like to form a rebuttal here to each of these eight points:

1   Listing rewards as monetary is just a simplification that can easily be changed or redefined as "gains," such that these gains may include other rewards such as prestige.
2   The general crime model used by economists is very easily transformed into models for specific crime types with varying factors impacting criminal choices.
3   The ability to avoid detection may be incorporated into economics-based rational choice models considering the probability of being caught, and this probability may be specified in any way defined by the person performing the modeling.
4   The employment choice model is a simplification, but this is an important factor to consider because, as assumed by much of environmental criminology, criminal events are simply a part of everyday life that is committed by those who are generally considered law-abiding citizens.
5   The economics-based rational choice model of crime can be modified to include a decision based on how much criminal versus legitimate activity to undertake.
6   No economist would try to convince you (I hope!) that there is a demand for personal victimization, but there is definitely a demand for victimization, generally speaking; stolen property is "demanded" by someone, the ability to illegitimately download music, movies, and games creates demand for people to make it possible.
7   Data availability is definitely an issue and there are many economic-based models that do not easily lend themselves to empirical verification, but this is not restricted to economics-based rational choice models of crime; with regard to unrealistic assumptions, these are sometimes made to render the problem solvable and these assumptions are usually made more realistic over time.
8   Optimization must be considered in any general framework for decision-making; rational choices are made when the individual makes the best/optimal choice based on the availability of information, sometimes referred to as limited or bounded rationality, discussed above (Simon, 1957, 1982).

One could argue that I am splitting hairs in this discussion, but I would argue that it is important. Many of the criticisms of the economics-based rational choice model are not as bad as they appear to be. Most often, these criticisms were actually dealt with in other economics research not found or in research published subsequently to these critiques. It is important to highlight that these criticisms are not as bad as they appear, because these original works on rational choice theory in environmental criminology are often read and cited today.

The general point to take from all this discussion is that rational choice theory in environmental criminology borrows a lot of ideas from rational offending approaches in sociology, criminology, economics, and cognitive psychology in order to formulate a set of decisions for criminal events. Rational choice theory in environmental criminology was put forth partially because of the frustration Ronald Clarke and Derek Cornish had with predominantly deterministic theories of criminality: "my neighborhood made me do it," "I come from a low socio-economic level household," "I have self-control issues," and so on. It is important to remember that the vast majority of offenders actually lead dominantly law-abiding lives and that not all people from relatively poor neighborhoods or from families without the appropriate social bonds run around committing criminal events. Therefore, there must be some things that lead people to make rational decisions to commit crime and, alternatively, some things that prevent people from making those very same criminal decisions.

The rational choice theory decision-making process put forth by Ronald Clarke and Derek Cornish has three fundamental choices regarding crime: the decision to be involved in crime, the decisions necessary for particular criminal events, and the decision to desist from crime. Clarke and Cornish also consider the choice of frequency in offending by offenders, but we will not consider that here, because I consider the other three choices most important for the purposes of this textbook.

The decision for the initial involvement in crime is shown in Figure 5.2. Immediately evident here is that rational choice theory, unlike routine activity theory and the geometric theory of crime discussed in Chapters 3 and 4, explicitly considers criminal motivation: psychological, upbringing, and social and demographic factors. The geometric theory of crime does recognize the importance of these factors, but they are not considered in any direct aspect of the theory and routine activity theory explicitly holds motivation constant.

It is also important to note that rational choice theory is always dealing with individuals: What happens to an individual's choices when you change the cost of crime? Routine activity theory, on the other hand, dealt with societal level changes in its original formulation to explain changes in crime rates. However, as discussed in Chapter 3, routine activity theory has been applied to the individual level. Therefore, routine activity theory may be applied at multiple levels of analysis, whereas rational choice theory is applicable for one level of analysis.

Additionally, rational choice theory does not try to explain criminal events from a causal perspective, in the sociological sense of the term. Ronald Clarke and Derek Cornish repeatedly state in their work that each crime type must have a different flowchart that deals with the specific nature of that crime type. Rational choice theory has its strength in understanding the criminal choice phenomenon as well as making predictions in regard to changes in behavior from modifying factors for a criminal event.

Regardless, it should be clear from Figure 5.2 that there are many factors that lead to someone deciding whether to commit a crime or not: psychological,

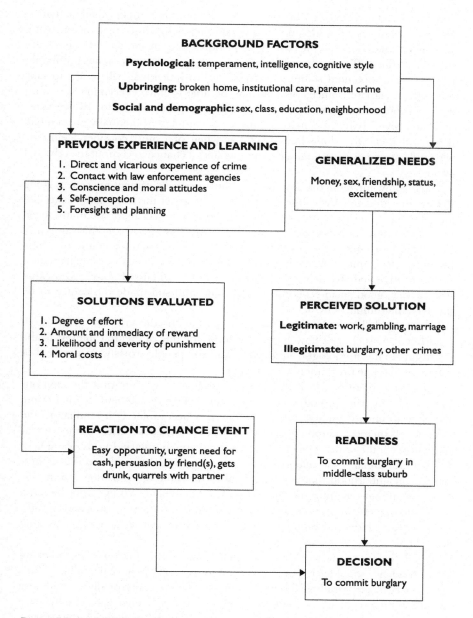

Figure 5.2 Initial involvement in crime.
Source: Adapted from Clarke and Cornish (1985).

familial, societal, economic factors, previous exposures to criminal activities, and the willingness to undertake illegitimate means to satisfy their needs. And, of course, many of the needs of any individual, including offenders, are socially defined. From these motivations and needs, a potential offender must evaluate potential solutions. Sometimes an individual will prefer to take the path of least resistance; yes you may be able to have everything you want if you become a surgeon, but are you willing to go to school for twelve years or more, give up income in that time to accumulate (potentially substantial) debt, and then work long hours? This is when one must consider legitimate versus illegitimate opportunities and, potentially, a chance to commit the criminal event.

Having any impact in the flowchart for the initial involvement in crime is going to be rather difficult. Very little can be done to impact the legitimate versus illegitimate opportunities of any given potential offender. Yes there are many social programs and support systems that aim to alleviate low socio-economic status and provide opportunities for the less fortunate, but we cannot count on these programs. Remember the sociological paradox, the context for the explanation within routine activity theory, and Norman Parker, discussed above, who came from a very good socio-economic background and still made the choice to be involved in criminal activities.

The second decision-making flowchart is that for the criminal event itself, Figure 5.3. As such, this flowchart tends to be the one of greatest interest to the environmental criminologist, in general, and the people working in the field of (situational) crime prevention, specifically.

This is the point at which the motivated offender will interpret the environmental cues in order to both create his or her crime template and use that crime template to choose suitable targets. Is the area accessible? Is it familiar to the offender? Is there a common police patrol or some form of security? In the context of Figure 5.3, the crime type of interest is residential burglary. In this example of residential burglary, the offender will generally choose a residence that is in a familiar neighborhood that is relatively affluent—note that this does not necessarily mean that the entire neighborhood will be affluent. No one appears to be home, no one else appears to be paying attention, and there is some sort of sufficient cover to hide and eventually break into the residence, potentially making some noise.

The desire for residential burglars to have some form of cover when breaking into a residence should get your attention. A lot of people believe that a high fence is necessary to keep residential burglars out of their yard. I personally see and hear about this on a regular basis. But, as stated above, a high fence will actually serve as an attractive feature for a residential burglar because, once inside that perimeter, no one can see you breaking into the residence. The best fence simply sets a boundary to be crossed such that other people will notice when someone has invaded that area, allowing them to ask: Who is that person inside so-and-so's yard? One of the best fences to have is the relatively old-fashioned white-picket

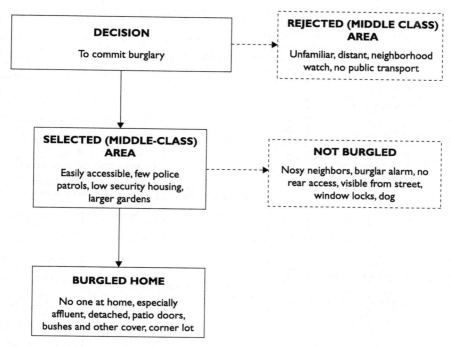

Figure 5.3 The criminal event.
Source: Adapted from Clarke and Cornish (1985).

fence. It is typically a low fence that cannot only be seen over, but seen through because the pickets have spaces between them. This is also when your nosy neighbor pays off, because s/he will notice the residential burglar before most others.

This example should make it clear why Ronald Clarke and Derek Cornish have stated these flowcharts must be crime-type-specific. Many of the factors for residential burglary will have no impact for an automotive theft, for example. Consequently, in order to understand the implications for a situational crime prevention strategy, the crime-type-specific factors need to be considered, especially those that do not carry over to other crime types.

In the last flowchart, Figure 5.4, the motivated offender is having his or her motivation questioned. Because of a series of potential external events, the offender must re-evaluate his or her readiness for crime, residential burglary in this case. In other words, the offender is essentially back at the first flowchart with new information. Some of the factors that lead to the offender questioning his or her motivation are simply occupational hazards that may have emerged one too many times: too many low-value crimes in a row, you lose your contact for selling your stolen items (the fence), you are bitten by a guard dog, or are even apprehended

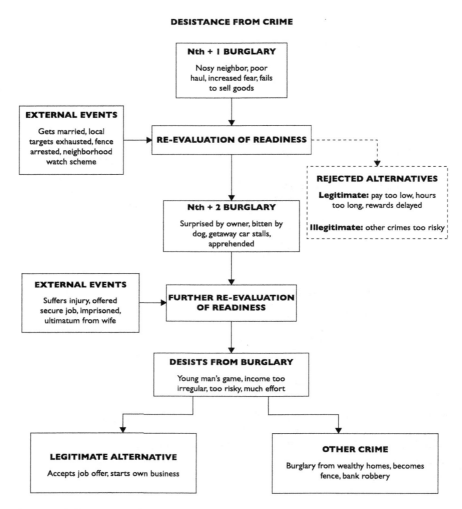

Figure 5.4 Desistance from crime.
Source: Adapted from Clarke and Cornish (1985).

by the police or some other form of security. But there are also just significant life events that begin to occur. We must remember that many offenders start their criminal career at a relatively early age, most often the teenage years (Gottfredson and Hirschi, 1990; Hirschi and Gottfredson, 1983). Consequently, significant life events are bound to happen for many offenders as they approach or enter adulthood: marriage or stable relationship, a good job offer, children, and so on. These turning points in one's life force the reconsideration of current activities, both illegitimate and legitimate. In the end of this flowchart, the offender must decide between a legitimate alternative or, perhaps, another crime type that does not carry the same risks as residential burglary.

That is the basic framework for rational choice theory in environmental criminology. And it is worth stating again that the focus of rational choice theory is on the heuristics of decision-making in a criminological context. These heuristics still follow the basic tenets of the economics-based rational choice model for crime, but without the formal mathematical modeling. Because rational choice theory is not a "causal" model in the sociological sense, it has not been as widely adopted in subsequent work as routine activity theory. However, rational choice has had a significant impact, as mentioned above, within the situational crime prevention literature and practice. We will not, however, go into any great detail within the (situational) crime prevention literature. Rather, we will now discuss the implications (and subsequent tests) of rational choice theory on (situational) crime prevention and its applicability in the most serious of violent offences.

Testing rational choice theory

As stated above, the rational choice theory of Ronald Clarke and Derek Cornish emerged out of Ronald Clarke's (1980, 1983) work on situational crime prevention. Moreover, rational choice theory had the purpose of developing a general framework in order to think about crime prevention and crime deterrence (Cornish and Clarke, 1987). The reason for this was because, prior to the conceptualization of rational choice theory, the predominant criticism of crime prevention activities, generally speaking, was that the increasing difficulty of committing a particular crime type at a particular place and time would simply lead to that crime being displaced elsewhere, hence the term "crime displacement"—we will discuss this in more depth below (Gabor, 1981; Reppetto, 1976). Consequently, rational choice theory was developed in order to show theoretically that most crimes are not functionally equivalent (Cornish and Clarke, 1986a, 1987). And this lack of equivalency mattered, not only for a specific crime type, but for the spatial and temporal dimensions of that crime as well. Why is this the case? One reason is that motivated offenders will seize the easiest opportunities first and "second best" may simply not be worth the effort (Felson and Clarke, 1998). This argument is no different than explaining why an individual does not drive to the other side of a municipality to shop for groceries when there is a grocery store in their own neighborhood or on their way home from their work commute. There are many classic examples of this behavior in the criminological literature. Patricia Mayhew and colleagues (1976) found that, when steering column locks were installed in all cars in West Germany, automotive thefts decreased by 60 percent, whereas the same locks being installed in Great Britain on new automobiles led to a displacement to earlier model automobiles that did not have this security measure; Paul Wilkinson (1977) found that added security measures reduced the hijackings of airplanes in the early 1970s; and, in the case of suicide, the detoxification of domestic gas supplies (a formerly common method of suicide in Great Britain, approximately 50 percent of cases) led to a 35 percent reduction in the national suicide rate (Clarke and Mayhew, 1988; Kreitman, 1976; Kreitman and Platt, 1984).

In order to put rational choice theory to the test in a more formal manner, Ronald Clarke and Derek Cornish put forth the concept of choice-structuring properties. These properties are "derived" from the fact that rational choice theory denies that potential offenders have a biological drive to commit criminal events. Rather, potential offenders choose specific crime types and, subsequently, particular criminal events for specific reasons, choice-structuring properties. And these are choice-structuring properties because these properties structure the nature of the choice made by the potential offender. So, whether or not a potential offender will switch to another crime type, location, time, and so on, is dependent upon the offender's preparedness to make that substitution.

These choice-structuring properties, as with rational choice in general, are specific to crime types and even situations. Ronald Clarke and Derek Cornish list some choice-structuring properties for two crime types: theft involving cash and illegal substance abuse. We will briefly cover the choice-structuring properties of theft involving cash for instructive purposes. Cornish and Clarke (1987) list eighteen choice-structuring properties for theft involving cash, including: expertise needed, the availability of suitable targets, solo versus co-offence, risk of apprehension, and so on. Of course these choice-structuring properties may be present for a number of other crime types and crime contexts, but the specifics of each choice-structuring property will be different. For example, the risk of apprehension is going to be very different when considering a bank robbery versus a residential burglary, similar for the availability of suitable targets and the expertise needed. Generally speaking, these choice-structuring properties focus on the opportunities, costs, and benefits of the alternatives available to a motivated offender. If we can alter these three factors, and assume that the net crime displacement is negative (even if some crime displacement occurs, it is less than the decrease in criminal events where the crime prevention initiative was put in place), there will be a net benefit to society for these (situational) crime prevention efforts.

We will go into more detail in Chapter 7, but the essence of situational crime prevention, as discussed above, is rooted in the term "situational." Situational refers to specific crime types, the location of the criminal event, the time of the criminal event, the specific nature of the target of crime, and so on. Situational crime prevention is an approach to crime prevention with the goal of reducing criminal opportunities. This approach is directed at very specific crimes (specific not only in the crime classification, but the time and place of criminal activity), seeks to modify the environment within which criminal events occur, making criminal events more difficult, more risky, and less rewarding (Clarke, 1992, 1997). Consequently, there is no panacea approach to preventing "crime." Rather, there is a set of principles to guide situational crime prevention activities:

1   increase the perceived effort
2   increase the perceived risks
3   reduce the anticipated rewards
4   reduce provocations, and
5   remove the excuses for crime.

This set of principles is further broken down into twenty-five techniques of situational crime prevention, that we will cover more in-depth in Chapter 7 (available on the Center for Problem-Oriented Policing URL: http://www.popcenter.org/25techniques/). And, as discussed in the context of rational choice theory, more generally, underlying all of these techniques is that potential offenders (or people, more generally) will respond to these activities in a heuristic fashion and reduce or, hopefully, eliminate their criminal activities.

One of the most common applications of rational choice theory is the analysis of impacts from (situational) crime prevention initiatives and the measurement of any crime displacement or diffusion of situational crime prevention benefits (Cornish and Clarke, 1986b, 1989). As outlined by Rob Guerette (2009) in a Center for Problem-Oriented Policing Tool Guide, there are five forms of potential crime displacement: temporal, spatial, target, tactical, and offence. Temporal displacement occurs when offenders simply change the time they commit their offences, hoping to avoid the crime prevention initiative; spatial displacement occurs when offenders begin to commit their criminal events in another location to avoid the crime prevention initiative; target displacement occurs when offenders switch from one target to another—single-family dwellings to apartments for residential burglary, for example—in order to avoid the crime prevention initiative; tactical displacement occurs when offenders alter the methods they use to commit the criminal event, such as stealing keys to commit an automotive theft because of increased strength in automobile security, in order to avoid the crime prevention initiative; and offence displacement occurs when offenders stop committing one crime type and start committing another crime type in order to avoid the crime prevention initiative altogether. There are clearly many ways in which crime displacement may be measured to capture its presence or lack thereof. Target, tactical, and offence displacement are difficult to identify using police data. However, temporal and spatial displacement are relatively easy to measure using police data, though there are some methodological issues that will be dealt with in Chapter 9. Consequently, much of the displacement literature focuses on spatial crime displacement, because it can be measured using data commonly available to criminological researchers.

In the 1990s there were three reviews of the literature on crime displacement (Barr and Pease, 1990; Eck, 1993; Hesseling, 1994). These empirical reviews covered research studies from Canada, United States, United Kingdom, and Continental Europe, all coming to the same general conclusions. First, there is very little evidence for perfect crime displacement, defined as all prevented criminal events occurring somewhere else. Second, whenever crime displacement did occur, it was most often less than the amount of criminal events presented. And lastly, the most common finding in these research studies was that there was no evidence for crime displacement. As with any research studies, these were not without their limitations. Most often, crime displacement was a secondary aspect of the empirical research studies under investigation—crime prevention was the primary focus of these studies. Consequently, there were a number of measurement issues that prevented any conclusive statements regarding the presence of crime displacement.

David Weisburd and colleagues (2006) sought to address these limitations in what is the most comprehensive analysis of crime displacement and crime diffusion to date, undertaken in Jersey City, New Jersey. Significant resources were dedicated to identifying the crime sites to study and deciding upon the crime types to investigate. Weisburd and colleagues decided to investigate drug crime and prostitution because of the economic nature of these crimes—they figured that if any types of crime would lead to displacement, these would. They investigated two crime sites with substantial levels of both criminal events and disorder and identified the surrounding areas that would serve as catchment areas for any displaced crime. As the title of their journal article should make clear, they wished to find out whether crime would literally move around the corner or not. The crime prevention intervention was a set of intensive police patrols that were implemented at the two crime sites, but not the catchment areas. This was followed by more than 6,000 "social observations" that were 20 minutes in duration—research assistants would watch and record criminal events and disorder activity in both the crime sites and the catchment areas. The researchers also conducted interviews and ethnographic field research to supplement their social observations. In the end, the results indicated that, at least in the case of drug crimes and prostitution, there was no evidence for any crime displacement—crime did not move around the corner. Moreover, the catchment areas in the study also experienced crime reductions such that Weisburd and colleagues were confident to say that a highly focused crime prevention initiative most likely leads to a diffusion of benefits. Because the catchment areas for this crime prevention initiative were restricted to the immediate area surrounding the crime sites, it is possible that crime displacement may have been identified if larger geographic units of analysis (neighborhoods, communities, etc.) were used.

Though an indirect test of rational choice theory, the crime displacement and crime diffusion literature definitely supports its predictions. The introduction of (situational) crime prevention initiatives such as intensive police patrols definitely alters the choice-structuring properties of any crime type. The fact that the number of criminal events decreased in the police patrol sites and their surrounding catchment areas showed that cost-benefit analyses would have been undertaken by potential offenders in the area. Lastly, we will briefly go over research into the use of rational choice theory to understand serious violent offending. Once again, this is an indirect "test" of the theory, but shows that rationality is at work even for those criminal events we consider irrational.

Eric Beauregard, Kim Rossmo, and Jean Proulx (2007) used rational choice theory to analyze the offending behavior of serial sex offenders. These researchers used qualitative data from sixty-nine serial sex offenders (with stranger victims) incarcerated in Canada to develop a descriptive model that contained nine phases. These nine phases—which we will not cover, for the sake of brevity—were organized by Eric Beauregard and colleagues into two categories: victim search methods and offender attack methods. These researchers were able to find that serial sex offenders used heuristic methods at every stage of the sexual offence. As such, those offenders whom most of us consider to be the most irrational actually behave in a rational manner. These offenders simply make different (rational) choices than we do based on the objectives they wish to achieve.

The purpose of this chapter has been to present and explicate rational choice theory as put forth in environmental criminology. Though this is not a causal theory, it provides a lot of insight into the decision-making processes of offenders. Research in this area clearly shows that rationality is operating in the background of even the most heinous crimes. And, as discussed in the following chapter, rationality is assumed to be operating within environmental criminological theories all the time. If offenders did not behave in a rational manner, we would not be able to predict their (criminal) actions and there would be no place for the field of (situational) crime prevention.

Review questions

1 What is a rational choice?
2 What is the primary difference between routine activity theory and rational choice theory when it comes to explaining crime?
3 Rational choice theory puts forth three distinct rational choices. What are they and how do they relate to crime?
4 Can a general rational choice model be applied to all crimes? Explain.
5 Rational choice theory is commonly used in situational crime prevention efforts. A common criticism of rational choice theory in this context is crime displacement. Why is crime displacement not that big an issue within rational choice theory?

References

Barr, R. and Pease, K. (1990). Crime placement, displacement and deflection. *Crime and Justice: A Review of Research*, 12, 277–318.
Beauregard, E., Rossmo, D. K., and Proulx, J. (2007). A descriptive model of the hunting process of serial sex offenders: A rational choice perspective. *Journal of Family Violence*, 22(6), 449–63.
Clarke, R. V. G. (1980). Situational crime prevention: Theory and practice. *British Journal of Criminology*, 20(2), 136–47.
Clarke, R. V. (1983). Situational crime prevention: Its theoretical basis and practical scope. *Crime and Justice: An Annual Review of Research*, 4, 225–56.

Clarke, R. V. (1992). *Situational crime prevention: Successful case studies.* New York, NY: Harrow and Heston.

Clarke, R. V. (1997). *Situational crime prevention: Successful case studies*, 2nd edition. Monsey, NY: Criminal Justice Press.

Clarke, R. V. and Cornish, D. B. (1985). Modeling offenders' decisions: A framework for research and policy. *Crime and Justice: An Annual Review of Research*, 6, 147–85.

Clarke, R. V. and Mayhew, P. (1988). The British gas suicide story and its criminological implications. *Crime and Justice: An Annual Review of Research*, 10, 79–116.

Cornish, D. B. and Clarke, R. V. (1986a). *The reasoning criminal: Rational choice perspectives on offending.* New York, NY: Springer-Verlag.

Cornish, D. B. and Clarke, R. V. (1986b). Situational prevention, displacement of crime and rational choice theory. In K. Heal and G. Laycock (eds.), *Situational crime prevention: From theory into practice* (pp. 1–16). London, UK: HMSO.

Cornish, D. B. and Clarke, R. V. G. (1987). Understanding crime displacement: An application of rational choice theory. *Criminology*, 25(4), 933–47.

Cornish, D. B. and Clarke, R. V. (1989). Crime specialisation, crime displacement and rational choice theory. In H. Wegener, F. Lösel, and J. Haish (eds.), *Criminal behavior and the justice system: Psychological perspectives* (pp. 102–17). New York, NY: Springer-Verlag.

Cromwell, P. F., Olson, J. N., and Avary, D. W. (1991). *Breaking and entering: An ethnographic analysis of burglary.* Newbury Park, CA: Sage Publications.

Eck, J. E. (1993). The threat of crime displacement. *Criminal Justice Abstracts*, 25(3), 527–46.

Felson, M. and Clarke, R. V. (1998). *Opportunity makes the thief: Practical theory for crime prevention.* London, UK: Home Office, Policing and Reducing Crime Unit Research, Development and Statistics Directorate.

Gabor, T. (1981). The crime displacement hypothesis: An empirical examination. *Crime and Delinquency*, 26, 390–404.

Goertzel, V., Goertzel, M. G., Goertzel, T. G., and Hansen, A. (2004). *Cradles of eminence: Childhoods of more than 700 famous men and women*, 2nd edition. Scottsdale, AZ: Great Potential Press.

Gottfredson, M. R. and Hirschi, T. (1990). *A general theory of crime.* Stanford, CA: Stanford University Press.

Guerette, R. T. (2009). *Analyzing crime displacement and diffusion*, Tool Guide no. 10. Washington, DC: Center for Problem-Oriented Policing.

Hesseling, R. B. P. (1994). Displacement: A review of the empirical literature. *Crime Prevention Studies*, 3, 197–230.

Hirschi, T. and Gottfredson, M. (1983). Age and the explanation of crime. *American Journal of Sociology*, 89(3), 552–84.

Klein, G. A. (1999). *Sources of power: How people make decisions.* Cambridge, MA: MIT Press.

Klein, G. A. (2004). *The power of intuition: How to use your gut feelings to make better decisions at work.* New York, NY: Doubleday.

Klein, G. A. (2009). *Streetlights and shadows: Searching for the keys to adaptive decision making.* Cambridge, MA: MIT Press.

Kreitman, N. (1976). The coal gas story: United Kingdom suicide rates, 1960–71. *British Journal of Preventive and Social Medicine*, 30(2), 86–93.

Kreitman, N. and Platt, S. (1984). Suicide, unemployment, and domestic gas detoxification in Britain. *Journal of Epidemiology and Community Health*, 38(1), 1–6.

Mayhew, P. M., Clarke, R. V., Sturman, A., and Hough, M. (1976). *Crime as opportunity.* Home Office Research Study no. 34. London, UK: HMSO.

Reppetto, T. A. (1976). Crime prevention and the displacement phenomenon. *Crime and Delinquency*, 22(2), 166–77.

Simon, H. A. (1957). *Models of man, social and rational: Mathematical essays on rational human behavior in a social setting*. New York, NY: John Wiley & Sons.

Simon, H. A. (1982). *Models of bounded rationality*, 3 vols. Cambridge, MA: MIT Press.

Weisburd, D., Wyckoff, L. A., Ready, J., Eck, J. E., Hinkle, J. C., and Gajewski, F. (2006). Does crime just move around the corner? A controlled study of spatial displacement and diffusion of crime control benefits. *Criminology*, 44(3), 549–91.

Wilkinson, P. (1977). *Terrorism and the liberal state*. London, UK: Macmillan.

Chapter 6

Pattern theory of crime

Introduction

In the previous three chapters covering routine activity theory, geometric theory of crime, and rational choice theory, we have considered an overall perspective that focuses on criminal events. This should be painfully obvious at this point. Additionally, aside from some of the considerations in rational choice theory, motivation exists and this motivation may have rather diverse sources such as social, cultural, biological, economic, and so on. This motivation for criminal events is present in order to meet certain goals that may be monetary profit, status, or even domination. Most often, criminal events come about because of ordinary non-criminal activities undertaken throughout the day. Therefore, one may stumble across a criminal opportunity that cannot be resisted. Or, alternatively, someone may actively seek out criminal opportunities and intersect with those who are undertaking non-criminal activities.

These resulting criminal events are best seen as the result of a decision-making process that is deemed, in most cases, rational—most likely limited or bounded rational using heuristics. Target suitability depends not only on the target itself, but the surroundings of that target. This, of course, is referring to the environmental backcloth: a house may be a very attractive target for a residential burglary because of all the goods inside, but it is well guarded with someone always home. And this suitability is also tied into the crime template. The crime template is developed from cues emitted from the environment that allow a potential offender to identify good targets versus bad targets. And these crime templates, though varying from crime type to crime type and place to place, are relatively fixed once they are established, though they do change and adapt if the environmental cue pattern changes.

The connectedness between these three environmental criminology theories should be apparent in these two relatively short paragraphs. Now we will cover the pattern theory of crime—that is, an attempt to synthesize these different theories within environmental criminology into one connected theory of crime, a metatheory.

Turning our attention to a *pattern* theory of crime, however, forces us to ask ourselves what a pattern actually is. The definition we will use here is a recognizable interconnectedness of objects, processes, or ideas. This interconnectedness may be physical (on a map, for example) or it may be conceptual, linking ideas in your mind. Sometimes patterns are obvious, but other times the information available must be scrutinized to discover the pattern because it is so subtle. Patterns matter, particularly for human activities, because we are creatures of habit. There are patterns to our daily lives, as discussed in the previous chapters, in the ways, times, and how we move through the urban (or rural) landscape. This is why criminal activity is neither randomly nor uniformly distributed across space. This is also why the environmental backcloth matters. The environmental backcloth consists of the economic, socio-cultural, legal, and physical surroundings that necessarily also includes the (routine) activities of the population. Therefore, the environmental backcloth is patterned.

Consequently, any theory of crime really should be able to explain criminal events with different, or changing, environmental backcloths because the patterns of daily life do change over time. This does not mean that all possible backcloths must be explicitly included in the theoretical framework, because that would effectively be an infinite number of environmental backcloths. But any theory of crime should allow for changes in that environmental backcloth. This is precisely what routine activity theory did through the incorporation of changed routine activities, a changed sexual composition of the workforce, and educational student body, and, of course, the changed inertia of consumer goods. The pattern theory of crime expands upon the flexibility of routine activity theory by showing its relationship to the other theoretical frameworks within environmental criminology.

Pattern theory of crime

The previous chapters on the theories within environmental criminology, and social disorganization theory, all contained a substantive section discussing metaphysics. This was done because metaphysics are an important aspect of theory, because anyone using a theory should know what it simply assumes to be true. No such section is necessary for the pattern theory of crime. This is the case because the metaphysical aspects of routine activity theory, geometric theory of crime, and rational choice theory all apply to the pattern theory of crime.

Figure 6.1 is the first of a set of flowcharts representing the pattern theory of crime. This flowchart shows a general representation of a criminal event. An individual is simply doing something, their current actions. It does not matter what these actions are, but for simplicity we shall assume that these are legal actions. Then something happens: the triggering event. These triggering events may be simple or complex, they may occur when the individual is alone or in a group, what is a triggering event for one individual may not be a triggering event for another, and they may have an immediate effect or start another process altogether. Such a triggering event could be stumbling across an opportunity that cannot be resisted (minimal search) or something resulting from peer pressure or some form of initiation, for example (broader search).

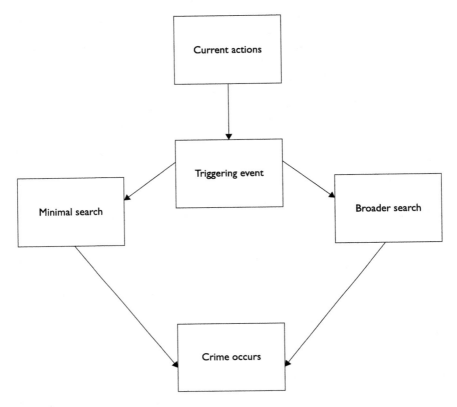

Figure 6.1 The general criminal process.
Source: Adapted from Brantingham and Brantingham (1993b).

Moving on to a more complex process, Figure 6.2 incorporates routine activity theory, geometric theory of crime, and rational choice theory—rational choice theory is operating in the background at all times. Routine activity theory is very easy to incorporate because routine activities represent the source of an individual's current actions. Of course, an individual's current actions will include non-routine activities from time to time, but it is important to recognize that non-routine activities are not reinforced in this representation.

Routine activity theory has another dimension that is tied to the geometric theory of crime through the concepts of activity space and awareness space. As discussed in Chapter 4 on the geometric theory of crime, we develop an awareness space because we spend significant portions of our time in particular places; consequently, our awareness and activity spaces are part and parcel of our routine activities. In fact, it could be argued that the geometric theory of crime is at least partially a spatial representation of routine activity theory. And because a potential offender will want to commit crime in areas where s/he is most comfortable, if at

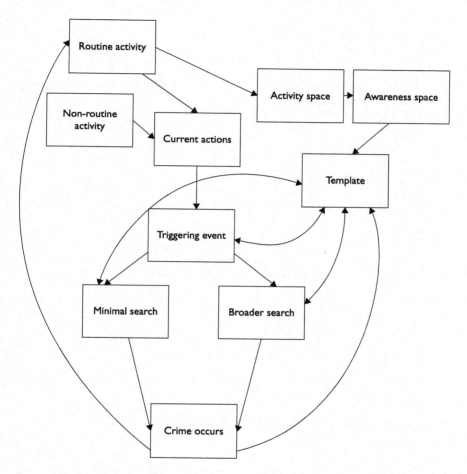

Figure 6.2 The general criminal process and activities.
Source: Adapted from Brantingham and Brantingham (1993b).

all possible, a potential offender's awareness space affects their crime template. At this stage, there are now two things feeding into the triggering event.

This is the stage in which the crime template "allows" us to perceive a triggering event as a triggering event: we are able to recognize an opportunity that is placed before us. This may appear to be tautological, but if an individual has such a restrictive crime template that the individual would essentially never commit a crime, an obvious criminal opportunity may not even be recognized. As shown in Figure 6.2, the connection between the crime template and the triggering event is bidirectional. This is because the successful recognition of a criminal opportunity (or not) will then impact the crime template such that the crime template is reinforced if the triggering event turns out to have been correct or the

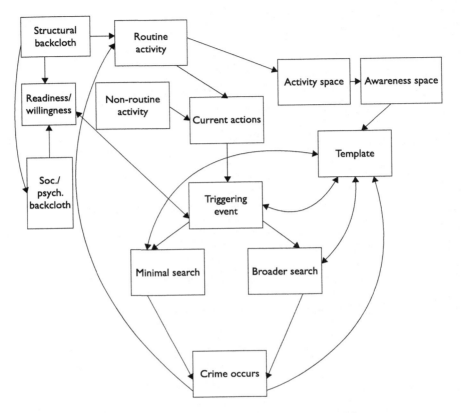

Figure 6.3 The general criminal process, activities, and motivation.
Source: Adapted from Brantingham and Brantingham (1993b).

crime template is modified because the triggering event turns out to have been incorrect.

Because of the triggering event, the search process begins a minimal or broader search process. Whether this search process is minimal or broader will be identified through the crime template. Simultaneously, the success or failure within each of these search processes again informs the crime template such that it is reinforced or modified. Finally, the criminal event occurs and has two effects. First, it either reinforces or modifies the crime template, in combination with the triggering event and the search process. Such reinforcements or modifications will help the offender identify "good" and "bad" targets in the future. And, second, the criminal event affects the offender's routine activities in at least three ways. First, if the particular criminal event was rooted in established routine activities and successful, then there would be no reason to modify the current routine activities. Second, if the particular criminal event was rooted in current routine activities and the routine activities were part of a broader unsuccessful search (this connection is not shown to keep the flowchart as simple as possible), there may be a need to alter routine activities because the area in which the unsuccessful event took place may need to be removed from the offender's awareness space. And third, if the particular criminal event were rooted in non-routine activities and the criminal event was a success, the offender may wish to modify his/her routine activities to incorporate these current actions.

The last flowchart, Figure 6.3, adds in the final complications related to the backcloths. The backcloths are used to show their impacts on routine activities as well as generating the motivation to commit criminal events. The structural, or environmental, backcloth's effect is the simplest to recognize. This is the backcloth that includes the built environment (roads, buildings, other infrastructure). Routine activities are necessarily undertaken within some sort of urban or rural landscape and that landscape is defined by where roads are, where workplaces are, and where recreational activities are located. So, we are at the mercy of urban planners, for better or worse.

This structural or environmental backcloth, primarily through the locations available for us to live in, will also affect our other backcloth: the social/ psychological/economic/legal backcloth. This, in turn, affects our motivations though readiness and/or willingness. As discussed above, this is incorporated within the crime template as well: an incredibly restrictive crime template really implies a lack of readiness and/or willingness to commit a crime. However, this link, though present, is more subtle and is left out of this flowchart for simplicity.

The importance of the pattern theory of crime

Though the three theories within environmental criminology are always presented together and the commonalities between the three theories may be apparent, the pattern theory of crime adds a lot of value in terms of theory by explicitly showing how these three theories are connected using the flow charts above. Moreover, the process of showing that all three of the theories within environmental criminology are connected and part of a general pattern of ideas is important for the understanding of the criminal event. The pattern theory of crime is important because it highlights the cohesiveness of the field of environmental criminology. The three theories within environmental criminology are concerned with the environment within which crime occurs: routine activity theory is concerned with changes or variations in the social environment that lead to changes in crime rates, the geometric theory of crime is concerned with the built environment and how it shapes the geographic pattern of crime, and rational choice theory is concerned with the cognitive environment that governs the choice-structuring processes of potential offenders. On their own, each of these theories significantly adds to our understanding of crime and the criminal event, but collectively they are able to provide a meaningful representation of the environment within which crime occurs.

The pattern theory of crime also reveals the benefits of a metatheory by revealing the increased complexity through the connections between the three theories. The pattern theory of crime emphasizes the dynamic nature of the decision-making process to commit a criminal event at a particular time and a particular place through the use of feedback loops. The crime template affects, and is affected by, the commission (or avoidance) of criminal events, which in turn affects our routine activities, activity space, and awareness space. A change at any point within this interconnectedness sends a ripple effect through the decision-making processes that encompass the pattern theory of crime, and its respective theories. Consequently, this interconnectedness is at the heart of this spatial-temporal investigation of crime and the criminal event. This is the recognition that change, or the dynamic nature of our environment, is inherent in our understanding of the criminal event. Recognizing this importance of change only serves to further legitimize the field of environmental criminology within the broader criminological literature. This is because the theories within environmental criminology seek to explain not only the old facts of criminal behavior, but new ones as well. As a result, it is important to understand where these theories of environmental criminology came from and how they are related so that we can see where they are going and how they are changing.

Review questions

1   According to crime pattern theory, a criminal event has two effects. State and explain what those effects are.
2   In the grand scheme of things, what does crime pattern theory do within environmental criminology?

Reference

Brantingham, P. L. and Brantingham, P. J. (1993b). Environment, routine, and situation: Toward a pattern theory of crime. In R. V. Clarke and M. Felson (eds.), *Routine activity and rational choice*, vol. 5 (pp. 259–94). New Brunswick, NJ: Transaction Publishers.

Chapter 7

Crime prevention

Introduction

Crime prevention has always been at the heart of environmental criminology. In fact, C. Ray Jeffery coined the term "environmental criminology" on the last page of his 1971 book, *Crime Prevention Through Environmental Design* (Jeffery, 1971, p. 279). As we will discuss below, crime prevention was based on theoretical frameworks quite different from what we call environmental criminology today. These theoretical frameworks were used to justify crime prevention activities. But, as you know well by now, environmental criminology has developed its own set of theories that are now the theoretical support for crime prevention. As such, crime prevention and environmental criminology theories have come full circle.

Before we get into too much discussion regarding crime prevention, it is important to recognize the different ways we can organize what we call crime prevention. Specifically, I am referring to the time frames involved for preventing crime. In 1976, Paul Brantingham and Frederic Faust published a journal article on just such an organizational structure. They borrowed an idea from the medical field and applied it to criminology: the primary, secondary, and tertiary levels of prevention. In the context of health, primary prevention involves aspects of life such as a good diet and exercise, a long-term view of health. Secondary prevention involves recognizing things like family history of disease and screening for early detection; secondary prevention has a short- to medium-term time horizon. And tertiary prevention is treatment that one receives when already sick. In this case, you are dealing with symptoms, and so on. Tertiary prevention has an immediate time horizon.

As shown by Brantingham and Faust, it is rather simple to adapt this model of prevention to crime prevention. Treatment, punishment, and placing people in prison is tertiary prevention. When this is done, only *further* crime is "prevented" because at least one criminal event must have been committed to be involved with this stage of the criminal justice system. Secondary prevention attempts to identify *potential* offenders and keep them busy in legitimate activities. This could, perhaps, be used to identify a potential offender and get him (usually a young male) involved in a local community club such as a Boys & Girls Club. And primary prevention would be along the lines of preventing crime from occurring in the first place. This may take several forms, but in the context of environmental criminology it most often involves the modification of the environment within which crime occurs—environmental design. The term "environment" can be quite broad or quite narrow, as discussed below, but it was quite distinct from the crime prevention methods that were dominant before C. Ray Jeffery published his research in this area. Examples of such crime prevention may include designing mass transit stations to prevent motivated offenders from hanging around to rob people, or designing a neighborhood such that it is difficult for non-residents to find their way in or out because of a convoluted street network.

This Primary–Secondary–Tertiary (PST) crime prevention model (see Table 7.1) proves to be very useful in helping to understand the place of many crime prevention initiatives. Different people have different definitions of what crime prevention is and having the PST model in place allows everyone to see where (or when) their crime prevention initiative fits. This may also prove to be instructive because with this general model of crime prevention in place, and the ability to see the time frame of any particular crime prevention initiative, it may lead to individuals altering their view of crime prevention. If, for example, someone or some agency is trying to implement or promote some policy for the purposes of primary prevention and find that the said policy is in the realm of secondary or even tertiary prevention, their views may be altered.

As will be clear below, crime prevention within environmental criminology spans all of the primary, secondary, and tertiary categories. However, crime prevention within environmental criminology is most often seen "in action" in the context of primary and tertiary prevention. The influential role of the environment

Table 7.1 The Primary–Secondary–Tertiary model of crime prevention

	Crime Prevention		
	Primary	Secondary	Tertiary
The general paradigm	• Environmental design • General social and physical wellbeing programs • Crime prevention education	• Early identification • Pre-delinquent screening • Individual intervention • Neighborhood programs	• Community treatment • Institutional treatment • Punishment • Training • Support • Surveillance • Institutional custody
Time horizon	Long	Short to medium	Immediate

Source: Adapted from Brantingham and Faust (1976).

on crime has been recognized for a very long time, predating environmental criminology by at least seventy years. Enrico Ferri, in his 1896 book *Criminal Sociology*, noted the importance of the built (and natural) environment in the following quotation:

> High roads, railways and tramways disperse predatory bands in rural districts, just as wide streets and large and airy dwellings, with public lighting and the destruction of slums prevent robbery with violence, concealment of stolen goods, and indecent assaults.

> (Ferri, 1896, p. 123)

This is a very clear statement that the built environment has a significant impact on the criminal event. The purpose of crime prevention, however, is not just to recognize this relationship, but to modify the built environment in order to prevent criminal events from occurring in the first place.

An important point to make at this juncture is that we must be careful how we modify the environment in order to prevent criminal events from occurring. There are those who take an extreme view of the importance of altering the environment: environmental determinists. This is a view of the world that states that the nature of our environment determines (without randomness) our behavior. This mode of thought existed in human geography in the early twentieth century, has appeared more recently in economics, and had its day in the relationship between housing and crime. Essentially, it was assumed that bad housing makes for bad behavior. Consequently, all we have to do to eliminate crime is to eliminate bad housing, particularly the slums, and provide good (public) housing for those who need it—this comes from the socialist architecture literature in the 1920s.

At this point in this textbook, I would hope you would be asking questions such as: Will this really work? Would simply replacing bad housing for good housing affect crime? Would this alter the levels of social organization in a neighborhood? Would it alter routine activities? Would the geography of opportunity really change in a positive manner? How would this alter the (rational) choices of offenders? Forgetting about the theoretical difficulties such a plan had, the plan to replace housing failed miserably, partially because slum replacement is expensive and partially because it only made things worse. Overall, the slum replacement projects were a disaster. They were tried in St. Louis, New York, and Chicago. In the end, social problems got worse, crime and victimization increased, the housing stock was devastated, and the projects became known as "dreadful enclosures," meaning that they were horrible places to live and spend your time in. In the end, these projects were abandoned and blown up.

Even if we forget about the huge costs involved for such an endeavor, it is critical to remember that the built environment is only one part of the criminal event. The built environment is an important part and it can be used to reduce and/or prevent criminal events, but this cannot be the only tactic. This is why the socialist architects failed: they thought that everyone would react in a very predictable way, but they did not. This is the danger of thinking that anything is deterministic. At best, we can hope for stochastic processes—in a stochastic process there is a deterministic component because we expect people to act in a particular way, on average, but we recognize that there is "randomness" in human behavior. Based on the material covered for rational choice theory, Chapter 5, there is no randomness, only individual rationality. However, for the purposes of understanding what will happen when a given crime prevention initiative will be implemented, we can consider these individual rationalities to be "random." The critical factor is simply recognizing that not all people will react to a crime prevention initiative in the same manner.

C. Ray Jeffery and CPTED

C. Ray Jeffery put forth his crime prevention through environmental design because of his frustration with the view of crime prevention in the 1960s, when he was working in this field. At this time, and continuing today, there were two approaches considered: the deterrence-punishment model and the treatment-rehabilitation model.

The police are the most visible aspect of the deterrence model. They operate under the assumption that if potential offenders are detected, arrested, and punished the criminal event volume (and corresponding rate) will decrease. This assumption originates from Jeremy Bentham, Cesare Beccaria, and the Classical School of Criminology: potential offenders have free will and, therefore, punishment can be a deterrent to criminal activity if it is swift and sure. However, in order for the police to be effective at this strategy they must, of course, be swift and provide the evidence of punishment for a broader society in order to act as a deterrent. Needless to say, the police get rather frustrated when criminals are released from the criminal justice system based on some legal technicality. As such, even if the police are swift and able to move criminals into the criminal justice system, it will become well known by criminals and non-criminals alike that they may be released on a technicality. Consequently, the view that the police are any threat becomes challenged.

How effective are the police? Though police presence has consistently shown in the recent empirical literature to have a deterrence effect on crime (Nagin, 2013; Ratcliffe et al., 2011; Weisburd et al., 2006), approximately 20–25 percent of property offences are cleared by an arrest. That simply means that 75–80 percent of property offences do not result in an arrest, let alone a charge. So, right from the beginning of the process any offender has a relatively low chance of getting caught for a property offence. In a recent report on the activities undertaken by the Royal Canadian Mounted Police (RCMP), 1983–2003, by researchers in British Columbia (Malm et al., 2005) it was found that the time taken for the police to handle a case increased radically during this time. In fact, the time spent per case increased between 50 and 1,000 percent, depending on the crime type—most of this increase related to paperwork. In the 1970s, a RCMP sworn member would spend 1.5 hours per day undertaking administration and paperwork, but by 2003 that had increased to 4 hours per day. It is unlikely that these burdens have decreased over the past decade. While on patrol, up to 80 percent of a police officer's time was spent doing "paperwork" on mobile terminals. Based on these necessary activities of the police, how much can we expect them to do?

The courts, much like the police, are only involved in the criminal process once a criminal event has been committed. Consequently, very few criminals actually make it through to the court system. So how can this be a meaningful way to prevent crime? Perhaps we can get more criminals into the court system? But how long does it take to get some cases to trial now? What happened to swift and sure punishment? How large a monstrosity would the court system have to be if arrest rates were only to double? Aside from being a significant benefit to graduates from criminology programs for employment, is this a feasible and optimal option?

Perhaps prison is a deterrent? Officially, depending upon the research study, less than 5 percent of criminals are in prison. Some estimates are as low as 2 percent. The threat of imprisonment is very weak, at best, and certainly not swift and sure.

So what are we left with? The police are not able to arrest enough people, the courts do not prosecute and convict enough people, and correctional facilities (prisons or otherwise) do not deter criminals. But what about those who actually make it through the system and go to some form of prison for their criminal events? Depending upon the study and the country involved in the study, anywhere from 50 to 75 percent of the prison population had been in prison before and would be in prison again. Many of these criminals were violent criminals as well.

In the 1970s, a National Advisory Commission on Standards and Goals in the United States concluded that punishment was a failure. Treatment was harsh, treatment was a failure, and recidivism continued unchanged (Jeffery, 1971). In spite of this "ruling" more than forty years ago, we still hear that the war on crime must be won and the most common "weapon" is building more prisons. Perhaps the treatment-rehabilitation model has fared better than the deterrence-punishment model?

The primary method of the treatment-rehabilitation model (in the context here, we are considering this model at the time C. Ray Jeffery wrote his book) is for the treatment of individuals or groups in therapy. This therapy may occur either inside or outside of prison. However, this therapeutic view of the world is fundamentally flawed for one important reason, that I argue is still an issue today. In a therapeutic case, success is deemed to have occurred if the individual or group adapts or adjusts well to the therapeutic environment. But it is the environment within which the "bad" behavior manifested itself that is the problem. Just as prisons are not capable of transferring their control over prisoners once they have been released into the outside world, neither can the therapist control the non-therapeutic environment. In the context of prison, it is ironic that a prisoner can be released early because of good behavior despite the fact that the individual was in prison (and will likely return to prison) because of bad behavior. These situations are analogous.

Because of the failures of these models, generally speaking—there have definitely been successes, but not at a systemic scale—C. Ray Jeffery wanted to put forth a different view of crime prevention. This different view had the goal of preventing criminal events from occurring in the first place, not after the criminal event had already occurred in hopes of preventing *further* criminal events. C. Ray Jeffery pioneered crime prevention as it is most often undertaken today, crime prevention through environmental design (CPTED). There are two other forms of crime prevention: Oscar Newman's crime prevention through urban design (CPTUD) and crime prevention through social development (CPTSD). We will not cover CPTSD here, but the interested reader may consult Canadian Council on Social Development (1984); this approach to crime prevention considers factors such as family, school, employment, drugs and alcohol, media, and health. These are clearly important aspects of good governance, more generally, and do not obviously fall under the umbrella of environmental criminology. In fact, as you will recall from Chapter 3 on routine activity theory, many of the factors that the CPTSD approach considers crime prevention were very good and/or getting better when crime rates were skyrocketing during the 1950s and 1960s. Regardless, even though CPTSD may not obviously be a part of environmental criminology, it does have a place within the PST Model. CPTSD would fall under primary crime prevention because it addresses general social and physical wellbeing. One could argue that CPTSD is part of the environment within which crime occurs, so it may be subsumed under the broad category of CPTED. Though C. Ray Jeffery does not consider CPTSD in his books, he does consider the work of Oscar Newman and CPTUD a subset of CPTED.

When C. Ray Jeffery developed CPTED, he assumed that there was a complex human–environment interaction and that this interaction produced probabilistic effects. This harks back to the attempts of crime prevention that assumed a deterministic process, discussed above. C. Ray Jeffery did not believe that there was a deterministic process, only a relationship. However, that relationship was strong enough to justify the implementation of changes in the environment to prevent criminal events. C. Ray Jeffery's CPTED environment is a complex idea, as it should be and is considered in the subsequent theories within environmental criminology—explicitly so in Chapter 4 on the geometric theory of crime. People interact with and adapt to their environment. Some environments make criminal events easier to commit than other environments, as evidenced by the nature of spatial crime patterns—criminal events are most often quite clustered in particular areas. As such, we should be able to modify existing environments to make non-criminal behavior the fittest adaptation. This simply means that potential offenders will undertake non-criminal activities if particular environments are developed and, hence, prevent criminal events; in other words, the environment can be made such that potential criminals never realize their criminal potential.

This work by C. Ray Jeffery was based on the assumption of experimental psychology, particularly within the field of behavioral learning theory based on the work of Ivan Pavlov and Burrhus Frederic Skinner—most people have heard of Pavlov's dog. Rooted in behavioral learning theory, Jeffery's CPTED approach emphasized the role of the physical environment in the development of pleasurable and painful experiences for the potential offender that would have the capacity to alter the behavioral outcomes of the potential offender. In the context of crime prevention, a pleasurable experience would be a successful commission of a criminal event and a painful experience would be an unsuccessful commission of a criminal event, with the latter either having the offender caught in some manner or simply not obtaining the desired outcome. In C. Ray Jeffery's original formulation of CPTED, he considered the stimulus-response model that put forth that the organism (people in the crime prevention context) learned from punishments and reinforcements in their environment. Consequently, Jeffery emphasized the use of material rewards and the use of the physical environment to control behavior. The primary idea was that by removing the reinforcements for criminal events, criminal events would be prevented. It is important to recognize here that C. Ray Jeffery focused on removing the reinforcements. In the stimulus-response model, in order to decrease the rate of occurrence of some phenomenon, one can provide an aversive stimulus (physical pain response) or remove the reinforcing stimulus (the pleasure response); the former is rather difficult to implement in a free society!

The stimulus-response model is a purely environmental model, meaning that there is no presence of genetic or biological aspects of behavior. Because of this, the stimulus-response model is at times referred to as the model of the empty organism. This is purely a nurture-based model of behavior that is successful through compliance to an authority of some form. But what happens to such compliance once the authority figure is gone? Did you behave differently when your parental units or guardians were not able to observe your behavior?

C. Ray Jeffery's environment was rather complex, including the physical design of places, but also the legal and societal situations. By controlling this environment the optimal choice for people would be non-criminal adaptations that would be engineered, but "good" behavior would not be internalized. The response in the stimulus-response model was an externally stimulated response. In other words, this view of environmental control did not socialize law-abiding citizens, but people who learned what they needed to do in order to get the reward they wanted or avoid certain punishment. You could argue that this was not a problem, per se, because if the environment was designed "properly" the desired response would occur. The trouble was that if the environment was not designed properly, it failed for some reason, or the environment changed because we are in a constant state of flux, we would be back to square one again.

In order to address this limitation of CPTED, in the second edition of his book C. Ray Jeffery incorporated the biosocial learning model, or biological behavioralism. As with the stimulus-response model, the biosocial learning model was an environmental model that had the physical environment affecting behavior, but in a far more complicated way. The complication was involved with the intervening organism, us. The biosocial learning model stated that the environmental conditions that led to behaviors occurred within and through the brain and the central nervous system. The important difference between the biosocial learning model and the stimulus-response model was that our actions, or reactions, were not simply hard-wired genetic code that manifested through instinct. Rather, we interpreted and reacted based on what we had learned. If all we had was a pure environmental approach there would be no room for individuality and we would essentially be moving back toward a deterministic model of behavior.

C. Ray Jeffery justified the importance of such an approach through a comparison of the various types of adaptation modes for different species on the planet. The adaption modes are taxes, reflex, instinct, learning, and reasoning. Taxes are very simple reactions to stimuli such as turning away from a bright light, reflexes are involuntary responses such as pulling your hand away from a hot surface after touching it, and instinct is an inborn pattern of activity of tendency to action that is common to a given biological species, such as a common fear of another particular species. Of course, we all use the adaptation modes of taxes, reflex, and instinct, but the primary adaptation modes for humans are learning and reasoning. Consequently, if there is any effort to change our collective behavior it must be rooted in a learning and reasoning perspective or it is bound to fail; hence the importance of rational choice theory within environmental criminology and crime prevention, more generally.

Though we no longer discuss the theoretical frameworks used to justify CPTED, stimulus-response and biosocial learning, it is important to know where this approach to crime prevention initially came from. This is similar to the metaphysics discussed for the theoretical frameworks within environmental criminology.

C. Ray Jeffery's model of crime prevention through environmental design is represented as a flowchart in Figure 7.1. The stream on the left of Figure 7.1 states that we should reward lawful behavior, remove the reward for crime, and impose certain enforcement. In its rawest sense, this stream is based on a stimulus-response model: in order to prevent crime, we either reward or punish and any enforcement of reward and punishment must be swift. As stated above, this view stems back to the Classical School of Criminology operating on pain and pleasure. But it is not quite that simple, because an adaptation does occur in which the person learns non-criminal activities. This is important for Jeffery because this adaptation is a biosocial learning process. Because of the increased cost of crime and decreased reward, the potential offender desists from criminal activity. The empirical crime prevention literature, briefly discussed in Chapter 5 on rational choice theory, repeatedly finds support for this hypothesis. The question is whether or not people

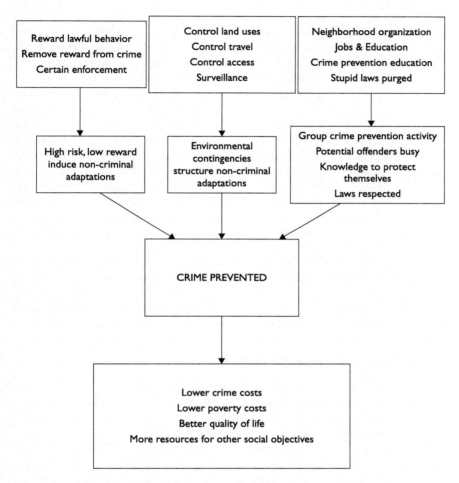

Figure 7.1 C. Ray Jeffery's crime prevention through environmental design.

continue to choose non-criminal adaptation once the situation reverts to its original state.

The middle stream is more of a long-term phenomenon that definitely has the potential to be along the lines of the biosocial learning model used in the second rendition of CPTED. This stream includes activities such as designing streets that make quick getaways rather difficult: a convoluted street network discourages criminal activity (residential burglary, in particular) relative to a Manhattan Grid street network (Beavon et al., 1994; Johnson and Bowers, 2010). This may be done not only through street design, but housing orientation and city planning that considers the placement of different land uses in an area. An example of this type of planning can include actions to separate potential offenders from potential victims through the design of a transit station; these locations often become hangouts for teenagers, so it is important to design the transit station such that the convergences of these two populations occur as little as possible (Felson et al., 1996). Again, the end goal is to create the environmental conditions such that non-criminal activities become the fittest adaptive behavior.

And lastly, the third stream is dominantly an education view of CPTED. Neighborhood organization sends an environmental cue to a potential offender that they will be watched if they enter the neighborhood: their actions will be noticed by a number of people in the neighborhood even if the potential victim of crime is not present. Jobs and education keep potential offenders busy, much like the community clubs keep youth busy and, hopefully, out of trouble. Crime prevention education keeps the public up to speed on classic and the most recently developed crime prevention initiatives—as discussed in Chapter 14, this becomes very important in the context of (near-)repeat victimization. Lastly, the purging of what Jeffery refers to as stupid laws is supposed to lead to people respecting the laws that are actually in place.

Overall, C. Ray Jeffery's crime prevention through environmental design posits continuous interacting effects between organisms and their environment that have reciprocal influences on one another. These continuous interacting effects operate at all levels of analysis from the cell to society and matter for genetics, the brain and nervous system, the individual, the group, the community, and society.

Oscar Newman and CPTUD

Oscar Newman's crime prevention through urban design (CPTUD) and the corresponding concept of defensible space came to be at approximately the same time as C. Ray Jeffery's CPTED. C. Ray Jeffery's book was published in late 1971 and Oscar Newman's book was published early 1972. Curiously, these two authors were both working at the same time in New York and even lived in the same area but did not know about each other's research. C. Ray Jeffery's research was based on more of a theoretical level, whereas Oscar Newman's research was based on the context of public housing in New York, but the concepts are relevant for all architecture. Oscar Newman started his book in a similar manner as C. Ray Jeffery did, proclaiming that the crime problem would not be solved with more police. However, Oscar Newman did not go off on a 200-page rant to support his claim. Rather, he went into practical applications of modifying the existing environment to prevent crime. This is likely one of the reasons why Oscar Newman's work received more attention than that of C. Ray Jeffery—C. Ray Jeffery acknowledged this in the second edition of his book, published in 1977.

Aside from the claim that more police would not solve the crime problem, Oscar Newman also stated that there was a lack of a social framework that allowed for a heterogeneous group of neighbors to take collective action against crime. He was clearly harking back to the Chicago School, social disorganization theory, in that a lack of social organization was conducive to crime. As we shall see, much of Newman's treatments for crime problem areas was to create or expand social organization in an area. Newman stated that the reason why this social framework did not emerge was not related to the issues that concerned social disorganization theory: population turnover and ethnic heterogeneity. Rather, it was because of the ways in which we had been building our cities, particularly since the end of the Second World War. As such, Newman believed that we needed to build neighborhoods that fostered the development of social cohesion through the development of what Newman called defensible space.

Defensible space, as defined by Oscar Newman, is a model of residential environments that inhibit crime by creating the physical expression of a social fabric that defends itself (Newman, 1972). So we have an environment that exhibits territorial behavior and a sense of community that translates into a safe, productive, and well-maintained place. In other words, defensible space develops an area that sends environmental cues to a potential offender who interprets these as showing that the area is not conducive to criminal activity. Consequently, I agree with C. Ray Jeffery that defensible space can be understood as a specific application of CPTED for one dimension of the environment: the architectural component of the built environment. Defensible space was intended to be a subtle establishment of boundaries that "outsiders" would interpret as territorial marking; these outsiders would be noticed by the residents even if only through their windows and the residents would be willing to act if necessary.

Two terms are worthy of specific definitions: "outsider" and "boundary." First, the outsider does not have to be someone from far away, just someone who does not have legitimate access to a particular area. Therefore, an outsider may literally be someone living two blocks away; those living in the area know who does and does not belong. Second, boundaries can be both real and symbolic. The real boundary is simple to understand, a fence for example. But the symbolic boundary tends to be far more subtle. Such boundaries could be a change in the surface of the walkway that symbolizes the movement from the public to the private sphere.

So how does one create defensible space? Oscar Newman identified four factors that were necessary to crease defensible space:

1 Create territoriality.
2 Provide natural surveillance.
3 Provide uniqueness of design to eliminate stigma and generate pride in residence.
4 Be cognizant of the geographic placement of "safe" and "unsafe" activities or areas.

When all of these factors are at least considered in an environment—they may not all be relevant in all cases—a defensible space would be created.

Territoriality is the capacity of the physical environment to create perceived zones of territorial influence. Because of the nature of its boundaries, territoriality will be quite clear in the context of a single-family detached home. These homes have their own plot of land, and when there is ownership there tends to be an increased interest in the presence of strangers. These homes will most often have fences, shrubs, bushes, and gates that mark off territory. However, it should be noted that just because you live in a single-family detached home does not mean that you have defined territoriality. All of the concepts of defensible space still need to be applied to this standard form of housing. But the point is that it is easier to establish territoriality and, hence, defensible space with the single-family detached home. And, as one moves to greater densities of housing such as row houses (townhomes), walk-up apartments, and high-rise apartments, the opportunity to define territory becomes increasingly difficult. This was what Oscar Newman saw as the primary problem in *some* of the public housing developments in New York.

An obvious question at this point is: How does one create territoriality? The first aspect of territoriality to consider is site design. For site design, there needs to be a strong signal to both residents and outsiders that the grounds the building is on, and the building itself, are for private use. This can be fairly easily done in a single high-rise that has a single entrance in the front with a doorman and, perhaps, some highly secure rear entrance for maintenance purposes. But, in the case of the housing projects studied by Oscar Newman and many townhouse and high-rise condominiums today, this is a rare phenomenon.

The second aspect of territoriality is what Newman calls the compositional versus the organic approach. This simply means that you do not want to consider each element in the complex as a separate entity—the compositional approach. Rather, you need to consider how the buildings and the grounds are organically interrelated. If you do not consider the interrelated nature of the various components of the complex, there may be "holes" in the site design such that the environmental cues perceived by a potential offender facilitate a criminal event.

And the third aspect of territoriality is street design. Though this is ideally undertaken at the original design process, it may also occur as a redesign, as has been the case, particularly in the United States. The redesign of the streets has the purpose of extending the territorial expression of the homes into the streets. The purpose of this action is to send a potential offender environmental cues repeatedly before they attempt to enter a residence, in the case of residential burglary. For some potential offenders, it may take a few "attempts" to send the environmental cue that this is not a good target for a criminal event. This can be done through the disruption of traffic flows by creating cul-de-sacs, for example, where children are more likely to play with their parental units or guardians watching. Alternatively, a whole portion of the street may be closed off to automotive traffic with the purpose of creating a play area for children and/or a communal area for everyone.

There are also smaller-scale methods to create territoriality that are mentioned by Oscar Newman, referred to as real and symbolic barriers—these have been discussed briefly above. Real barriers are walls, fences, locked gates, and doors; symbolic barriers are more subtle, including designs such as open gateways, a short run of steps, vegetation, or, as mentioned above, a change in the walking surface such as moving from concrete sidewalks to paving stones. Symbolic barriers send a signal to a person that they are moving from a public space (where their presence cannot be questioned) to a semi-public or semi-private space (where their presence can be questioned). Once again, this ties back to the environmental cues and the subsequent interpretations of a potential offender. In this sense, even some real barriers have the properties of symbolic barriers; a meter-high wall or fence with a gate is a real physical barrier, but it is hardly preventing people from entering because most people could simply step over the wall or fence. The point is that territory has been marked such that a person must make a conscious effort to cross over that boundary even though it really cannot keep them out.

Natural surveillance, in its most basic sense, is all about the site design of the area to facilitate people watching over their territory. This may be having your eyes on the street or a nosy neighbor, but the important aspect here is that the potential offender must get the environmental cue that s/he will be watched. Clearly, natural surveillance is necessarily related to territoriality because residents must be willing to act. If something were to happen, such as an outsider being noticed, residents must be willing to let that outsider know they are being watched, possibly with the authorities on their way—direct confrontation is not necessary. In order to accomplish this, the residents must necessarily develop territorial feelings with the willingness to defend that territory. The residents must understand that unwanted activity is actually occurring in their space, the residents need to have some form of identification or relationship with the victim (person or property), and the residents must believe that they are able to alter the course of events in their favor.

The uniqueness of design to eliminate stigma and generate pride in residence can be summarized in one word: image. Image relates to both territoriality and natural surveillance because the whole purpose of surveillance is to give residents the knowledge to be able to intervene, to some extent, once an outsider is identified. The point here is that housing, whether it is owned, rented, or provided by the government, should generate pride in residence.

And lastly for the development of defensible space is milieu, being cognizant of the geographic placement of "safe" and "unsafe" activities or areas. Safe and unsafe in this context can be thought of as preventing criminal events and facilitating criminal events, respectively. In any site design it may not be possible to address every single crime prevention issue, or they may at times be in conflict with one another. For example, it is generally a good idea to have entrances to a building close to places with high levels of pedestrian and automotive traffic. This is often done so that potential offenders cannot hide in the shadows of an isolated area waiting for suitable targets. However, by placing the entrance on the main road with pedestrian and automotive traffic, the risk of an outsider gaining access to the building increases. As such, the site designers and the residents must be aware of this situation. One potential solution to this issue is to put a highly used facility in the building by the front door so it can view those who come in and out of the building. Another example is that of the provision of neighborhood parks. Neighborhood parks can be a great facility in a residential neighborhood because there is a place for children to play. However, parks can also be great places to commit criminal events such as selling drugs or prostitution. Such activities may only emerge if there is no territorial aspect to the neighborhood park. One neighborhood park design that may prove to not be conducive to criminal events is one that can only be entered from one side, is relatively shallow, and is flanked by residences on the other sides. This would provide a lot of natural surveillance and, potentially, more territorial behavior, because the park may be seen as an extension of the yards of the residents.

With this view of how Oscar Newman views the establishment of defensible space, these ideas may now be summarized, like those of C. Ray Jeffery, in a flowchart, Figure 7.2. The stream on the far right in this flowchart, target hardening, is often considered in the realm of CPTED but it is included here as well because you can actually harden a target (making it more difficult to victimize) through architectural change. Probably the best way to think of this is through milieu and the geographic placement of safe and unsafe areas. Consider the example of the neighborhood park, discussed above, that is flanked by residences on three sides and all aspects of the neighborhood park are visible from all of those residences. A potential offender will most likely view this park as a bad place to commit criminal activity, of whatever type, so the potential offender perceives a hardened target and moves on. In this situation the hardened target is a place rather than a thing.

The second stream from the right, new territorial cues, is clearly related to the two streams on the left—I actually consider these two streams on the left one interrelated stream. They are related because they both invoke territoriality. However, territoriality can take two forms: passive and active. The stream of new territorial cues invokes passive territoriality. These new territorial cues are passive in this context because I am referring to the environmental/territorial cues that are interpreted by the potential offender through his/her perceptions of the environment that s/he has entered. Consider walking into one area that has a very sterile look to it, no marking of territory, property is damaged, graffiti, and litter. Such an area would not represent pride in ownership. Now consider walking into an area that is clean, well kept, and has territorial markers that are both real and symbolic (fencing, walls with open walkways, and a change in the walking surface, etc.). All of these property aspects indicate that you have moved from a public space to one that is either semi-public or semi-private. These are passive territorial cues that signal increased risk to a potential offender who then (hopefully) chooses non-criminal adaptations.

The last stream, the two boxes on the left, are what I consider to be the most important and are represented by the two most important dimensions of defensible

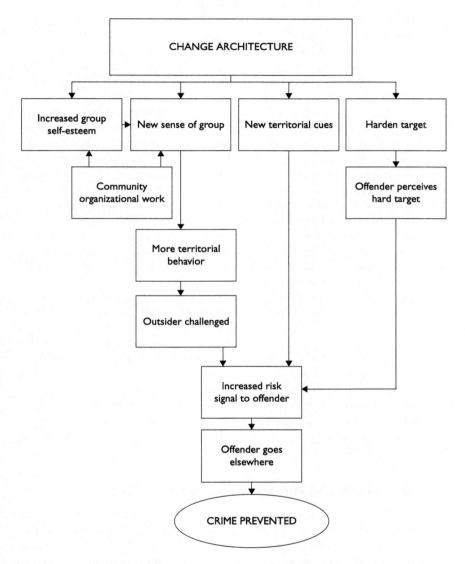

Figure 7.2 Oscar Newman's crime prevention through urban design.

space: territoriality and natural surveillance. This is the active form of territoriality because of one of the subsequent boxes in the flowchart: an outsider is challenged. And recall from above that this does not have to be a direct confrontation with a potential offender. Rather, this is the willingness to act, being seen in a window with a telephone in your hand with a focus on the behavior of the (potential) offender, for example. A change in architecture brings out an increased level of group self-esteem and a new sense of group. This may be in part because of a new image of the building that unifies the residents.

The primary way in which this prevents criminal events is through the establishment of territorial behavior, increased surveillance through the creation of zones of territorial influence (site design, an organic approach, street design, real and symbolic barriers), and convincing the residents that their actions make a difference. Subsequently, people begin to act in a territorial manner with direct impacts on criminal activity in the neighborhood. Therefore, the most critical box in this stream, and arguably the whole flowchart, is community organizational work. Without community organizational work, crime prevention activities are going to be limited both in terms of scope (how broadly the efforts will work) and for how long they will work. You cannot simply change a bit of architecture and expect a lot of change. This is why I do not focus much on the passive form of territoriality. Yes, passive territoriality alone may have an impact, but eventually potential offenders are going to realize that it is superficial. So, think of architecture as not having a direct deterministic impact on criminal activities. Architecture has an indirect impact through what it does to the residents, community organizational work.

This brings us back to Oscar Newman's statement that started his work on defensible space: there is a lack of a social framework that allows for a heterogeneous group of neighbors to take collective action against crime (Newman, 1972). So, it is not the architecture, per se, it is the creation of a social framework such that neighbors will take collective action that impacts criminal activity in their neighborhood. Consequently, when defensible space "fails" to have an impact on criminal activity it is because that social framework had not been generated, perhaps only passive territoriality for a short period of time. Rather than having an impact on the decision-making processes of a potential offender resulting in non-criminal adaptations, the potential offender interprets the environmental cues as not being a deterrent to criminal activity.

Marcus Felson and the changing metropolis

One aspect of crime prevention that has been discussed in the context of situational crime prevention, discussed further below, is that crime prevention initiatives must be specifically designed for the situation at hand. This means that different crime types will, most often, have different crime prevention initiatives to prevent their occurrence. This also means that crime prevention initiatives may vary from place to place and time to time. Considering a longer-term time frame, Marcus Felson articulated the importance of crime prevention activities in the ever-changing city (Felson, 1987).

Marcus Felson's story with regard to crime prevention is one of urban change. This means there are some parallels with his routine activity changes affecting crime rates. However, his claim here is that with urban change there must also be changes in the way we try to prevent criminal events. Felson identified three stages of the urban landscape to understand this urban change: community, metro-reef, and metro-quilt.

The community was a very small area where you lived your life. Aside from your commute to work, everyone in the community shopped, went to school, and recreated in this small area. And criminal events were dominantly in the zone in transition. This was not to say that there were no criminal events in these neighborhoods, but they had all of the ingredients to prevent a lot of criminal events, particularly from outsiders. This was simply because everyone knew each other and if you (or your children) did something "bad," word traveled fast. Shortly after the Second World War, the proliferation of the automobile changed the nature of how we moved throughout the day. Though school (elementary, middle, and high schools) would still have been close to or within the neighborhood, most often our shopping and recreation left the community. Think of the consequences of a shopping mall emerging. Consequently, the collection of small communities that used to dominate our urban landscape had given way. This means that the ecology of crime had changed and, by necessity, so does our study and prevention of crime.

This next stage in the development of the urban landscape is what Marcus Felson called a set of streets that act as the sociocirculatory system of the modern metropolis (Felson, 1987). In the metro-reef, the streets now link everything together, not the community. Therefore, internal community ties break down. Neighbors no longer talk as much as they had because each of them would be too busy running around the metropolis. Consequently, by this time the streets had become much more in the realm of the public domain. Of course, streets would most often have been public in the truest sense of the word, but to use Oscar Newman's terminology they probably would have been better viewed as semi-public because the actions of people on community level streets were scrutinized by those who lived in the streets; you could not do whatever you wished with anonymity. Marcus Felson called this metropolis with streets acting as the sociocirculatory system the metro-reef. In this urban landscape the street network provides the means for subsistence and is truly the means of urban growth. As such, economic and social life would cling to the street network like coral would cling to a reef, hence the term. For crime prevention, the efforts and initiatives that worked in the past—essentially the supervision of youth by those who lived in the community—no longer worked, because the youth could move beyond the reach of those surveying them into the realm of anonymity with very little effort. This is a situation in which private and semi-private space were shrinking and public space was rising, relatively speaking. But now, for Marcus Felson, we are moving into yet another urban form and that form is what he calls the metro-quilt.

In order to motivate this concept, Marcus Felson introduced the concept of the facility. The easiest example of such a place is a shopping or recreation center. These facilities have privatized formerly public services such as security, sewers, and communications. Consequently, the primary difference from the previous urban landscape was that these facilities had increased both semi-public and semi-private spaces.

What these facilities do is attempt to provide a haven from excess traffic, parking difficulties, and other undesirables that are consequences of the metro-reef such as criminal events. And what Marcus Felson saw happening, at least potentially, was the community being replaced by these facilities, because facilities were growing in both size and in frequency. Shopping malls are growing ever larger and including more and different forms of shopping and entertainment. Movie theaters now tend to be a part of larger entertainment centers, sometimes within shopping malls, being "bundled" with other recreational activities such as bowling and drinking establishments. The primary implication of these facilities is that they do not foster a sense of community. And because of the privatization of space there are implications for crime prevention.

Marcus Felson refers to this new metropolitan form as the metro-quilt because the metropolis now represents a patchwork of facilities that are connected through the street network. The street network is only a part of the urban landscape because people need it to move to and from the different facilities. The implications for crime prevention are that these privately built facilities can be built in such a way that there is limited access but also that they direct the flows of different people. One of the "goods" for sale in a shopping center can be a safe environment to shop within, rather than a dimly lit street with your automobile parked a few blocks away. Areas can be built to attract youth and hopefully keep them away from the temptation of criminal opportunities, keeping them busy otherwise while they are under surveillance. It is not necessary to keep people physically separated, but design the facilities in such a manner that the people will separate themselves.

This latter idea harks back to the ideas of C. Ray Jeffery, that people are rational and that you can alter the environment in such a manner that non-criminal activities are the optimal choice. Because of this altered environment, criminal events are prevented. The key factor for Marcus Felson (1987) was that crime prevention initiatives are never static. The time frame that Felson operated at for this particular article is relatively long, but recognizing the importance of a changing situation is critical.

Ronald Clarke and situational crime prevention

The last aspect of crime prevention we are going to discuss in this chapter is situational crime prevention. This aspect of crime prevention has been mentioned a number of times already, particularly in Chapter 5 in the context of rational choice theory. Situational crime prevention, though applied by many, was developed by Ronald Clarke (1980, 1983, 1992, 1997). Situational crime prevention has three primary characteristics. First, as mentioned previously, it is directed at specific forms of crime, arguably very specific forms of crime. Residential burglary has many factors that can contribute to this offence that are very different from the factors that may contribute to theft from vehicle. It makes no sense to attempt to prevent theft from vehicle using the same initiatives as for residential burglary. Also, "very specific" can refer to theft from vehicle occurring at a particular place and a particular time. In other words, situational crime prevention is very situational. Second, situational crime prevention involves the manipulation of the immediate environment for that very specific crime type in an effort to have non-criminal behavior as the fittest adaptation. Moreover, these manipulations, or changes, will be made as permanently as possible such that the undesirable criminal behavior does not again become the fittest adaptation. And third, the first two factors are undertaken in order to reduce the opportunities for criminal events and increase the risks of criminal events in such a manner to be perceived by most (if not all) offenders. Situational crime prevention may be used from very simple applications such as target hardening (locking doors and windows, installing stronger doors and windows, burglar alarms, etc.) to neighborhood efforts such as block/neighborhood watch to the coordination of public transportation with the location of drinking establishments and their closing time (Clarke, 1983).

Most often, situational crime prevention would be classified as tertiary crime prevention because it begins after a problem has been identified. After all, the first two factors of situational crime prevention refer to very specific crime types (very difficult to predict *a priori*) and the manipulation of the immediate environment within which those very specific crime types occur. Consequently, one of the most common criticisms of situational crime prevention is that it does not address the "root causes" of crime. Whenever you hear such a criticism, it usually is coming from someone with a sociological or psychological background who is referring to underlying problems in our social fabric or some form of psychological disturbance. This is not to say that such factors are not important components within crime prevention, more generally. In fact, many, if not most, of the sociological factors would fall under the category of primary crime prevention and would be recognized as a part of C. Ray Jeffery's crime prevention through environmental design. But what this should force us to ask is the following: What are the root causes of crime?

Recall from Chapter 3 on routine activity theory that crime (property and violent) skyrocketed while socio-economic conditions improved greatly—the sociological paradox. This alone should cause one to question a sole focus on these factors for the prevention of crime. This is, perhaps, why the use of crime prevention through social development (CPTSD) is not nearly as widespread as CPTED and CPTUD. So what are the root causes? Should we be asking about something that is plural, or singular? In 1998 Marcus Felson and Ronald Clarke published a paper titled *Opportunity Makes the Thief: Practical Theory for Crime Prevention*. In this work, Felson and Clarke argued that opportunity is the root cause of crime. They are obviously referring to theft, given the title of the paper, but this idea can be carried over to almost any crime type. No matter how extreme the behavior, criminal or otherwise, an opportunity must be present in order to act out that behavior. Even in the context of a rather severe mental health condition, paranoid schizophrenia, patients have been found to act differently depending upon the neighborhood context and how the neighborhood tolerated particular behaviors (Lycan, 1991). Recall from Chapter 4, on the geometric theory of crime, that we all have a crime template; if the right *opportunity* came along we would seize that opportunity. However, the *right* opportunity never comes along for many people because we are not willing to take the risk. But for those who are willing to take the risk, we must modify the opportunities for crime in order to reduce the level of criminal activity.

We are not going to finalize the discussion regarding the root causes of crime here, but needless to say environmental criminologists favor the opportunity explanation rather than sociological or psychological ones. And because there are unique opportunity characteristics for all crime types (including variations of the same crime type in different locations and times), there is no panacea approach to preventing "crime." In an effort to address this complexity, Ronald Clarke has put forth the following, in order to organize how situational crime prevention may be put into practice:

1   Increase the perceived effort.
2   Increase the perceived risks.
3   Reduce the anticipated rewards.
4   Reduce provocations.
5   Remove the excuses for crime.

These principles of situational crime prevention are broken down into the 25 techniques of situational crime prevention that were expanded upon from 16 opportunity-related techniques described by Ronald Clarke in his 1997 book. The 25 techniques of situational crime prevention are shown in Table 7.2. As should be clear, these 25 techniques will vary significantly from crime type to crime type: concealing targets (technique #11) will be very different for residential burglary than theft from vehicle.

The best way to think of these situational crime prevention techniques is from a cost-benefit perspective. If benefit > cost, a criminal event will occur, but if benefit < cost, a criminal event will not occur. Considering the five primary categories, situational crime prevention attempts to do one or more of: 1) increase the perceived effort (increase cost), 2) increase the perceived risks (increase cost), 3) reduce the anticipated rewards (decrease benefit), 4) reduce provocations (decrease benefit), and 5) remove the excuses for crime (increase cost). It really is that simple and, as research in this area continues to show (see Clarke, 1997), situational crime prevention works. And, as mentioned in Chapter 5, on rational choice theory, the empirical evidence is against the displacement of crime.

Clearly, situational crime prevention assumes that it is dealing with a rational offender. Otherwise, there is no point in trying to alter the relative benefits and costs of a particular type of crime such that an offender chooses differently. Recall that even the most violent and "irrational" criminal events have embedded within them many rational decisions (Beauregard et al., 2007).

Table 7.2 Ronald Clarke's situational crime prevention

Increase the effort	Increase the risks	Reduce the rewards	Reduce provocations	Remove excuses
1. Target harden	6. Extend guardianship	11. Conceal targets	16. Reduce frustrations and stress	21. Set rules
2. Control access to facilities	7. Assist natural surveillance	12. Remove targets	17. Avoid disputes	22. Post instructions
3. Screen exits	8. Reduce anonymity	13. Identify property	18. Reduce emotional arousal	23. Alert conscience
4. Deflect offenders	9. Utilize place managers	14. Disrupt markets	19. Neutralize peer pressure	24. Assist compliance
5. Control tools/weapons	10. Strengthen formal surveillance	15. Deny benefits	20. Discourage imitation	25. Control drugs and alcohol

Source: Adapted from Clarke (1997), Felson and Clarke (1998), Center for Problem-Oriented Policing (2013).

Most recently, Ronald Clarke has published an article asking "so what?" with regard to what has been achieved by the research that has considered the impact of opportunity on crime. Clarke (2012) makes the following seven claims:

1   Criminally disposed people will commit more crimes if they encounter more criminal opportunities.
2   Regularly encountering such opportunities can lead these people to seek even more opportunities.
3   At the point of deciding to commit a crime, opportunity plays a more important role than dispositions.
4   The existence of easy opportunities for crime enables some people to lead a life of crime.
5   People without pre-existing dispositions can be drawn into criminal behavior by a proliferation of criminal opportunities, and generally law-abiding people can be drawn into committing specific forms of crime if they regularly encounter easy opportunities for these crimes, especially in their occupations.
6   The more opportunities for crime that exist, the more crime there will be.
7   Reducing opportunities for specific forms of crime will reduce the overall amount of crime (p. 6).

These claims have very clear and strong implications for situational crime prevention. This all ties back to C. Ray Jeffery and altering the environment (preferably building/designing it right the first time) in order to make non-criminal choices the fittest adaptation.

Review questions

1　Why did Jeffery think that altering the environment could alter crime?
2　CPTUD separates the actions of insiders (residents) and outsiders. What effects does Newman think architecture has on these two groups?
3　What is the key factor in making CPTUD work that was absent with architectural determinism?
4　In a general sense, what is the significance of the metro-reef and metro-quilt for crime prevention?
5　How does the existence of "facilities" change crime prevention?
6　Explain the importance of "situational" in situational crime prevention.

References

Beauregard, E., Rossmo, D. K., and Proulx, J. (2007). A descriptive model of the hunting process of serial sex offenders: A rational choice perspective. *Journal of Family Violence*, 22(6), 449–63.

Beavon, D. J. K., Brantingham, P. L., and Brantingham, P. J. (1994). The influence of street networks on the patterning of property offences. *Crime Prevention Studies*, 2, 115–48.

Brantingham, P. J. and Faust, F. L. (1976). A conceptual model of crime-prevention. *Crime and Delinquency*, 22(3), 284–96.

Canadian Council on Social Development (1984). *Crime prevention through social development: A discussion paper for social policy makers and practitioners*. Ottawa, ON: Canadian Council on Social Development.

Center for Problem-Oriented Policing (2013). 25 Techniques of Crime Prevention. Washington, DC: Center for Problem-Oriented Policing. Available online at http://www.popcenter.org/25techniques/ [accessed June 12, 2013].

Clarke, R. V. G. (1980). Situational crime prevention: Theory and practice. *British Journal of Criminology*, 20(2), 136–47.

Clarke, R. V. (1983). Situational crime prevention: Its theoretical basis and practical scope. *Crime and Justice: An Annual Review of Research*, 4, 225–56.

Clarke, R. V. (1992). *Situational crime prevention: Successful case studies*. New York, NY: Harrow and Heston.

Clarke, R. V. (1997). *Situational crime prevention: Successful case studies*, 2nd edition. Monsey, NY: Criminal Justice Press.

Clarke, R. V. (2012). Opportunity makes the thief. Really? And so what? *Crime Science*, 1, Article 3.

Felson, M. (1987). Routine activities and crime prevention in the developing metropolis. *Criminology*, 25(4), 911–31.

Felson, M. and Clarke, R. V. (1998). *Opportunity makes the thief: Practical theory for crime prevention*. London, UK: Home Office, Policing and Reducing Crime Unit Research, Development and Statistics Directorate.

Felson, M., Belanger, M. E., Bichler, G. M., Bruzinski, C. D., Campbell, G. S., Fied, C. L., Grofik, K. C., Mazur, I. S., O'Regan, A. B., Sweeney, P. J., Ullman, A. L., and Williams, L. M. (1996). Redesigning hell: preventing crime and disorder at the Port Authority Bus Terminal. *Crime Prevention Studies*, 6, 5–92.

Ferri, E. (1896). *Criminal sociology*. New York, NY: Appleton.

Jeffery, C. R. (1971). *Crime prevention through environmental design*. Beverly Hills, CA: Sage Publications.

Jeffery, C. R. (1977). *Crime prevention through environmental design*, 2nd edition. Beverly Hills, CA: Sage Publications.

Johnson, S. D. and Bowers, K. J. (2010). Permeability and burglary risk: Are cul-de-sacs safer? *Journal of Quantitative Criminology*, 26(1), 89–111.

Lycan, C. A. (1991). *Rational choice and mental illness in a clinical population: A study of treatment compliance*. Seattle, WA: Washington State University.

Malm, A., Pollard, N., Brantingham, P. J., Tinsley, P., Plecas, D., Brantingham, P. L., Cohen, I., and Kinney, B. (2005). *A 30 year analysis of police service delivery and costing: "E" Division*. Abbotsford, BC: University College of the Fraser Valley.

Nagin, D. S. (2013). Deterrence: A review of the evidence by a criminologist for economists. *Annual Review of Economics*, 5, 8.1–8.23.

Newman, O. (1972). *Defensible space: Crime prevention through urban design*. New York, NY: Macmillan.

Ratcliffe, J. H., Taniguchi, T., Groff, E. R., and Wood, J. D. (2011). The Philadelphia Foot Patrol Experiment: A randomized controlled trial of police patrol effectiveness in violent crime hotspots. *Criminology*, 49(3), 795–831.

Weisburd, D., Wyckoff, L. A., Ready, J., Eck, J. E., Hinkle, J. C., and Gajewski, F. (2006). Does crime just move around the corner? A controlled study of spatial displacement and diffusion of crime control benefits. *Criminology*, 44(3), 549–91.

Part III

The practice of environmental criminology

As should be clear from Part II of this textbook, the theories within environmental criminology have been around long enough to be well developed with, for the most part, a substantial amount of empirical validation. However, there is much more to environmental criminology than theory. This should be obvious at this stage because of Chapter 7, covering crime prevention. Even if this was the only reach of the theories within environmental criminology, there is a wide array of research and practice in this area, with much more work to be done, that has the improvement of society as its primary motivation. But this is not the case.

Though one could argue that many of the applications of environmental criminology have their roots in crime prevention activities, and they do to varying extents, the practice of environmental criminology extends far beyond theory and its original incantation of crime prevention. In Part III of this textbook we will cover a number of the applications of environmental criminology in eight chapters, though many of these chapters include more than one application of environmental criminology.

The first of these chapters, Chapter 8, covers the area of crime measurement. Crime measurement is a concern for all criminologists, but there is at least one additional dimension to crime measurement within environmental criminology because we use spatially referenced crime rates. These crime rates have two components to them, both of which have a spatial component. Chapter 8 covers the material on this issue with regard to spatially referenced crime rate calculations. Additionally, an alternative statistic of criminal activity, the location quotient, is presented as well as a number of aggregation concerns that matter, particularly, for environmental criminology: ecological stability; the aggregation of individual crime types into classifications such as property crime, violent crime, and all crime; and the temporal aggregation of daily, weekly, or monthly crime data into yearly aggregates. These are all common practices but may be particularly problematic within environmental criminology because the underlying spatial patterns of crime may change for different crime types and different seasons of the year.

Chapter 9 addresses spatial issues that are of particular importance to spatial crime analysis. Because most data used within environmental criminology are spatially referenced, there are a number of additional data concerns and choices that must be made within any analysis. At which scale should the data be analyzed? What are the limitations of my inference? As discussed in previous chapters, the theories within environmental criminology predict that criminal events will be clustered in particular places and follow a distance decay pattern—see Chapter 4 on the geometric theory of crime, in particular. Generally speaking, this means that places with high levels of criminal events will be surrounded by other places with high levels of criminal events, but as one moves further away from places with high concentrations of criminal events the level of criminal events falls such that places with low levels of criminal events are surrounded by other places with low levels of criminal events. This is referred to as (positive) spatial autocorrelation and has a number of implications for statistical analyses. Lastly, because of the nature of the units of analysis in much of environmental criminology (census tracts, neighborhoods, etc.), there is an entire branch of statistics that is available, local indicators of spatial associations. Though entire books could be written on each of these topics, they are all introduced below in the context of environmental criminology.

In Chapter 10, the topic of hot spots of crime is discussed. Hot spots are a popular topic in the media but are often misunderstood. In this chapter we will cover the standard definition of a hot spot, some methodological issues surrounding the measurement of hot spots, and some of the common forms of measuring hot spots, primarily kernel density estimation because of its widespread use. Lastly, a related method called risk terrain modeling will be discussed. Risk terrain modeling is a theoretically informed method for identifying risk (surprise!), that is most useful as a supplement to more traditional methods of hot spot analysis.

The temporal dimension of criminal events is discussed in Chapter 11. As discussed earlier in this textbook, environmental criminology is concerned with asking where and when a criminal event occurred. This chapter begins with a theoretical model that shows how closely related time and space are when considering criminal events. Moreover, a temporal theory of crime generates very similar spatial patterns as those shown in Chapter 4. Subsequently, this chapter will cover some of the temporal regularities of crime. These temporal regularities occur over the course of the day, the week, the season, the year, even the decade.

Chapter 12 begins when Chapter 11 ends, the crime drop. This chapter reviews the standard explanations for the crime drop of the 1990s and beyond. After this review, criteria for assessing the explanations for the crime drop are explained and used to assess the standard explanations. Finally, an approach that considers the role of environmental criminology is reviewed, one that is able to address many of the limitations of previous attempts to explain this phenomenon.

Chapter 13 covers geographic profiling. Geographic profiling is an application of environmental criminology theories that is used as an investigative tool, particularly in serial criminal events. The method itself is explained in this chapter as well as a number of its specific applications. Additionally, geographic profiling has been moving into exciting areas of new research, being applied to counterinsurgency, counterterrorism, biology, zoology, and epidemiology. These new applications of geographic profiling are useful on a number of fronts. First, most are simply interesting in and of themselves. Second, these new applications show the utility of the thinking within environmental criminology in alternative fields that deal with the predatory behavior of animals. And third, through the application of geographic profiling to other contexts that involve predatory behavior (primarily in animal populations), more data become available for the application of geographic profiling to human behavior.

The topics of repeat victimization and near-repeat victimization are covered in Chapter 14. The Pareto principle, commonly referred to as the 80–20 rule, states that for many phenomena, approximately 80 percent of the effects are attributed to approximately 20 percent of the causes. This principle is commonly invoked in colloquial settings as well as in economics (wealth distributions), business, and health care. The Pareto principle is also present in the context of criminal events and, most probably, is an underestimate—for example, 1 percent of street segments accounted for 23 percent of crime in Seattle, Washington. In this chapter, the topic of repeat victimization is covered that encompasses the same individuals or structures (think of homes for residential burglaries) being victimized over and over again; the topic of near-repeat victimization refers to the same areas being victimized over and over again, but not necessarily the same home—most research in the near-repeat victimization literature investigates residential burglary. The phenomena themselves, and their methodological limitations, are covered.

Lastly, Chapter 15 covers the topic of crime and place. The crime and place literature focuses on the continued use of the micro-spatial unit of analysis such as the street address, street intersection, or the street segment. This last chapter harks back to Chapter 1, which outlined the trajectory of spatial criminology over the past 200 years being the repeated finding of spatial heterogeneity within the status quo spatial unit of analysis of the time. This literature, as we know it today, began twenty-five years ago and is the specific research focus of a small number of spatial criminologists.

Chapter 8

Crime measurement

Introduction

We are bombarded by crime statistics in contemporary society. Whether we hear about crime statistics through the traditional media, social media, or discussions with colleagues, friends, and neighbors, crime statistics are everywhere: crime is going up, crime is going down, or crime is higher/lower relative to other places in the country. How reliable is this information that is so freely available? Many scholars are split between those who accept or reject the quantification of social phenomena. This divide may, in part, be because there are those who simply mistrust data and/or data representation. We have all heard the well-known adage from Benjamin Disraeli: there are lies, damned lies and [then there are] statistics (cited in Twain, 1906). This general mistrust of statistics is compounded because of "journalists and politicians, among others, [who] often issue declarations about crime rates, . . . [without encouraging the public] . . . to think critically about what the crime rate measures really are" (Sacco and Kennedy, 2002, p. 92)—Pallone (1999) was highly critical of nightly newscasts reporting on crime. Despite the fact that the media give crime rates so much attention (Sacco, 2000) that may or may not be accurate, knowledge of criminal activities, generally speaking, is important because "[w]e may factor information about crime rates into our decisions about whether we will buy a home in a particular neighbourhood, vacation in a particular place, or allow our children to attend a particular school" (Sacco and Kennedy, 2002, p. 94). It is particularly problematic when academics, politicians, and the media no longer make broad statements regarding general public risk about crime and begin to make inferences from conventional crime rates to personal risk; most often this is an ecological fallacy, an issue in spatial crime analysis that is discussed in Chapter 9.

Sources and limitations of criminal event data

One of, if not the, most common criminal event data sets used in criminology relates to "official" crime data. These data are collected by national or subnational criminal justice agencies such as the Federal Bureau of Investigation (FBI) in the United States and the Canadian Centre for Justice Statistics in Canada. Of these data, the most well-known, -cited, and -used official crime data are from the Uniform Crime Reporting (UCR) system—see Mosher et al. (2011) for a detailed history of the UCR. The UCR began in 1930 in the United States and 1962 in Canada; reporting through the UCR is voluntary in the United States but nearly all law enforcement agencies do provide their data to the FBI, and responding to the UCR survey is mandatory in Canada (FBI, 2013; Statistics Canada, 2012).

Another form of official crime data that is particularly common within environmental criminology is calls for service data. Calls for service data have become increasingly popular and available since the late 1980s and represent requests made for police service through an emergency service such as 911, requests for police service made directly to the respective police detachment, and internal calls for service made by police officers (Sherman et al., 1989). Calls for service data are, at times, criticized for not truly representing criminal events, because a call for service does not necessarily mean a founded crime report. As such, calls for service data are sometimes referred to as police activity data. Despite this concern with calls for service data, the possible inclusion of some unfounded calls would be dwarfed by the volume of calls never even reported to the police—the calls for service data I have used in my own research from the Vancouver Police Department and the Royal Canadian Mounted Police allow for the identification of unfounded calls for service, and this identification will likely be available within the data from many law enforcement agencies.

One of the biggest concerns regarding the use of any official crime data is that it may not be representative of actual crime, a concern that goes back to at least the early 1800s (Bulwer, 1836). In Canada, in 2009, 31 percent of total criminal victimization was reported to the police, down from 34 percent in 2004, and from 37 percent in 1999 (Perreault and Brennan, 2010)—these data are drawn from the Canadian victimization survey. There is also substantial variation across the following individual crime types: sexual assault, robbery, physical assault, residential break and enter (residential burglary), motor vehicle/parts theft, theft of household property, vandalism, and theft of personal property. As shown in Table 8.1, property crimes have much greater levels of reporting to the police, particularly those crimes that would require insurance claims because of greater economic losses: residential break and enter and motor vehicle/parts theft. The reasons listed for not reporting a crime to the police range from "not important enough" (almost 70 percent) to "fear of publicity or news coverage" (approximately 5 percent).

The primary method of data gathering to address this issue of non-reporting criminal events to the police is to undertake criminal victimization surveys. Small victimization surveys, often called self-report data, are instructive but tend to lack an appropriate control group (non-victims of crime) or cover a relatively small geographic area preventing any generalizations regarding broader trends. Large-scale victimization surveys, most often undertaken at the national level—General Social Survey in Canada, National Crime Victimization Survey in the United

Table 8.1 Percent of self-reported victimizations reported to the police

Crime type	1999	2004	2009
Total victimization	37	34	31
Sexual assault	n/a	8	n/a
Robbery	46	46	43
Physical assault	37	39	34
Total violent victimization	31	33	29
Break and enter	62	54	54
Motor vehicle/parts theft	60	49	50
Household property theft	32	29	23
Vandalism	34	31	35
Total household victimization	44	37	36
Theft of personal property	35	31	28

Source: Perreault and Brennan (2010).

States, and the British Crime Survey in the United Kingdom—are also instructive with the ability to make generalizations through national coverage and an appropriate control group. However, because the sample size does not vary significantly as the population of interest decreases, they are not feasible for most applications of environmental criminology. For example, according to the sample size calculator available at Raosoft.com, considering common parameter choices regarding the confidence level and margin of error, a population of 5,110 requires a sample of 358 for inference to be made—this is the average number of persons in a Vancouver census tract for the 2011 Census of Population in Canada. With there being 118 census tracts in Vancouver for the 2011 census, that would require a total sample of 42,244. In order to be able to have the same confidence level and margin of error for inference at the level of the Canadian province, similar to the General Social Survey, a sample of 30,681 is necessary. If a smaller spatial unit of analysis was required or desired in the analysis such as the dissemination area—the Canadian equivalent to a block group in the United States—the total sample required for Vancouver would be over 225,000. Needless to say, a victimization survey for a municipality at a scale relevant to much of the literature within environmental criminology would be a tremendous undertaking.

Despite the difficulty in obtaining (potentially) more representative criminal event data through a victimization survey, this is an important avenue of future research. Within environmental criminology we must assume that the police data we use are representative of the real world. In particular, because of the strong focus on spatial patterns within environmental criminology, we must assume these spatial patterns are similar. If not, much of the research based on such data may be spurious. At this time I am only aware of one research study that has attempted to investigate the similarity of spatial patterns between police data and victimization data. In an analysis of data in Vilnius, Lithuania, Vania Ceccato and Nijole Lukyte (2011) found that the spatial patterns of police data and victimization data were not similar at all. Though the victimization data used by these authors were too coarse to be able to draw very strong conclusions, the implications of this finding are incredibly significant. Therefore, some form of victimization survey at a municipal level is necessary in the future of environmental criminology. The difficulty will be overcoming the sampling issue discussed above because of the implication for costs in terms of time and money.

Regardless of these concerns, police data are what we have to work with most of the time and have proven to be incredibly instructive. Most often, however, we do not analyze raw police data. It has been well known for many years that criminal events tend to cluster in urban centers, typically the parts of the city that have a lot of commercial area and a significantly large daytime population (Schmid, 1960a, 1960b). Because of this phenomenon urban areas with large populations will have more criminal events and appear more dangerous than smaller areas with fewer people. As such, a method of normalizing police criminal event data is necessary in order to compare victimization across space. This is accomplished with the crime rate, probably the most widely used statistic in (environmental) criminology. The crime rate is a great statistic to be used in any analysis, but as we shall see in the following section, it has concerns in its calculation that go beyond the concerns involving police criminal event data, discussed above.

Spatially referenced crime rates

The calculation of crime rates is almost always spatially referenced. This is simply because of the nature of the calculation. A crime rate has three components, as shown in Equation 8.1: the number of criminal events (the numerator), the population at risk (the denominator), and a scalar. Despite the discussion above regarding the reliability of criminal event counts available to the police, the numerator in crime rate calculations is not usually a contentious issue, at least at a conceptual level. The scalar is simply used to transform the crime rate into a statistic with meaningful units. For example, crime rates per 1,000 are common in a lot of research within environmental criminology that is conducted at the neighborhood, or census tract, level, whereas crime rates per 100,000 are more common at the national or subnational (states and provinces) levels. There is nothing contentious regarding the scalar because it simply transforms the crime rate into a comparable statistic: comparable across time or different places. And because crime counts and populations at risk must be defined spatially (within which boundaries?) I use the term "spatially referenced crime rates," but this term more specifically refers to crime rates in the environmental criminology literature. The population at risk has the function of normalizing the crime rate such that risk can be inferred. As mentioned above, places with more people have been shown to have more crime, so this must be controlled for if the crime rate is to be a meaningful statistic for criminological research, teaching, and policy. Consequently, the population at risk is a contentious component within crime rate calculations.

$$\left(\frac{Crime\ count}{Population\ at\ risk}\right) * Scalar \qquad\qquad (8.1)$$

Consider a rather simple example of why the selection of the population at risk can be considered both contentious and critically important for understanding crime patterns. Are all people equally likely to be a victim of a criminal event? No. Are all people likely to be a criminal offender? No. This is particularly true with violent crime and young males, a topic that Neil Boyd (2000) has thoroughly investigated. Given that "no" is the answer to both of these questions, why do we then use the total population (young and old, males and females) in almost all crime rate calculations? The United States Bureau of Justice Statistics has published offender-based crime rates for years and there is some research on this issue (see O'Brien, 1989).

In some earlier research in collaboration with Greg W. Jenion and Michelle Jenion, I calculated the traditional Canadian homicide rate using the total Canadian population as the population at risk as well as a modified homicide rate that used the number of 15–30 year old males as the population at risk. These two crime rates, 1961–1999, are plotted in Figure 8.1—these data from Andresen

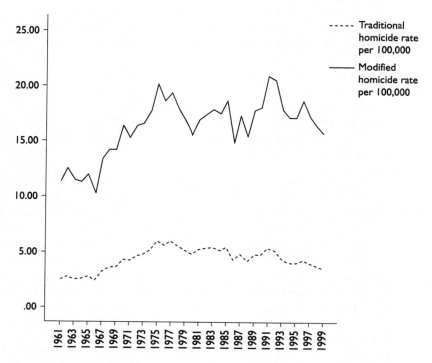

Figure 8.1 Traditional versus modified homicide rates, Canada, 1961–1999.
Source: Adapted from Andresen et al. (2003).

et al. (2003) are dated now, but the trend is all that matters. Clearly apparent from Figure 8.1 is that the trends of these two crime rates are substantially different. The traditionally calculated homicide rate increased until the mid-1970s and has been on a steady decrease that continues to this day. The modified homicide rate, however, also increased until the mid-1970s but has trended flat (remained constant), with a fair degree of volatility since then. The point of this discussion is to show that a theoretically informed alternative crime rate calculation reveals a substantially different trend from the traditional crime rate. This is not to say that the traditionally calculated crime rate is of no use or provides a misleading interpretation of the state of criminal activity, but that we must take caution when interpreting such crime statistics that use very general populations at risk that are not tailored to the known facts regarding criminal offending and victimization.

The importance of critically considering the population at risk in crime rate calculations goes back to the work of Sarah Boggs in 1965. In this seminal work, she showed the utility of alternative denominators (populations at risk) in victim-based crime rate calculations. Boggs was interested in calculating crime rates that considered the environmental opportunities that were specific to each crime type—a population at risk. She stated that this was necessary for a crime rate to be a meaningful statistic: we vary the numerator for each crime rate calculation, so why not the denominator as well? Keith Harries (1981, 1991) reiterated these statements that a crime rate only has the *potential* to be a meaningful statistic.

This, of course, forces us to ask the following question: What are the appropriate denominators for different crime types? Some of these may be open to interpretation, but here is a short list: 1) the number of residential housing units for residential burglary; 2) the number of commercial outlet units for commercial burglary; 3) the number of equivalent parking spaces in a given area for automotive theft; and 4) the number of people present for violent crime. All of these possibilities represent actual populations that are at risk of victimization for these crimes. So what did Sarah Boggs find? Using a correlation statistic, Boggs found that traditionally calculated crime rates and alternatively calculated crime rates were at times very similar, but other times quite different. For example, the correlations were significantly high between traditional and alternative crime calculations for: residential night burglary, residential day burglary, forcible rape, and criminal homicide-aggravated assault—highway robbery also had a high correlation coefficient. On the other hand, automotive theft for joyriding, automotive theft for permanent retention, and business robbery all had very low magnitude correlation coefficients, whereas non-residential night burglary, grand larceny, and non-residential day burglary all had negative correlation coefficients. Needless to say, sometimes the alternative calculations may matter and other times they may not.

But does this issue really matter? Is this not simply an academic curiosity? Yes Sarah Boggs found statistically significant and meaningful results, but her results may have been specific to her data. Some subsequent research undertaken by

Lawrence Cohen and colleagues in 1985 claimed that it did not matter whether crime rates were calculated using traditional or alternative populations at risk because they were often so highly correlated. This is to be expected for residential units and residential populations because where there are more homes there are usually more people. If this is true, generally speaking, any gains in insight will be small and costly in terms of money and/or time—most, if not all, alternative populations at risk will not be readily accessible in the census, for example. It is important to note that the proponents of alternative populations at risk do not deny this, for some crime types. Sarah Boggs (1965) found that it mattered very little for five of the eleven crime types under analysis. But the point is that this will not be the case for all comparisons.

The outcome of the research in this area, up until recently, has led to a lot of theoretical discussions and, perhaps, token references to the work of researchers such as Sarah Boggs, but very little in terms of practice. Because of the high cost in terms of time and money in obtaining alternative populations at risk—the primary exception would be the number of housing units available in the census—the conventional crime rate calculation has largely been the status quo. This has changed recently because of the availability of a relatively inexpensive population at risk measure that was available at a spatial scale useful to criminological research.

These data are an ambient population database developed and provided by Oak Ridge National Laboratory (2003)—these data have been free for non-commercial use. The ambient population data, LandScan, are an estimate of the population for a 1 square kilometer area at any given time of the day and for any given day of the year—the actual area depends on how far the location is from the equator. Because it is an average over a 24-hour period and for any given day of the year, such data will underestimate the daytime population, especially at certain times of the year, such as the season of summer (particularly in relatively cooler climates), and major shopping times of the year, such as back to school and Christmas. However, at least in principle, such a population estimate will be superior to the resident population most commonly used in environmental criminology and social disorganization theory research—the resident population is easily available from any census. This is obviously the case for violent crime types that, by definition, require the presence of at least two individuals but also for other crime types such as automotive theft, because of our car culture here in North America: where there are people, there are cars. Such data may also be useful for residential burglary because the ratio of the ambient to the resident population could provide an indication of which neighborhoods are being vacated during the day. The obvious question to ask now is: How is the ambient population calculated?

As outlined by Jerome Dobson and colleagues (2000, 2003, 2004), four factors were used to calculate the ambient population: roads, slope, land cover, and nighttime lights—some of the more recent data produced by Oak Ridge National Laboratory include other factors such as land use and other census information, but it is only available for the United States whereas the LandScan data had been available globally. Transportation networks, particularly road density, are excellent indicators of where people actually are. Consider the road density of an urban center versus a rural area. Slope is important because humans tend to settle on relatively flat terrain. This obviously is not always true, but it is a tendency. Land cover such as desert, water, wetlands, urban, and rural are also important for the locations of human settlement for obvious reasons. And lastly, nighttime lights have been found to be the best global indicator of where people work, live, and recreate. For a visual indication of nighttime lights see the Visible Earth web page maintained by NASA: http://visibleearth.nasa.gov.

In 2010, Greg Jenion and I published an article with preliminary results of a comparison between the ambient population data from Oak Ridge National Laboratory and the resident population from Canada's Census of Population. In that article we used 1996 data and the enumeration area as the spatial unit of analysis. In the maps presented below, I have updated the data to 2001 and used dissemination areas from the census—dissemination area is just the new name for enumeration area, starting in the 2001 census. What should be clear in Figure 8.2a

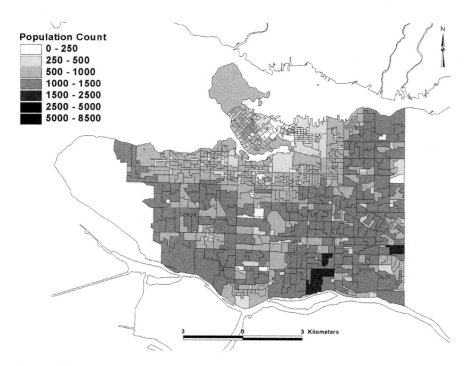

Figure 8.2a Resident and ambient populations, Vancouver, 2001.

a) Resident Population

Source: Andresen (2013a).

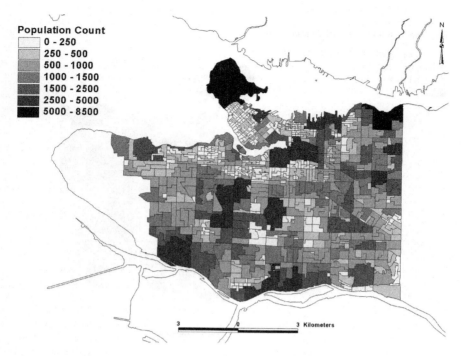

Figure 8.2b Resident and ambient populations, Vancouver, 2001.
b) Ambient Population
Source: Andresen (2013a).

is that the census resident population is distributed quite evenly. This should come as no surprise, because that should be the goal of the census in order to be able to make meaningful interference later. There is a moderate "concentration" of the resident population in the southern portion of the city, but this is partially because the northern coastal region of the city consists of downtown and the majority of commercial and industrial areas. The ambient population is presented in Figure 8.2b, and clearly shows that there are concentrations of population in these data. Also notable here is that the legend categories are the same for both maps—see Monmonier (1996) for methods to avoid and be cautious of when viewing maps. There are concentrations of the ambient population in very predictable places: major arterial routes, shopping centers, educational facilities, and part of the central business district. These comparative patterns are even more apparent in Figure 8.3, that represents the ratio of the ambient population (numerator) and the resident population (denominator). Those places that have values greater than 1.1, and especially places with values greater than 2, attract more populations during the day.

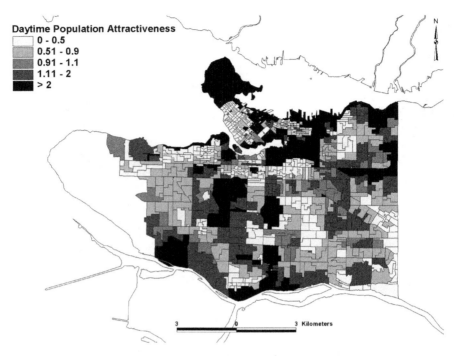

Figure 8.3 Daytime population attractiveness, Vancouver, 2001.
Source: Andresen (2013a).

Considering the data and analysis in Andresen and Jenion (2010), there are many differences between these two data sets. First, the ranges of the two population variables are very different with dissemination areas: both have 0 as the minimums, but the resident population has a maximum of 1,850 persons and the ambient population has a maximum of 8,250 persons. And the correlation coefficient for comparing the two population variables, $r = 0.54$, is moderate in magnitude and statistically significant. Thus far, these two population variables do cause concern for their similarity, but there could have been a much lower correlation coefficient between them. Using a regression framework to predict the ambient population using the resident population, the results did not look promising. In such a comparison, the ideal situation is to have a very high coefficient of determination (as close to 1 as possible), r^2, and an estimated coefficient that is also close to 1; this is desirable because having a high value for the coefficient of determination means that any predictions will be more precise and having an estimated coefficient that is close to 1 indicates that the two populations move one-to-one. The results are not particularly promising: the estimated coefficient is 1.16, quite close to 1, but the r^2 is 0.287, indicating that there is a lot of "noise" in the regression, so one cannot be too confident in the precision of any predictions. Overall, the substitutability of these two population variables does not look that promising, but it could be a lot worse. Let us move on to a comparison of violent crime rates before any judgment is made.

Figure 8.4 shows the resident-based violent crime rate and the ambient-based violent crime rate; violent crime includes assault, fighting, hold-ups, homicide, robbery, sexual assault, and stabbing. Violent crime was chosen as the crime type to present here because it is the most obvious crime type to "test" the ambient population: a violent crime requires the presence of two or more people. Figure 8.4a shows that the resident-based violent crime rate was at its greatest levels in and around the central business district in Vancouver, the northern peninsula shown on the map. Violent crime is also greater in those areas that include major arterial roads and on the east side of Vancouver. The ambient-based violent crime rate map, Figure 8.4b, reveals a subtle but important change from the resident-based violent crime rate map using the same legend categories. Most areas have experienced a decrease in violent crime rates with an increase and westward shift of the high crime area in the central business district. When

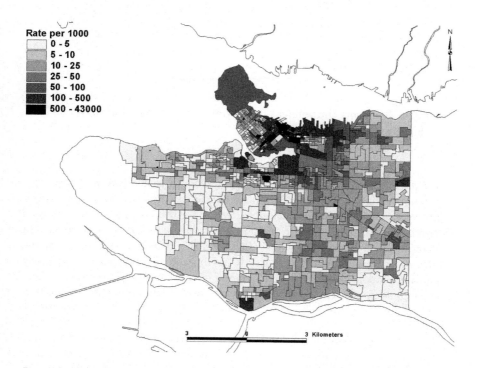

Figure 8.4a Resident- and ambient-based violent crime rates, Vancouver, 2001.
a) Resident-based violent crime rate
Source: Andresen (2013a).

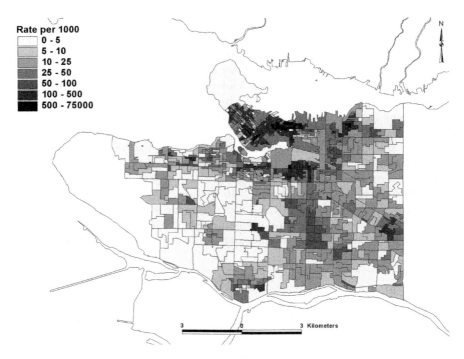

Figure 8.4b Resident- and ambient-based violent crime rates, Vancouver, 2001.
b) Ambient-based violent crime rate
Source: Andresen (2013a).

compared empirically, the violent crime rates do not fare nearly as well as the raw population variables. The correlation coefficient between the two crime rates is statistically significant, but very close to zero, $r = 0.09$. Using the resident-based violent crime rate to predict the ambient-based violent crime rate, the coefficient of determination is very low, $r^2 = 0.007$, and the estimated coefficient for the resident-based violent crime rate is 0.152. Consequently, despite a statistically significant relationship, the two violent crime rates are essentially unrelated: there is a lot of noise in the regression results and the two violent crime rates do move in the same direction (positive estimated coefficient) but hardly in a one-to-one manner.

In some other research involving the ambient population at the census tract and enumeration/dissemination area spatial units of analysis, I have shown how using the ambient population impacts the results in spatial crime analysis. For example, the use of ambient-based crime rates (automotive theft, burglary, and violent crime) tends to lead to the retention of more theoretically justified variables, more realistic magnitudes for the statistically significant variables in the analysis, better goodness-of-fit (greater levels for the coefficient of determination), and better concordances with theoretical expectations in the realms of social disorganization theory or routine activity theory (Andresen, 2006a, 2006b, 2011a). Perhaps the most striking impact from the use of the ambient-based crime rates is in the context of local spatial statistical analysis—this will be covered in detail in Chapter 9. In an analysis using local Moran's I to investigate local clustering of crime (see Anselin, 1995), though the general patterns of where high crime and low crime clusters were located were essentially the same, the details changed significantly, leading to the identification of different areas that may have been experiencing crime problems, and vice versa (Andresen, 2011a, 2011b, 2013a). And lastly, in an analysis of ambient-based crime rates at the municipal level, I was able to find that the ranking of municipalities based on the level of their respective crime rates changed substantially in some cases (Andresen, 2010). In fact, the municipality of West Vancouver (the wealthiest municipality in the Metro Vancouver region) was ranked fourteenth out of fifteen municipalities for crime considering a resident-based crime rate calculation; however, that ranking increased to seventh considering an ambient-based crime rate calculation. This result makes perfect sense because almost 80 percent of the working population in West Vancouver leaves the municipality during the day for work—nine of the fifteen major municipalities in the Metro Vancouver area had 75 percent or more of the working populations leaving their home municipality to go to work almost twenty years ago (Andresen, 2010), a number that has likely increased in recent years.

To summarize the importance of this research, it needs to be remembered that many people, especially those who study (environmental) criminology, may factor information regarding crime rates into the decisions regarding the purchase of a home, locations for vacations, or the schools we send our children to (Sacco and Kennedy, 2011). Consequently, we need to ask whether or not conventionally calculated crime rates using the resident population are an accurate portrayal of those places in which we choose to live, work, and recreate. The importance of this issue extends far beyond public opinion regarding such choices. If we test a theory, within environmental criminology or not, using the characteristics of people who sleep in a neighborhood, census tract, or dissemination area (census block group) we may not be understanding the characteristics of that area at all. People take their characteristics with them when they leave their home (income, age, family composition), so how can we properly test theory unless we can assume that neighborhoods maintain their characteristics when their residents leave? Given that there is no substantive relationship between the resident-based and ambient-based crime rates, at least in one context, it may be the case that any confirmation or rejection of a theory would be in error if the ambient population could provide a better population at risk. And, in the context of public policy, any of these policies that are based on theories that have been confirmed by conventionally calculated crime rates might be misinformed.

An alternative to the crime rate: the location quotient

As thoroughly discussed in the preceding section, the calculation of spatially refer-enced crime rates has two potential sources of measurement issues: the criminal event counts available through police data and the population at risk. There is another statistic that could be used independent of, or in conjunction with, the spatially referenced crime rate, particularly for spatial crime analyses. This statistic only requires criminal event data and has been used in environmental criminology for over twenty years now—the location quotient. The location quotient is a specifically geographic statistic that measures the over- or underrepresentation of some (criminal) activity in a spatial unit of analysis relative to the entire study area, and has its roots in the geography literature used since the 1940s (Isard et al., 1998). The location quotient is calculated as follows:

$$LQ_{in} = \frac{C_{in} / C_{tn}}{\sum_{n=1}^{N} C_{in} / \sum_{n=1}^{N} C_{tn}} \tag{8.2}$$

where C_{in} is the count of crime i in sub-region n, C_{tn} is the count of all crimes in sub-region n, and N is the total number of sub-regions. In the context of crime, the location quotient is a ratio of the percentage of a particular crime type in a sub-region relative to the percentage of that same particular crime type in the region as a whole; neighborhoods or census tracts within a city, for example. If the loca-tion quotient is equal to 1, the sub-region has its proportional share of a particular crime type; if the location quotient is greater than 1, the sub-region has a disproportionately greater share of a particular crime type; and if the location quotient is less than 1, the sub-region has a disproportionately lesser share of a particular crime type. For example, if a sub-region has a location quotient of 1.50, that sub-region has 50 percent more of that crime type than expected given the percentage of that crime type in the region as a whole. Therefore, it may be said that this sub-region "specializes" in that particular crime type. Miller et al. (1991) provided the following classifications that are useful for interpreting the location quotient: very underrepresented areas, $0 \leq LQ \leq 0.70$; moderately underrepresented areas, $0.70 < LQ \leq 0.90$; average represented areas, $0.90 < LQ \leq 1.10$; moderately overrepresented areas, $1.10 < LQ \leq 1.30$; and very overrepresented areas, $LQ > 1.30$.

Paul Brantingham and Patricia Brantingham (1993c, 1995b, 1998) first introduced the location quotient into criminological research in the early 1990s—Barr and Pease (1990) did discuss the possibility of using the location quotient in crime analysis but did not actually perform such an analysis. Curiously, despite its initial use being more than twenty years ago, its adoption as a standard criminological measurement has been slow.

Brantingham and Brantingham (1993c, 1995b, 1998) used the location quotient to measure the crime mix and specialization within the municipalities of British

Columbia, focusing on violent crime; they compared the location quotient results to those for crime counts and spatially referenced crime rates. In their analyses, larger municipalities had the highest counts, as would be expected. But, also expected, after controlling for the population at risk, the large municipalities no longer ranked at the top of the list—larger municipalities were now commonly at the bottom of the ranked list. In the comparison of spatially referenced crime rates, the smaller hinterland municipalities topped the rank list. When considering the location quotient, another ranking emerged: some municipalities with high crime rates also had high-valued location quotients, and some municipalities that had low crime rates had high-valued location quotients. Therefore, there were municipalities that had a low risk of criminal victimization generally speaking (low crime rates), but specialized in violent crimes when considering the location quotient.

The phenomenon of a sub-region, however defined, specializing in a particular crime type when the risk of criminal events is generally low is interesting in itself. Such a result may allow a researcher to investigate a curious result that emerged when considering crime rates. For example, in the context of illegal drugs in the United States, George Rengert (1996) expected the north-central region of the United States to have the greatest proportions of marijuana crimes (of all drug-related crimes) because of a lack of a coastline and its agricultural base. George Rengert expected this relationship because heroin and cocaine were expected to have a greater need to be close to international transportation networks on the coast. However, Rengert (1996) found that the spatial pattern of marijuana crimes effectively followed the same spatial pattern as heroin and cocaine when using the crime rate: the north-central region of the United States was ranked last. In an attempt to further understand this result, Rengert (1996) used the location quotient to consider crime specialization and its impact on the spatial pattern of illegal drug crimes: other regions of the United States had greater volumes and corresponding crime rates of marijuana crimes than the north-central region, but if one were to commit a drug crime in the north-central region it would most likely be related to marijuana. This is precisely what George Rengert found in his research.

Curiously, the location quotient appeared to be absent within criminological research for approximately ten years, aside from one study that used the location quotient as a component in a composite index. In this more recent research, Eric McCord and Jerry Ratcliffe (2007) used the location quotient to measure crime intensity across neighborhoods. They found that drug markets tended to cluster close to pawnshops, drinking establishments, and mass transit stations. I performed an inferential analysis (spatial regression) using the location quotient as a dependent variable and found that if independent variables were interpreted as attractors of a particular crime type, the location quotient was predicted rather well considering social disorganization theory and routine activity theory (Andresen, 2007). In some circumstances there were differences in the theoretical interpretations of the estimated parameters relative to an analysis considering crime rates. At times, these differences were subtle: the estimated parameters had the same sign, but how one interpreted the results changed. In other contexts, the expected sign was opposite compared to a crime rate (a negative relationship between burglary and the unemployment rate, for example) that required a completely different, but theoretically justified, explanation.

In 2008, Jerry Ratcliffe and George Rengert published a journal article that used the location quotient to identify areas with greater intensities of shootings, relative to the city as a whole. In a Canadian context, I investigated the phenomenon of crime rates in Canadian provinces increasing as one moves east to west—crime rates in the territories are even higher than in the western provinces (Andresen, 2009a). This is a phenomenon that has existed for at least sixty years and is poorly understood. In this analysis, I used the location quotient to show that just because all crime rates are greatest in the west did not mean that western provinces specialized in all crime types. Rather, crime specialization was present in all provinces for at least two crime types in each province. This analysis showed that crime concentration (crime rates) did not necessarily imply crime specialization (location quotients). This does support the historical fact that the risk of criminal victimization is greatest in the west. However, if an individual is going to be a victim of crime, the western provinces are not disproportionately more violent than other areas in Canada. The western provinces simply have more of everything. And, most recently, Block et al. (2012) used the location quotient in the context of automotive theft in the United States. They found that U.S. states and counties that contained or were near heavily trafficked borders and ports specialized in automotive theft; Block et al. (2012) hypothesized that this indicated the presence of a "theft for export" problem in these areas. Perhaps most interesting was that these were not always areas that had high rates of automotive theft.

I strongly believe that the utility of the location quotient is that it identifies different patterns because it is an alternative measure of criminal activity. In my previous book, I outlined the spatial patterns of crime rates versus location quotients within Vancouver, British Columbia, Canada (Andresen, 2013a). I found that the spatial patterns for crime rates and location quotients were somewhat similar for a number of crime types. However, notable differences emerged when considering crime specialization versus risk of victimization. In the case of assault, a crime rate map indicated that assaults were concentrated in skid row. This is an expected result, particularly in the context of social disorganization theory and that skid row in Vancouver is in the zone in transition. However, when considering the location quotient, the east side of Vancouver (and the north east side in particular) exhibited significant assault specialization. What did this mean? In order to answer this question, both the crime rate and the location quotient needed to be considered. First, the risk of victimization from an assault is greatest in Vancouver's skid row. But, if an individual is going to be a victim of an assault, it is more likely to be on the east side of Vancouver relative to the west side of Vancouver. A number of similar differences in the spatial patterns of crime emerged for other crime types (robbery, sexual assault, theft, theft from vehicle, and theft of vehicle), but these differences were not always in the same places.

Arguably the most interesting application of the location quotient in Vancouver is burglary. The burglary crime rate map, Figure 8.5a, indicates that burglary had its greatest risk in and around the central business district and skid row. Similar to assault, this is the standard prediction from social disorganization theory. However, the location quotient map, Figure 8.5b, shows that burglary specializes more frequently within the relatively affluent west side of Vancouver. Clearly evident from Figure 8.5a, this is the area in which burglary rates are the lowest. This result does not mean that burglary is actually more frequent on the west side of Vancouver than the crime rate map indicates. Rather, it indicates that if an individual is going to be a victim of a criminal event on the west side of Vancouver it is most likely going to be a residential burglary. There is no research to support the following claim, but it has been hypothesized that this may explain the fear of crime in low crime neighborhoods: the burglary rate may be low, but everyone whom an individual speaks to about criminal victimization has referred to a burglary, so other residents in the neighborhood begin to fear that crime.

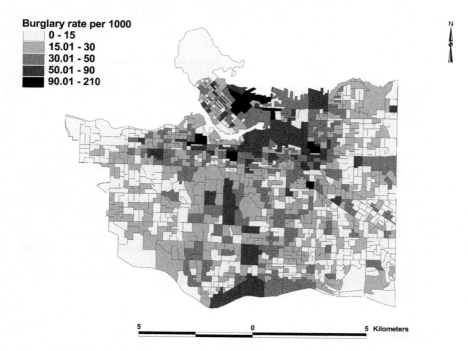

Burglary rate per 1000
- 0 - 15
- 15.01 - 30
- 30.01 - 50
- 50.01 - 90
- 90.01 - 210

Figure 8.5a Burglary crime rate and location quotient, Vancouver, 2001.
a) Burglary crime rate
Source: Andresen (2013a).

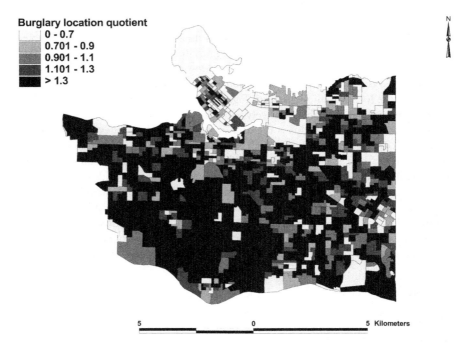

Burglary location quotient
 0 - 0.7
 0.701 - 0.9
 0.901 - 1.1
 1.101 - 1.3
 > 1.3

Figure 8.5b Burglary crime rate and location quotient, Vancouver, 2001.
b) Burglary location quotient
Source: Andresen (2013a).

In all of the applications of the location quotient reviewed above, the researchers were forced to ask different questions, or ask questions differently, with regard to the spatial pattern of crime, sometimes subtle and sometimes not. Because they asked these questions differently, I argue that this allowed the researchers to obtain a better and deeper understanding of the (spatial) phenomena of crime. Consequently, the use of alternative measures of crime such as the location quotient, particularly in a spatial context, should not be used to replace spatially referenced crime rates, but to supplement spatially referenced crime rates for a more in-depth understanding of the spatial dynamics of crime.

Crime stability and crime aggregation issues

The discussions above all relate to how we measure crime, or count criminal events. The critical importance of this subject matter needs little justification. However, these are far from the only concerns to deal with in the measurement of crime. Once we have accepted the limitations of criminal event data, decided if criminal events will be represented as counts, a form of rate, or a specialization statistic such as the location quotient, we must still make other decisions that could potentially impact (i.e., bias) our results. In this section, we will review some of my recent research that has investigated issues on the topics of crime stability and crime aggregation.

Because of data limitations and because of standards or common practice, we proceed in our (spatial) crime analyses with a number of assumptions, some explicit and others implicit, regarding crime stability and crime aggregation. Using a spatial point pattern test that I developed—see Andresen (2009b) for the details of the test itself—the appropriateness of these assumptions is investigated. In most cases, there is little justification of continuing to invoke these assumptions, particularly when the data are commonly available now that do not require these assumptions to be made.

The first assumption investigated here is in regard to crime stability—referred to as ecological stability in the social disorganization theory research. In 2011, Nicolas Malleson and I published a journal article that investigated the stability of crime patterns over time—we will revisit this article in Chapter 15 when we discuss the crime and place literature. As discussed in Chapter 2, on social disorganization theory, the stability of crime patterns over time, ecological stability, is important because if the spatial patterns of crime are not stable, then any relationships found may only be relevant for that particular year under analysis. This is not necessarily a problem for the development of theory and/or public policy. If spatial crime patterns do change but change because of the underlying factors explained by theory—the opportunities for criminal events move, spatially—then generalizing is not a problem. However, if the factors explained by social disorganization theory and routine activity theory, for example, do not change and the spatial crime pattern does change, then using these theories to inform public policy decisions would be erroneous.

Because of the support the various theories within environmental criminology have had over the years, this situation is unlikely. Yes, it is possible that our theories may not be able to explain *all* of the changes in the spatial patterns in crime, but if we can explain a good portion of those changes we are in a good position to legitimately inform good public policy to address various criminal event concerns. A more likely problematic situation would emerge if the criminal event data and the data representing the underlying theoretical factors (census data, for example) are not available for the same year. Even if we know there are subtle changes in the spatial patterns of crime from year to year, such changes may be enough to lead to spurious inference.

Such a situation is actually rather common in the environmental criminology literature and the geography of crime literature, more generally. Researchers do not always have the choice of which year of criminal event data they obtain from a police detachment and the census data are only available every five years (Canada) and ten years (United States and United Kingdom)—though different years of availability may be present in other countries, a census that gathers detailed information on the population is typically not available more frequently than every five years because of the costs associated with gathering these data. Consider a country in which the census is conducted every ten years. This means that a researcher may have as many as nine years' difference between census data and criminal event data—census data for the year 2000 and criminal event data for the year 2009, for example. Such a situation is potentially problematic because there may have been changes to the spatial patterns of crime by 2009 that cannot be accounted for using the 2000 census data; as discussed above, this may lead to spurious inference.

In our analysis of Vancouver, Canada, Nicolas Malleson and I found that ecological stability cannot be assumed except for a small number of cases. The spatial point pattern test we used generates an Index of Similarity that ranges from 0 to unity. The closer to unity, the more similar the spatial point patterns. We considered an Index value of 0.80 or greater to indicate that two spatial point patterns are similar—see Andresen and Linning (2012) and Andresen and Malleson (2013a) for discussions of this value. We compared the years 1991, 1996, and 2001, because those are census years within Canada, for the crimes of assault, burglary, robbery, sexual assault, theft, theft of vehicle, and theft from vehicle. As such, each crime type was tested for similarity across each of the available years: 1991–1996, 1996–2001, and 1991–2001. The spatial units of analysis were census tracts, dissemination areas, and street segments. Census tracts are very common spatial units of analysis in environmental criminology; dissemination areas are geographically smaller, being similar to the census block group in the United States' census; and street segments represent each block face on every street and has become a common spatial unit of analysis in the crime and place literature (to be further discussed in Chapter 15). There were 110 census tracts, 1,011 dissemination areas, and 11,730 street segments in Vancouver for 2001.

In the context of census tracts, none of the results of the spatial point pattern test revealed similarity even close to the threshold Index value of 0.80. The highest magnitude Index values were close or essentially equal to 0.50 for sexual assault. Curiously, the longer time span of 1991–2000 did not consistently generate Index value results that were lower than the other five-year time spans. The dissemination area results exhibited more promising results. Both robbery and sexual assault had Index values that were approaching the threshold value of 0.80. However, aside from these two crime types, all Index values were still below 0.40. In an analysis of street segments, robbery and sexual assault both exceeded the critical threshold Index value of 0.80, with sexual assault exceeding 0.90 for all comparisons. The remaining Index values were greater than 0.50 in all other crime types except for theft from vehicle.

These results are discouraging for the use of different years of criminal event and census data. Only in the case of robbery and sexual assault at the street segment level is there consistency over time in the spatial point patterns. This is particularly discouraging, because census data are not available for this level of geography. Consequently, it is critical to minimize, ideally eliminate, any differences in the years for census data and criminal event data.

The second assumption investigated here is that of aggregating individual crime types into statistics such as property crime, violent crime, and all crime. In 2012, I investigated this phenomenon in a journal article with Shannon Linning considering both Vancouver, Canada and Ottawa, Canada. This comparison of two different cities in the same analysis proved to be very useful in identifying underlying tendencies regarding this aggregation. As with the previous study, we used census tracts, dissemination areas, and street segments; Ottawa is a geographically larger city than Vancouver, consisting of 184 census tracts, 1,275 dissemination areas, and 32,789 street segments. Rather than comparing the spatial patterns of crime across time, in this article we analyzed the similarity of various crime types with each other: assault and burglary, for example. For Vancouver, we used 2001 criminal event data for the crime types listed above plus the aggregate of those crime types; for Ottawa, we used 2006 criminal event data for the crime types of commercial burglary, residential burglary, total burglary, commercial robbery, individual robbery, other robbery, total robbery, theft of vehicle, and total crime, with total crime being the aggregate of these crime types.

In the context of Vancouver, we found that there was almost no similarity between the spatial patterns of the various crime types for census tracts. Of the possible twenty-eight comparisons, the Index of Similarity only exceeded 0.30 on four occasions. Though there were changes in the same set of comparisons using dissemination areas, the qualitative results were essentially the same: very low (if any) similarity between the spatial patterns of the various crime types—the Index value for robbery and sexual assault was approaching the critical threshold value of 0.80. Only in the analysis of street segments did the Index begin to increase in magnitude. However, the threshold of 0.80 was only surpassed in one case: robbery and sexual assault. The results for Ottawa were more encouraging. The census tract results were basically the same as Vancouver, indicating that the spatial patterns of individual crime types were rather different. The results for the dissemination areas were promising for the various classifications of robbery, indicating that the various classifications of robbery took place in similar areas with Index values all at 0.85 or greater. And the street segment analysis for Ottawa has the most promising results, with no Index value being less than 0.87. This indicates that at this level of geography the aggregation of individual crime types is not problematic in Ottawa.

There is at least one implication that may be drawn from these results. In the case of Vancouver, only robbery and sexual assault could be aggregated together to form a "violent crime" statistic. In Vancouver these two crime types only occurred in just over 5 percent (robbery) and just under 3 percent (sexual assault) of the street segments in the entire city. This is an incredible concentration of criminal events. In Ottawa, all of the crime types investigated occurred in just under 10 percent of all the street segments in the entire city; aside from total burglary, all of the individual crime types were concentrated within less than 5 percent of street segments. Again, this is an incredible concentration of criminal events. The implication is that if criminal events, of any crime type, are highly concentrated, that concentration takes place in the same area. Consequently, it is less likely that any spatial bias will be imposed on any aggregations of crime types. In Vancouver this may only take place for two crime types at the street segment level, but in Ottawa this may take place for robbery at the dissemination area or smaller and for all crime types (listed above) if the spatial unit of analysis is street segment. Of course, this is an hypothesis that must be tested in other contexts.

Overall, the implication here is that in most cases it is not advisable to aggregate individual crime types to any sort of statistic if the spatial pattern of crime is of interest. This is a common practice within environmental criminology. I have committed this act myself! More research is needed in this area, but similar to the stability of spatial crime patterns, the aggregation of individual crime types may lead to spurious inference because the spatial patterns of the individual crime types are so dissimilar—the overall spatial crime pattern muddles the individual spatial crime patterns.

Lastly, Nicolas Malleson and I published a journal article in 2013 investigating the aggregation of criminal event data to yearly observations. This article falls within the seasonality of crime literature that is further discussed in Chapter 11. However, the results of the work on the seasonality of crime with Nicolas Malleson has implications that deserve discussion here as well. Aside from the seasonality of crime literature, it would be unusual to see a research article or book chapter investigating the spatial patterns of crime at different times of the year. There is a small literature that does investigate this phenomenon, discussed in Chapter 11, but this research is not the norm. Most often, an entire year of criminal event data is analyzed with a (corresponding) year of census data. Or, in the few instances of longitudinal data analysis, yearly observations are used, or the seasonality within the data are not the primary interest.

In this work with Nicolas Malleson, we specifically investigated the similarity of spatial patterns comparing yearly aggregate criminal event data with the four seasons in Vancouver for the crime types listed above. We again used the spatial point pattern test discussed above, using census tracts, dissemination areas, and criminal event data for Vancouver in 2001. Overall, we found the presence of seasonality in most crime types, but the nature of that seasonality pattern did differ. For example, assaults had the expected seasonality trend in that assaults peaked in the summer. Theft, theft from vehicle, theft of vehicle, and burglary tended to peak in the fall or later in the year, and robbery and sexual assault had little evidence for a seasonal trend.

The general pattern of the previous work in Vancouver, discussed above, is present here as well. For most crime types the Index of Similarity was less than 0.60, especially in the analyses of census tracts. Most often, the dissemination area results were better, but not by much. Only for the crime types of robbery and sexual assault did the dissemination area results consistently exceed the critical threshold Index value of 0.80, particularly when considering the various seasons compared with the yearly aggregated data—robbery was very close to 0.80 in this latter case, greater than 0.75, but not quite at the threshold value.

The interpretation of these results appears to be the same as with the other research discussed above. If a crime type is sufficiently concentrated in space, it may be aggregated to a yearly aggregate without imposing any spatial bias. This may occur because whenever these criminal events occur (different seasons or different years) they always occur in the same places.

This brief review of these issues should make it clear that we cannot simply continue to invoke these assumptions (and others) when we analyze (spatial) crime patterns. This is particularly true in the case of spatial crime analysis and environmental criminology because of the additional dimensions of space and time explicit in the type of research that is undertaken.

The future of crime measurement

As indicated earlier in this chapter, probably one of the most important future research projects regarding crime measurement is a neighborhood level victimization survey for a number of crime types that will allow for a comparison of the spatial similarity of victimization criminal event data and police criminal event data. If such research finds that the spatial patterns are similar (enough), then we do not have to be concerned regarding any inferences made using police criminal event data. If, however, the spatial patterns are dissimilar enough to cause concern, we must do two things: 1) revisit all that we think we know based on the study of police data, and 2) attempt to devise a methodology for modifying the spatial patterns of police criminal event data such that they are more representative of the overall spatial patterns of actual criminal event data. Even if a "perfect" methodology cannot be determined, some methodology that could be developed would minimize the bias in any empirical research using police criminal event data. This is similar to the ambient population data: it may not be the perfect population at risk measurement, but it will reduce the bias present from employing the resident population data from the census.

In the context of spatially referenced crime rates, there is a need for applications of the Oak Ridge National Laboratory data in other contexts, primarily other locations. The research undertaken to date, using Vancouver, has proven to be most instructive. However, it is possible that these ambient population data may not be as useful in different locations. For example, the ambient population data from Oak Ridge National Laboratory may only be useful to spatial crime analysis for municipalities that are sufficiently large. Additionally, there are other sources for ambient population data that may be instructive in a spatial crime analysis context. The SENSEable City Lab at MIT (http://senseable.mit.edu), for example, uses cellular phone call data to estimate where people are. Additionally, with the proliferation of mobile technologies, more generally, applications such as Facebook and Twitter that use location data may be used to get a better understanding of where the population at risk may be. Moreover, the data obtained from mobile devices may allow for measurements of the population at risk for different days of the year and different times of the day. However, the use of such data may raise significant privacy concerns.

Research on the alternative measures of crime should involve a broader application of the location quotient. The purpose of this broader application is to continue to supplement the spatially referenced crime rate. Moreover, the crime rate and location quotient are not the only available measures that can be applied to the study of criminal events and their spatial dynamics. Future research should investigate other alternatives to be found in other disciplines such as economics or geography. Though the spatial patterns of a number of different specialization measures are similar, there are many readily available measures that may be applied to criminological research (Andresen, 2014).

And, lastly, we need to continuously question the assumptions we invoke when undertaking (spatial) crime analysis, particularly within environmental criminology. As discussed above, we cannot simply assume any of the following: ecological stability, spatial homogeneity, the similarity of spatial patterns for different crime types and their aggregations, and the similarity of spatial patterns within the same crime type but at different times of the year. As is most often the case, these statements are not controversial when they are made. The most common response is: of course that is true. But we still invoke these assumptions, sometimes unconsciously, simply because so many researchers before us did. We need to stop doing this and continue to question that which we assume to be true in order to advance crime science.

Review questions

1   In the context of spatial criminology, what is the most important implication of the dark figure of crime?
2   Why is the population at risk so important for spatially referenced crime rate calculations?
3   What have been the impacts of the ambient population in spatial crime analysis? State and briefly discuss three of them.
4   What are the general implications of using an alternative population at risk with the impacts you cited in question 3?
5   What is the location quotient and what does it measure?
6   Does an area with a high crime rate necessarily specialize in a particular crime type? Explain.
7   Explain the situation in which ecological instability is problematic and why.
8   Is it important for criminal event data and data representing theoretical factors to be measured in the same year? Explain.
9   Is it a good idea to aggregate individual crime types into aggregate crime types such as property crime and violent crime? Why or why not?
10   Why might it be problematic to analyze criminal event data aggregated to yearly observations?

References

Andresen, M. A. (2006a). Crime measures and the spatial analysis of criminal activity. *British Journal of Criminology*, 46(2), 258–85.

Andresen, M. A. (2006b). A spatial analysis of crime in Vancouver, British Columbia: A synthesis of social disorganization and routine activity theory. *Canadian Geographer*, 50(4), 487–502.

Andresen, M. A. (2007). Location quotients, ambient populations, and the spatial analysis of crime in Vancouver, Canada. *Environment and Planning A*, 39(10), 2423–44.

Andresen, M. A. (2009a). Crime specialization across the Canadian provinces. *Canadian Journal of Criminology and Criminal Justice*, 51(1), 31–53.

Andresen, M. A. (2009b). Testing for similarity in area-based spatial patterns: A nonparametric Monte Carlo approach. *Applied Geography*, 29(3), 333–45.

Andresen, M. A. (2010). Diurnal movements and the ambient population: An application to municipal level crime rate calculations. *Canadian Journal of Criminology and Criminal Justice*, 52(1), 97–109.

Andresen, M. A. (2011a). The ambient population and crime analysis. *Professional Geographer*, 63(2), 193–212.

Andresen, M. A. (2011b). Estimating the probability of local crime clusters: The impact of immediate spatial neighbors. *Journal of Criminal Justice*, 39(5), 394–404.

Andresen, M. A. (2013a). *The science of crime measurement: Issues for spatially-referenced crime data.* New York, NY: Routledge.

Andresen, M. A. (2014). Measuring crime specializations and concentrations. In D. Weisburd and G. Bruinsma (eds.), *Encyclopedia of criminology and criminal justice.* New York, NY: Springer-Verlag, 3010-3023.

Andresen, M. A. and Jenion, G. W. (2010). Ambient populations and the calculation of crime rates and risk. *Security Journal*, 23(2), 114–33.

Andresen, M. A., Jenion, G. W., and Jenion, M. L. (2003). Conventional calculations of homicide rates lead to an inaccurate reflection of Canadian trends. *Canadian Journal of Criminology and Criminal Justice*, 45(1), 1–17.

Andresen, M. A. and Linning, S. J. (2012). The (in)appropriateness of aggregating across crime types. *Applied Geography*, 35(1/2), 275–82.

Andresen, M. A. and Malleson, N. (2011). Testing the stability of crime patterns: Implications for theory and policy. *Journal of Research in Crime and Delinquency*, 48(1), 58–82.

Andresen, M. A. and Malleson, N. (2013a). Crime seasonality and its variations across space. *Applied Geography*, 43, 25–35.

Anselin, L. (1995). Local indicators of spatial association—LISA. *Geographical Analysis*, 27(2), 93–115.

Barr, R. and Pease, K. (1990). Crime placement, displacement and deflection. *Crime and Justice: A Review of Research*, 12, 277–318.

Block, S., Clarke, R. V., Maxfield, M. G., and Petrossian, G. (2012). Estimating the number of U.S. vehicles stolen for export using crime location quotients. In M. A. Andresen and J.B. Kinney (eds.), *Patterns, prevention, and geometry of crime* (pp. 54–68). New York, NY: Routledge.

Boggs, S. L. (1965). Urban crime patterns. *American Sociological Review*, 30(6), 899–908.

Boyd, N. (2000). *The beast within: Why men are violent.* Vancouver, BC: Greystone Books.

Brantingham, P. L. and Brantingham, P. J. (1993c). Location quotients and crime hot spots in the city. In C. R. Block and M. Dabdoub (eds.), Workshop on crime analysis through computer mapping, *Proceedings* (pp. 175–97). Chicago, IL: Criminal Justice Information Authority.

Brantingham, P. L. and Brantingham, P. J. (1995b). Location quotients and crime hot spots in the city. In C. R. Block, M. Dabdoub, and S. Fregly (eds.), *Crime analysis through computer mapping* (pp. 129–49). Washington, DC: Police Executive Research Forum.

Brantingham, P. L. and Brantingham, P. J. (1998). Mapping crime for analytic purposes: Location quotients, counts and rates. In D. Weisburd and T. McEwen (eds.), *Crime mapping and crime prevention* (pp. 263–88). Monsey, NY: Criminal Justice Press.

Bulwer, H. L. (1836). *France, social, literary, political*, vol. 1, book 1, *Crime*. London, UK: Richard Bentley.

Ceccato, V. and Lukyte, N. (2011). Safety and sustainability in a city in transition: The case of Vilnius, Lithuania. *Cities*, 28(1), 83–94.

Cohen, L. E., Kaufman, R. L., and Gottfredson, M. R. (1985). Risk-based crime statistics: A forecasting comparison for comparison for burglary and auto theft. *Journal of Criminal Justice*, 13(5), 445–57.

Dobson, J. E. (2003). Estimating populations at risk. In S. L. Cutter, D. B. Richardson, and T. J. Wilbanks (eds.), *The geographical dimensions of terrorism* (pp. 161–7). New York and London: Routledge.

Dobson, J. E. (2004). The GIS revolution in science and society. In S. D. Brunn, S. L. Cutter, and J. W. Harrington, Jr. (eds.), *Geography and technology* (pp. 573–87). Dordrecht: Kluwer Academic Publishers.

Dobson, J. E., Bright, E. A., Coleman, P. R., and Bhaduri, B. L. (2003). LandScan: A global population database for estimating populations at risk. In V. Mesev (ed.), *Remotely sensed cities* (pp. 267–79). London and New York: Taylor and Francis.

Dobson, J. E., Bright, E. A., Coleman, P. R., Durfee, R. C., and Worley, B. A. (2000). LandScan: A global population database for estimating populations at risk. *Photogrammetric Engineering and Remote Sensing*, 66(7), 849–57.

Federal Bureau of Investigation. (2013). Uniform Crime Reporting Statistics. Available online at http://bjs.gov/ucrdata/ [accessed May 8, 2013].

Harries, K. D. (1981). Alternative denominators in conventional crime rates. In P. J. Brantingham and P. L. Brantingham (eds.), *Environmental criminology* (pp. 147–65). Beverly Hills, CA: Sage Publications.

Harries, K. D. (1991) Alternative denominators in conventional crime rates. In P. J. Brantingham and P. L. Brantingham (eds.), *Environmental criminology* (pp. 147–65). Prospect Heights, IL: Waveland Press.

Isard, W., Azis, I. J., Drennan, M. P., Miller, R. E., Saltzman, S., and Thorbecke, E. (1998). *Methods of interregional and regional analysis*. Aldershot: Ashgate Publishing Limited.

McCord, E. S. and Ratcliffe, J. H. (2007). A micro-spatial analysis of the demographic and criminogenic environment of drug markets in Philadelphia. *Australian and New Zealand Journal of Criminology*, 40(1), 43–63.

Miller, M. M., Gibson, L. J., and Wright, N. G. (1991). Location quotient: A basic tool for economic development studies. *Economic Development Review*, 9(2), 65–8.

Monmonier, M. (1996). *How to lie with maps*, 2nd edition. Chicago, IL: University of Chicago Press.

Mosher, C. J., Miethe, T. D., and Hart, T. C. (2011). *The mismeasure of crime*, 2nd edition. Los Angeles, CA: Sage Publications.

O'Brien, R. M. (1989). Relative cohort size and age-specific crime rates: An age-period-relative-cohort-size model. *Criminology*, 27(1), 57–78.

Oak Ridge National Laboratory (2003). *LandScan Global Population Database*. Oak Ridge, TN: Oak Ridge National Laboratory. Data available online at http://www.ornl.gov/sci/gist/ [accessed July 2, 2013].

Pallone, N. J. (1999). Editor's notebook: On numerators in search of denominators: An exhortation toward caution in interpreting "reductions" in crime "rates." *Journal of Offender Rehabilitation*, 28(3/4), 145–54.

Perreault, S. and Brennan, S. (2010). *Criminal victimization in Canada, 2009*. Ottawa, ON: Statistics Canada.

Ratcliffe, J. H., and Rengert, G. F. (2008). Near repeat patterns in Philadelphia shootings. *Security Journal*, 21(1/2), 58–76.

Rengert, G. F. (1996). *The geography of illegal drugs*. Boulder, CO: Westview Press.

Sacco, V. F. (2000). News that counts: Newspaper images of crime and victimization statistics. *Criminologie*, 33(1), 203–23.

Sacco, V. F. and Kennedy, L. W. (2002). *The criminal event: An introduction to criminology in Canada*, 3rd edition. Toronto, ON: Nelson.

Sacco, V. F. and Kennedy, L. W. (2011). *The criminal event: An introduction to criminology in Canada*, 5th edition. Toronto, ON: Nelson.

Schmid, C. F. (1960a). Urban crime areas: Part I. *American Sociological Review*, 25(4), 527–42.

Schmid, C. F. (1960b). Urban crime areas: Part II. *American Sociological Review*, 25(5), 655–78.

Sherman, L. W., Gartin, P., and Buerger, M. E. (1989). Hot spots of predatory crime: Routine activities and the criminology of place. *Criminology*, 27(1), 27–55.

Statistics Canada (2012). Uniform Crime Reporting Survey (UCR). Ottawa, ON:

Statistics Canada. Data available online at http://www23.statcan.gc.ca/imdb-bmdi/pub/indexU-eng.htm [accessed July 2, 2013].

Twain, M. (1906). Chapters from my autobiography. *North American Review*, 183, 321–30.

Chapter 9

Spatial issues with crime analysis

Introduction

As outlined in the previous chapter, there are many issues that must be addressed, or at least acknowledged, when undertaking some form of (spatial) crime analysis. However, even if all of those crime measurement issues are addressed to a greater or lesser extent there are still other issues that relate to the spatial analysis itself. In this chapter, we will not cover subject matter that relates to crime mapping, per se. For information on that topic, I refer the reader to a publication published by the United States National Institute of Justice in 1999: *Mapping Crime: Principle and Practice*, by Keith Harries. Though this publication is now fifteen years old, it covers a lot of the fundamentals of crime mapping that do not change and is available free for download: https://www.ncjrs.gov/html/nij/mapping/pdf.html. Rather, in this chapter we will cover a few of the "bigger" issues with regard to spatial crime analysis. Specifically, we will cover: ecological fallacy, modifiable areal unit problem, spatial autocorrelation, local analysis, and visualization.

This approach is taken here because the technical aspects of spatial crime analysis more generally, and crime mapping specifically, change very quickly with newly available software and methods (Harries, 1999). However, the issues discussed below are constantly present within spatial crime analysis. In fact, many of the new techniques that emerged within spatial analysis have the purpose of addressing these issues with spatial data.

Ecological fallacy

The ecological fallacy occurs when statistical data are interpreted in such a manner that inference regarding individuals is deduced from relationships identified at the level of groups of individuals. More generally, the ecological fallacy occurs when one assumes that a statistical relationship found at one level of analysis is present for "smaller" units of analysis that are within the original level of analysis: provinces or states within a country, regions within a province or state, municipalities within a province or state, neighborhoods within a municipality, individuals within a neighborhood. To speak colloquially, that which is true for the whole is assumed to be true for all of the parts; the atomistic fallacy states that what is true of the part is also true of the whole. Though this is technically true, on average, it is fallacious to assume such relationships to be true for all of the parts within the whole. We have already indirectly discussed the presence of the ecological fallacy in this book. In Chapter 1, and elsewhere, the trajectory of spatial criminology was said to have been moving to ever smaller spatial units of analysis. This trajectory is usually couched in terms of spatial heterogeneity. And the presence of spatial heterogeneity recognizes the potential for making the ecological fallacy. An example from my own research, in the context of spatial crime analysis, is discussed below.

In 1950, William Robinson published the seminal article on the ecological fallacy. Robinson defined an individual correlation as a statistic involving subjects that are indivisible; an individual person is a prime example here. Further, he defined an ecological correlation as a statistic involving a group of subjects that are divisible; a census tract or neighborhood are good examples here because both are divisible into individuals, housing units, and blocks. In his article, Robinson showed the mathematical relationships between individual and ecological correlations. Specifically, he showed the conditions in which an individual correlation and an ecological correlation would be equal; however, he stated that there was no evidence for these conditions to hold.

In an effort to investigate the implications of the ecological fallacy in the context of areal (census) data, Stan Openshaw published an article (1984a) employing a number of statistical methods. Through his various analyses, Openshaw was able to show that the ecological fallacy was important for areal census data, but the severity of any problems that emerged depended upon the method of analysis, how results were interpreted, and which variables were employed in the analysis. Moreover, the differences between individual and ecological correlation coefficients cannot be known *a priori*.

In 2013, Nicolas Malleson and I published a book chapter on the degree of spatial heterogeneity within various spatial units of analysis. We considered data from both Vancouver, Canada and Leeds, England—the same crime types as with the previous research. Though many researchers acknowledge the importance of spatial scale, spatial heterogeneity, and the modifiable areal unit problem, discussed further below, there is very little research on the effects of these issues, particularly in the context of spatial crime analysis. As stated previously, the overall trajectory of spatial units of analysis in spatial criminology over the past 200 years has definitely been a decrease in the geographic size of the spatial units of analysis—relatively large spatial units of analysis are still being used, and are still considered to be instructive. Whenever spatial units of analysis decrease in geographic size there is often reference to spatial heterogeneity within the larger spatial unit of analysis: there is much variability of crime patterns within census tracts, for example (Sherman et al., 1989). However, we were unaware of any studies that quantified the degree of spatial heterogeneity within larger spatial units of analysis.

The analysis was undertaken to see if the changes in the spatial pattern of crime over time for census tracts were the same as the corresponding changes for dissemination areas, using the spatial point pattern test discussed above—middle layer super output areas and output areas for the data in Leeds, England. Most often, we found Index values less than 0.60, indicating a substantial degree of spatial heterogeneity within geographically smaller spatial units of analysis. What this clearly showed was that any inferences, specifically regarding change over time, at the level of the census tract cannot be assumed at the dissemination area, or equivalent. This is quite clearly an example of the potential for the ecological fallacy in crime analysis. As discussed in the crime and place literature—see Chapter 15— this is even more prevalent at the level of the micro-place: street addresses, street intersections, and street segments. Perhaps most interesting was that in a few cases, the smaller spatial units of analysis within the larger units had nothing in common with those larger units with regard to the type of change occurring. A close investigation of the data showed that this occurred because the differences from year to year in the smaller units of analysis were very low in magnitude and not big enough to indicate a statistically significant change, but when all those low magnitude changes were aggregated to one larger spatial unit of analysis, statistical significance was achieved.

The good news regarding the ecological fallacy is that it is easy to avoid: do not make any statistical inference at a level different from your analysis. At times, however, this is easier said than done, because we do not think in terms of neighborhoods causing crime, especially within a course in environmental criminology. Rather, we think about individuals making choices, so it is easy to do colloquially and commit the ecological fallacy. In this example, what we need to do is think of the results in a probabilistic manner. Neighborhoods do not cause crime, but certain conditions within a neighborhood may alter the probabilities that an individual would be an offender. Some may argue that I am walking on thin ice with this last statement, but I am not saying that individuals coming from a particular neighborhood are criminals because of a statistically significant relationship found at the neighborhood level. The lesson here is that the ecological fallacy is omnipresent in spatial crime analysis, it unpredictably impacts the results in an analysis depending upon a number of factors, but it can be avoided as long as inference is made with care. The same cannot be said regarding the modifiable areal unit problem.

Modifiable areal unit problem

Though researchers were aware of the modifiable areal unit problem previously, in 1984 Stan Openshaw published a pedagogical guide (1984b) that is often viewed as the starting point of serious academic scholarship on this issue—Gehlke and Biehl (1934) found that the magnitude of correlation coefficients increased as areal units were successively grouped into larger geographical units. The modifiable areal unit problem, commonly referred to using its acronym MAUP, is an issue for spatial analysis, including spatial crime analysis. The MAUP is similar to the ecological fallacy because it is a result of data aggregation. Specifically, the MAUP emerges because data (usually) gathered at a micro-level are arbitrarily aggregated into a set of spatial units. Census data are a prime example here: census data are gathered at the level of the individual and the household, then aggregated to spatial units such as block groups (United States), output areas (United Kingdom), dissemination areas (Canada), and census tracts. The census units are defined based on population counts and street boundaries for comparability across space and time (past and future censuses), but the census units themselves are arbitrary in the sense that they are not defined in such a manner to represent actual neighborhoods, for example. In this sense, these census units are modifiable because they can be redefined simply by changing the boundaries and they are areal because they represent some unit of area. We will get to the problem shortly.

There are two primary ways in which the MAUP may manifest itself. First, and most common, is from using spatial units of analysis that are of different geographic sizes. This is referred to as the scale problem. For example, an analysis may use both of: dissemination areas and census tracts (Canada), block groups and census tracts (United States), or output areas and middle layer super output areas (United Kingdom). In each of these cases, census data are represented at different scales, with one spatial unit of analysis covering a smaller area and a lesser population than the other—dissemination areas, block groups, and output areas fit within census tracts, census tracts, and middle layer super output areas, respectively. The second primary way in which the MAUP emerges is through a spatial shift in existing boundaries. This is referred to as the zoning problem. In this situation, the size and dimension of all the spatial units of analysis do not change, they are simply placed on the study area in a different place; think of a set of square grids on a map that are all the same size that you "drag" to a different location on the map. Both of these situations will lead to different aggregations of the micro-level data—in the grid example, the aggregations could be exactly the same if the grid was shifted exactly the distance of the grid width.

A priori, this is not necessarily a problem. The problem in the MAUP emerges because research consistently, though not exclusively, shows that different aggregations of micro-level data have led to different results. Moreover, there has not been the recognition of any systematic patterns that would allow for the prediction and correction of the MAUP (Openshaw, 1984b). This is a significant problem in any analysis of aggregated spatial data because a statistical relationship may be identified that is only an artifact of the spatial data aggregation rather than an underlying (social) process that can be impacted through public policy. One notable exception, briefly mentioned above, is that, as the number of spatial units of analysis decreases and the geographic size of the spatial units of analysis necessarily increases, the magnitude of correlation coefficients also increases. This is a pattern that emerges within the scale problem. This is an important result that clearly ties itself to the ecological fallacy, showing the potential problems with making individual level inferences from aggregate data. However, it should also be noted that Stan Openshaw (1984b) showed through a redefinition of spatial units of analysis that correlation coefficients could be altered from 0.99 to −0.99 by invoking the zoning problem. Consequently, because of the presence of the scale problem and the zoning problem, one may not only get the magnitude of a correlation coefficient wrong, but also its sign—Stan Openshaw also identified a similar problem using other, multivariate statistical methods.

In 1991, Stewart Fotheringham and David Wong published a journal article that investigated the MAUP in a multivariate context, extending the research of Stan Openshaw into more commonly used statistical methods in (geographical) social sciences. Specifically, these authors sought to demonstrate that statistical estimates in a multivariate context, regression, were not reliable because of the MAUP. Needless to say, they were able to demonstrate this unreliability, even referring to their results as "depressing." In the context of the scale problem, for example, they showed that the estimated coefficient in a regression could increase in magnitude approximately nine times by reducing the number of spatial units of analysis from 800 to 25. This may sound like an unreasonable reduction in the number of spatial units of analysis, but in the case of Vancouver, Canada, in 2006 there were 1,011 dissemination areas defined by Statistics Canada and 24 neighborhoods defined by the City of Vancouver. Fotheringham and Wong go on to state that it was possible for them to find almost any result through different aggregations of the data and that the effects of the MAUP within a multivariate (regression) analysis were more unpredictable than with the analyses presented by Stan Openshaw (1984b).

These empirical studies of the MAUP definitely do not bode well for spatial crime analysis because it uses these same forms of data, most often. Turning to some criminological examples, in 2002 John Wooldredge published a journal article investigating aggregation issues (MAUP) for crime. In his research study, Wooldredge analyzed 1932 individuals, 129 census tracts, and 48 official neighborhoods in Cincinnati for the crime of domestic assault using a regression analysis with over 30 variables. When statistically significant, Wooldredge effectively found that there were no differences with the results when comparing census tracts to official neighborhoods. Consequently, overall it makes little difference which spatial unit of analysis was used. Wooldredge did find, however, that census tracts were more favorable than official neighborhoods in a few contexts. Some of these advantages likely emerged simply from having more observations in the data and, subsequently, more variation. In most cases, this allows for better precision in statistical estimates.

John Hipp published a journal article in 2007 that investigated the importance of spatial units of analysis not only for criminological studies, but neighborhood level studies more generally. Hipp spoke more directly to the geographical literature in this article. He stated that we need to consider more natural spatial units of analysis that make sense for the process or relationship being measured— Openshaw (1984b) also called for such aggregations of spatial data. Hipp argued that researchers need to consider the theoretical relationships they are analyzing in order to choose which spatial unit of analysis is appropriate. For example, just because it may make sense to measure housing prices at the neighborhood level does not mean that the unemployment rate should also be measured at the neighborhood level. These distinctions depend on theory. And when we know that different sizes of spatial units of analysis impact the results, we must choose spatial units of analysis appropriately if we wish to properly inform public policy.

In some of my own research already discussed in Chapter 8 (Andresen, 2011a), I found results similar to those of Wooldredge (2002). In a spatial regression context there was very little difference in the nature of estimated coefficients when comparing census tracts to dissemination areas if both variables were statistically significant. One difference that did emerge was that the dissemination area model retained more statistically significant variables. However, as alluded to in the context of Wooldredge's study, this was likely just a consequence of having more observations and variability in the dissemination area model: 990 dissemination areas versus 110 census tracts in that particular analysis.

The lesson to be learned here is that you should never "trust" strong statements based on research that has only been conducted at one spatial scale. Though some research has indicated that it does not matter which spatial unit of analysis is used—Wooldredge (2002) stated that it is irrelevant—this research has its limitations. Wooldredge (2002) was an analysis of one municipality and one relatively rare (within police statistics) criminal event: domestic assault. My own work that indirectly investigates the MAUP, Andresen (2011a), was again only for one municipality with one aggregated crime type (violent crime).

Though this may not always be a possibility because of data access and restrictions, a researcher should undertake their analysis using at least two different spatial units of analysis—most often this will be at two different spatial scales. This will at least provide some indication if the results can be considered robust because they are qualitatively similar, or not. If statistically significant changes occur when the spatial units of analysis change, and those statistically significant changes are also meaningful (modify interpretations), much caution should be taken when making inference. However, if it makes little difference which spatial units of analysis are used, then at least some confidence may be exhibited when presenting results. However, it is always important to keep in mind that Stan Openshaw and Fotheringham and Wong found that modifying spatial units of analysis could lead to a full spectrum of results. As such, just because a theory or public policy is supported by a spatial analysis does not necessarily mean that the relationship is actually there.

Spatial autocorrelation and its impact on analyses

If things were not already bad enough with measurement issues and the modifiable areal unit problem, there is one further "big" issue for the analysis of spatial (crime) data: spatial autocorrelation. A very common assumption in statistical analyses is independence. Independence simply means that the occurrence of one event does not impact the probability of another event. For example, if you roll a 6 on a fair die, you cannot use that information to make a prediction on the number that will emerge on the next roll—the probability of any given value is always 1/6. The assumption of independence in statistical analyses is not a requirement, per se, but if this assumption holds then the statistical analysis is much more straightforward.

A common example of when independence is not a reasonable assumption is with time series data: daily, monthly, quarterly, or yearly time series. An excellent, though not perfect, predictor of the temperature on any given day is the temperature the day before. Time series data are very common in academic research. Research in areas such as finance, macroeconomics, climate, and even criminology commonly employ time series data. Because of the lack of independence of such data, in most cases, whole subfields in statistics and econometrics have emerged to address this lack of independence, termed autocorrelation.

It should be perfectly clear from the title of this section that time series autocorrelation is not the only form of autocorrelation. Though (environmental) criminologists do undertake analyses with time series data that require time series statistics/econometrics, more common in environmental criminology is the presence of spatial autocorrelation. Similar to the presence of autocorrelation in a temporal context, in the presence of spatial autocorrelation if a researcher knows the value of some variable for one spatial unit, that information can be used to make predictions regarding the values of other spatial units of analysis nearby. Needless to say, there are subfields of spatial statistics and spatial econometrics that are incredibly extensive in the development of statistical methods to address the issue of spatial autocorrelation.

Spatial autocorrelation can take two forms: positive and negative. In positive spatial autocorrelation, Figure 9.1a, neighboring spatial units of analysis have similar values. In this particular case, the reference spatial unit of analysis has a value of "10," and neighboring values are similar, but decrease according to a distance decay pattern—see Chapter 4. Negative spatial autocorrelation, Figure 9.1b, has neighboring spatial units of analysis being very different. If the reference spatial unit of analysis has a high value, its neighboring spatial units of analysis will have low values. This is shown in Figure 9.1b with the spatial autocorrelation occurring as values radiate out from the center reference spatial unit of analysis with a value of 10.

In most social contexts, data exhibit positive spatial autocorrelation, including crime. This pattern was evident in the previous chapter in Figure 8.4 with dissemination areas: dissemination areas close to one another in and around the central business district had high-valued crime rates (both resident- and ambient-based), with those crime rates decreasing further away from the central business district. This is a common spatial pattern of crime that dates back at least to the original work on social disorganization theory in Chicago. Consequently, if any analysis used data that are spatial and did not acknowledge spatial autocorrelation and use

4	6	5	4	6
6	8	8	9	5
5	7	**10**	7	6
4	9	7	8	6
5	6	4	6	5

a) Positive spatial autocorrelation

10	9	10	9	8
8	2	2	3	9
9	4	**10**	4	8
10	4	2	3	9
8	9	10	10	8

b) Negative spatial autocorrelation

Figure 9.1 Spatial autocorrelation.

the appropriate spatial statistical technique, particularly in a regression context, the results may be spurious.

Generally speaking, the consequence of ignoring spatial autocorrelation in a statistical context is that relationships between variables will appear to be stronger than they really are. In a regression context, in the presence of (positive) spatial autocorrelation the standard errors of the estimated coefficients are underestimated. This simply means that variables may appear to be statistically significant when they are not, leading to the retention of more variables in the statistical model, and depending on the modeling strategy this may also lead to greater levels for goodness of fit. This all means that your results will appear to be "better" than they really are.

What this all means is that if a researcher is using spatial data, s/he should always test for the presence of spatial autocorrelation. If spatial autocorrelation is present, s/he should use the appropriate spatial statistical method that is designed for such data or "filters out" the spatial autocorrelation so statistical results are representative of underlying social processes, not spatial proximity. In the context of regression analysis, there are two primary spatial statistical methods: the spatial-lag model and spatial-error model. We will not get into the statistical details of these methods here, but the spatial-lag model filters out the spatial autocorrelation for the dependent variable, whereas the spatial-error model filters out the spatial autocorrelation for the dependent variable and the independent variables. There are a number of statistical diagnoses that can be made to determine if a spatial-lag or spatial-error model is appropriate. A simple way to think about the different models is that the spatial-error model is better able to address spatial autocorrelation because it is filtered out of all the variables and because of the nature of social science data (positive) spatial autocorrelation is almost always present.

Local spatial (crime) analysis

Much of spatial crime analysis is the application of "global" spatial statistical methods. Though I did not explicitly discuss the previous section in this manner, it was all basically in a global context. Global, in this sense, means that one estimated parameter in a regression analysis is used to describe the relationship between two variables, unemployment and crime, for example. But is it reasonable to assume that changes in unemployment impact a relatively wealthy neighborhood in the same way as a relatively impoverished neighborhood? A "global" relationship? Having the unemployment rate increase from 3 percent to 4 percent (a 33 percent increase) may be a big deal in the relatively wealthy neighborhood, but an increase from 13 percent to 14 percent in the relatively impoverished neighborhood would probably go unnoticed. Once such an example is pointed out, it almost sounds ridiculous to undertake a statistical analysis that would generate results such as this. But this is what regression analysis does: parameters are estimated to represent the average impact of one variable on another. This is very interesting information that may be used to inform theory and/or public policy, but it cannot be expected to work equally well in all places.

In local spatial (crime) analysis, rather than trying to understand similarities at a global level (one value representing all spatial units of analysis), the focus is to try to understand the differences across the study area (one value for each of the spatial units of analysis)—spatial nonstationarity. This may be thought of as searching for exceptions to the rule, with the rule being a global relationship. These local exceptions can then be mapped to look for patterns to better understand the underlying processes being studied. Indeed, it is very unlikely that spatial stationarity will be present in any application in the social sciences.

In a journal article published in 1997, Stewart Fotheringham outlined three reasons why we should question any assumption of stationarity in a spatial data analysis. First, just by random chance when sampling across space there will be variations across space within the phenomenon under study. Though important from a statistical perspective, random variations are not particularly interesting. Second, for a variety of reasons there are variations in some relationships across space. Some factors may matter more in particular locations. The simplest examples of this are based on socio-economic status that also varies across space. This matters in the instance of unemployment and crime, used as an example of this above. In this example, the impact of unemployment on crime was discussed as being positive (unemployment goes up so crime goes up) but just with different magnitudes, but it is entirely possible that a statistical relationship may be positive for one spatial unit of analysis and negative for another. And third, we may find that spatial nonstationarity is present because of statistical model misspecification—omitted variable bias. This is a possibility in any statistical analysis that occurs because the researcher omits a variable that is important to the process being studied, or because the relationship between two variables is represented incorrectly—the relationship is assumed to be linear when it is quadratic, for example.

Probably one of the most well-known local spatial statistics used in spatial crime analysis falls under the category of a local indicator of spatial association (LISA), developed by Luc Anselin in a journal article published in 1995. By the nature of the last two letters in its acronym, spatial association, a LISA is a local statistic for measuring the clustering of spatial units of analysis. A LISA is defined by Anselin as any statistic that indicates for each observation (spatial unit of analysis) the degree of spatial clustering, and that the sum of all the LISA statistics is proportional to a global indicator of spatial association (Anselin, 1995). As such, the primary criterion for a local spatial statistic to be a LISA is for it to be related to another global statistic. In the case of Anselin (1995) these two statistics are Moran's I and local Moran's I. Moran's I is the most common global statistic used to test for spatial autocorrelation, ranging from -1 (perfect negative spatial autocorrelation) to $+1$ (perfect positive spatial autocorrelation)—the value of the statistic, because it is a global statistic, represents spatial autocorrelation for the entire study area. Local Moran's I, on the other hand, is a local statistic used to test for the presence of spatial autocorrelation for each spatial unit of analysis. Luc Anselin's development of the local Moran's I goes further to classify each spatial unit of analysis based on the local Moran's I value of its neighbors. For example, if a spatial unit of analysis is classified as high crime and is surrounded by other spatial units of analysis that are high crime, it is part of a High-High cluster. In addition to local Moran's I indicating no statistically significant spatial clustering, there are the following classifications: High-High, High-Low, Low-High, and Low-Low. As one would expect, the latter three LISA classifications in a criminological context represent high crime areas surrounded by low crime areas, low crime areas surrounded by high crime areas, and low crime areas surrounded by low crime areas. High-High and Low-Low LISA classifications represent positive spatial autocorrelation, whereas High-Low and Low-High LISA classifications represent negative spatial autocorrelation.

As stated above, many of the applications of spatial analysis methods in the study of crime are global, with local spatial crime analysis being a relatively small subset of this literature. Despite this subset of the spatial crime analysis literature being relatively small, it has proven to be quite instructive in a few different ways. First, LISA has been used as an exploratory spatial data analysis technique. In exploratory spatial data analysis, LISA has proven to be a powerful tool to be used for investigating spatial randomness at the local level: the degree of spatial interdependence in homicide (Morenoff et al., 2001) and collective efficacy (Morenoff et al., 2001; Sampson et al., 1999), for example. With the identification of statistically significant spatial interdependence (clusters) in crime, this can then be compared to places with or without any spatial interdependence within collective efficacy (Morenoff et al., 2001). Analyses such as these, though exploratory, may be able to reveal why global relationships are not identified in a study area—the relationships are only present at the local area in particular places—or, as discussed below, to identify why a result is opposite of theoretical expectations. Second, LISA may be used to inform subsequent statistical analyses. For example, a LISA analysis may be used to identify areas that are substantively different from each other, sometimes referred to as spatial regimes. Different spatial regimes indicate the necessity to undertake separate statistical analyses because the estimated parameters (or even entire models) are expected to be different for each spatial regime. Two examples of using LISA in this manner investigated homicide (Baller et al., 2001) and suicide (Baller and Richardson, 2002), providing a statistical justification for undertaking multiple spatial regression models. And third, a LISA analysis may be used as the primary statistical methodology. In such a situation, a LISA analysis may be used to identify and/or test theoretical processes and trajectories. Though exploratory in nature, Messner et al. (1999) analyzed county-level homicide rates using a LISA in order to identify a diffusion process (i.e. a statistical representation of a phenomenon that moves across space). Cohen and Tita (1999) used a LISA to differentiate between two forms of diffusion (contagious and hierarchical). Griffiths and Chavez (2004) used a LISA to show that census tracts that behaved similarly across time with regard to crime exhibited statistically significant clustering. And in some of my own research I showed how a statistical method (multinomial logistic regression) could be used to identify the four different LISA classifications of spatial clustering (Andresen, 2011b). Some of these results are shown in Figures 9.2–9.4.

Figure 9.2 shows the mapped results of local Moran's I for automotive theft in Vancouver, Canada. Figure 9.2a does not really show any information that has not been identified in previous maps, such as those in Chapter 8: there is a cluster of high crime (High-High) in the central business district and skid row and a cluster of low crime (Low-Low) in Vancouver's west side and a few areas in Vancouver's east side. The results of the LISA using dissemination areas as the spatial unit of analysis, Figure 9.2b, exhibits the usefulness of a LISA analysis as well as the impact of the modifiable areal unit problem. Only the central business district (western portion of the High-High cluster on the peninsula) and skid row are shown in Figure 9.2b. In both areas, there are now some Low-High local crime clusters representing negative spatial autocorrelation. These Low-High local crime clusters, particularly in the central business district and especially the large local crime cluster, are in recently gentrified areas (Lees et al., 2007). These

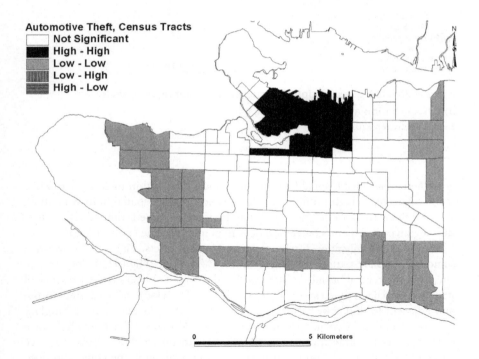

Figure 9.2a LISA classifications, Vancouver, 2001, automotive theft.

a) Census tracts

Source: Andresen (2011b).

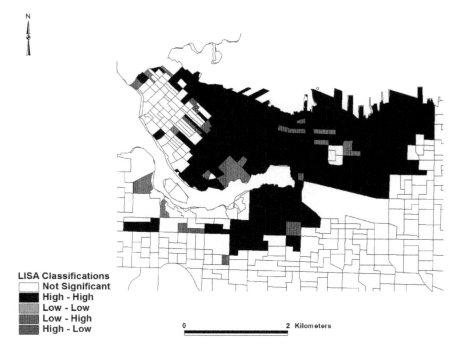

N

LISA Classifications
☐ Not Significant
■ High - High
▨ Low - Low
▧ Low - High
▤ High - Low

0   2 Kilometers

Figure 9.2b LISA classifications, Vancouver, 2001, automotive theft.
b) Dissemination areas
Source: Andresen (2011b).

gentrified areas have been able to maintain low crime within their borders while being adjacent to high crime areas, hence the negative spatial autocorrelation. Because these areas are relatively small, more than contained within census tracts, this negative spatial autocorrelation does not emerge in the census tract analysis.

The LISA classification for burglary and census tracts, Figure 9.3a, shows a somewhat similar pattern to that of automotive theft (High-High local crime cluster in the central business district and skid row) but also shows the presence of negative spatial autocorrelation, particularly Low-High local crime clusters within and adjacent to skid row. Figure 9.3b shows the LISA classifications of burglary for dissemination areas just to the southeast of skid row. The Low-High local crime clusters are quite apparent in this area of Vancouver, showing that negative local spatial autocorrelation is hardly a rare phenomenon in the context of positive global spatial autocorrelation.

And lastly, the LISA classifications for violent crime and census tracts are shown in Figure 9.4a. Similar to automotive theft, Figure 9.2a, this census tract map

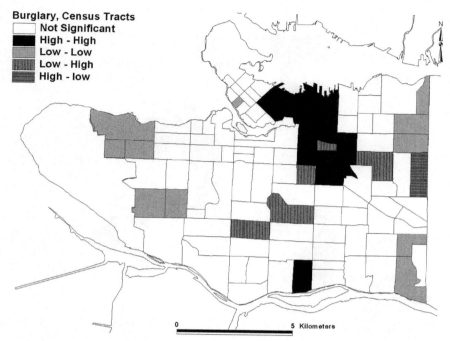

Figure 9.3a LISA classifications, Vancouver, 2001, burglary.
a) Census tracts
Source: Andresen (2011b).

shows a High-High local crime cluster in the central business district and skid row as well as a Low-Low local crime cluster on the west side of Vancouver. However, at the census tract level, Low-High local crime clusters are also apparent in the central business district largely in the gentrified areas of the central business district. The LISA classifications of violent crime for dissemination areas is similar to Figure 9.2b in that it shows the presence of Low-High local crime clusters not only in the central business district but also in skid row.

Another local spatial statistical method that is instructive is geographically weighted regression. At this time, "geographically weighted regression" (GWR) has only been used a handful of times in criminological contexts, but it would prove to be a useful analytical technique if used more frequently, particularly within environmental criminology. GWR was developed specifically for use with spatial data by Stewart Fotheringham and his colleagues (Brunsdon et al., 1996; Fotheringham et al., 1997, 2002). It is a conceptually simple statistical method that identifies local parameters in a regression context. The most common form of output with GWR is a map of estimated parameters that shows the variations in estimated relationships.

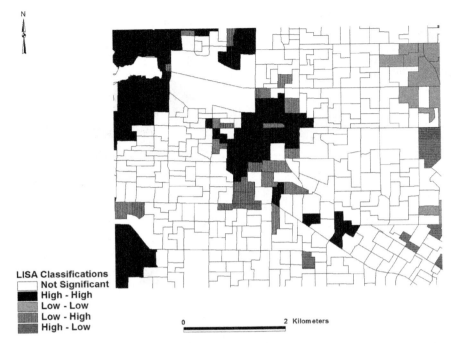

LISA Classifications
☐ Not Significant
■ High - High
▨ Low - Low
▦ Low - High
▨ High - Low

0 ▬▬▬▬▬▬▬ 2 Kilometers

Figure 9.3b LISA classifications, Vancouver, 2001, burglary.
b) Dissemination areas
Source: Andresen (2011b).

An interesting application of GWR to spatial crime analysis was an article published by Meagan Cahill and Gordon Mulligan in 2007. In their analysis of violence in Portland, Oregon, Cahill and Mulligan compare the output from a global statistical model to the output from a GWR. Though the global regression and GWR results were consistent in many ways, at least qualitatively, they did find some very interesting and striking results. Perhaps most interesting was the relationship between their measure of social (dis)advantage and its impact on violent crime. Their global statistical analysis generates a counterintuitive (positive) result: as social advantage increases, so does violent crime. However, in the GWR, most areas did exhibit a negative parameter estimate, as expected. Only a small number of areas had the unexpected positive estimated parameter, but they had extremely high levels of advantage/affluence. Consequently, these few areas were able to impact the estimated global parameter—a few extreme values severely impacted the average relationship, a relatively common concern in statistical analyses in general, and a reason to always plot/map/visualize your data. This shows the importance of understanding why spatial nonstationarity must be

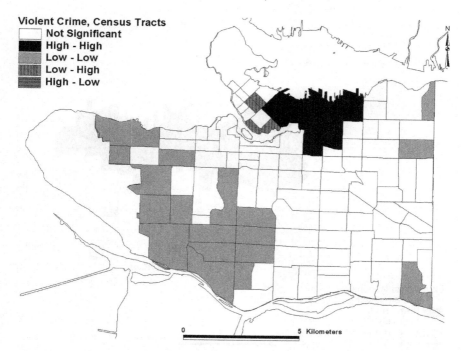

Figure 9.4a LISA classifications, Vancouver, 2001, violent crime.
a) Census tracts
Source: Andresen (2011b).

considered in a spatial analysis, specifically, and the importance of local spatial analysis, more generally.

It should be clear from this section that local spatial relationships are important to understand, particularly in a spatial crime analysis context. Despite the fact that local spatial relationships are interesting in and of themselves, they also prove to be important for exploratory spatial data analysis, testing theoretical expectations, and understanding the nuances of criminal event phenomena.

Visualizing crime

The last topic to discuss in the context of spatial analysis is how to visualize spatial data. One of the advantages of spatial (crime) data is the ability to represent it in another form not possible with non-spatial data, the map. Map design, cartography, is a topic that is often covered by multiple undergraduate courses in geography departments. Consequently, there is no attempt here to cover all of that material—see Dent (1998) and Fotheringham (1999) for a representative textbook and review article of some visualization techniques, respectively. Rather, a few

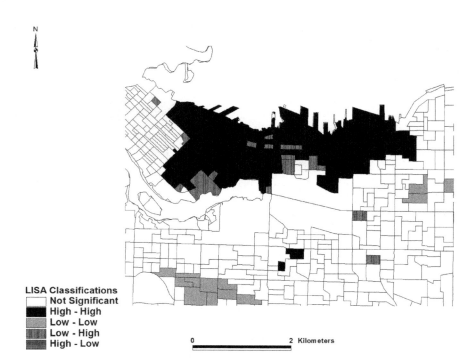

Figure 9.4b LISA classifications, Vancouver, 2001, violent crime.
b) Dissemination areas
Source: Andresen (2011b).

cautions about data visualizations of spatial data and an intriguing visualization technique are briefly presented.

In the second edition of his 1996 book, *How to Lie with Maps*, Mark Monmonier outlined how maps can be made to purposefully or accidentally mislead the reader. The contexts of these misrepresentations include advertising, municipal planning and development, politics, and the military, among others. For example, in order to show the impact, or lack thereof, from some initiative two maps may be made that use different legend categories for the same phenomenon, before and after the initiative. By using different legend categories, the inference one may make from the map can completely change. In Chapter 8, when maps were used to show the differences in the ambient population and residential population counts, as well as the ambient-based and resident-based crime rates, the same legend categories were used. In these cases, the actual numbers were used to show they were the same from map to map, but the legend categories could simply be "Low to High" with completely different classifications that could not even be seen without having access to the original data. Even if there is nothing devious being done with regard to the legend categories, the cartographer may also use particular colors to (de-)emphasize particular aspects of the map. Needless to say, any and all maps must be interpreted with caution, especially if some aspect of the map stands out upon first visualization.

The data visualization technique I wish to briefly discuss here is the cartogram. Most often, data visualization of areal units such as census tracts, are shown using choropleth maps. These are simply maps that represent the spatial units of analysis as they would be seen from the air, and each of the spatial units of analysis is shaded or colored based on the value of a variable of interest. This is shown for violent crime in Vancouver, Canada in Figure 9.5a. Anyone familiar with Vancouver would likely recognize the municipality even if there were no information regarding its name or its location. The individual spatial units are called polygons and represent one or both of the shape of the polygon on the ground or its area; this all depends on the projection used for the map—the projection is the method of transforming the curved Earth onto a flat sheet. Consequently, the

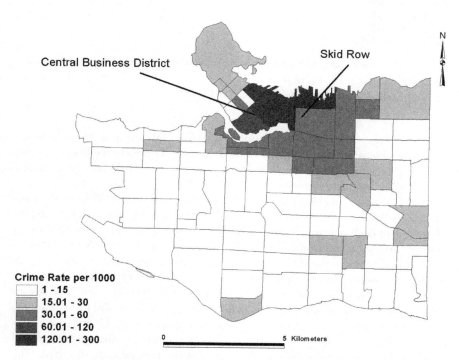

Figure 9.5a Crime rate and cartogram maps, Vancouver, 2001, violent crime.
a) Census tracts, choropleth map
Source: Andresen et al. (2009).

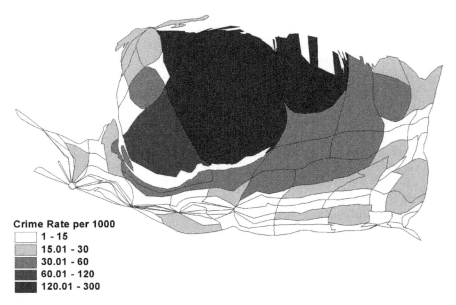

Crime Rate per 1000
- 1 - 15
- 15.01 - 30
- 30.01 - 60
- 60.01 - 120
- 120.01 - 300

Figure 9.5b Crime rate and cartogram maps, Vancouver, 2001, violent crime.
b) Disemination areas, cartogram
Source: Andresen et al. (2009).

choropleth map can only represent one variable of interest at a time, unless the other variable is the shape or area of the polygons. There are methods of super-imposing other graphs and figures on the map to visualize other data, but the "core" of the map can represent a single variable.

Cartograms are an alternative representation of the data that allow for the visualization of two variables simultaneously. Rather than using land area to represent the shape of each polygon, another variable is used instead. This may be done in one of two ways: noncontiguous and contiguous cartograms. Noncontiguous cartograms maintain the shapes of the spatial units of analysis but vary their size based on another variable, population, for example. In order to maintain the shape of each spatial unit of analysis they can no longer be connected. The advantage of the noncontiguous method is that it is still easy to recognize most (if not all) of the spatial units of analysis for subsequent interpretation. Contiguous carto-grams preserve the locations of the neighbors for each of the spatial units of analysis. Because of this property the shapes of the polygons are distorted. The advantage of this type of cartogram is that the changes in the resulting maps can be quite dramatic, but the disadvantage is that it becomes rather difficult to inter-pret the cartogram unless the researcher is well aware of the study area such that location can still be recognized.

Why would we want to visualize criminal event data in such a manner? By the nature of crime rate calculations (see Chapter 8), a high magnitude crime rate can emerge because of two situations. First, the criminal event volume may be very high leading to a high crime rate because there are simply a lot of criminal events in that area. Alternatively, the population at risk may be very low, leading to a high crime rate, because there are some criminal events but so few people that the risk of victimization is high. In the cartogram for violent crime, Figure 9.5b, these two different types of scenarios can be identified. Rather than using area to determine the size of each polygon, the criminal event count is being used. In this map, both criminal victimization risk (crime rate) and crime frequency (crime count) can be identified at the same time without the need for other data.

Because Figure 9.5b is a contiguous cartogram, Vancouver has become quite distorted, making some of the map difficult to interpret. However, the cartogram quite clearly shows that Vancouver's skid row not only has a high risk of criminal victimization but also a high volume of criminal events, and the opposite on both counts for the west side of Vancouver. Other possibilities of representation could have the crime rate or criminal event count determining the shape of the polygons, with the location quotient being represented as the color shading (Andresen et al., 2009).

Though the cartogram adds one more possibility for how to lie with maps, it shows the power of visualization for conveying spatial patterns. Though there may be a number of additional concerns with spatial data causing one to question the representation of spatial data, generally, there are just as many (if not more) opportunities to represent spatial data in an instructive manner. In the end, the added dimension of spatial data brings both costs and benefits. However, because of its continued and increasing use in the social sciences, not just spatial and environmental criminology, researchers are clearly confident the benefits outweigh the costs.

Review questions

1   Define the ecological fallacy and the atomistic fallacy, providing examples of each.
2   Why is the modifiable areal unit problem a problem?
3   What is spatial autocorrelation and why does it matter in statistical analyses?
4   Why would local spatial statistical techniques be useful for spatial crime analysis?
5   Why would geographically weighted regression be useful for spatial crime analysis?
6   What is the primary visualization benefit of cartograms?

References

Andresen, M. A. (2011a). The ambient population and crime analysis. *Professional Geographer*, 63(2), 193–212.

Andresen, M. A. (2011b). Estimating the probability of local crime clusters: The impact of immediate spatial neighbors. *Journal of Criminal Justice*, 39(5), 394–404.

Andresen, M. A. and Malleson, N. (2013b). Spatial heterogeneity in crime analysis. In M. Leitner (ed.), *Crime modeling and mapping using geospatial technologies* (pp. 3–23). New York, NY: Springer.

Andresen, M. A., Wuschke, K., Kinney, J. B., Brantingham, P. J., and Brantingham, P. L. (2009). Cartograms, crime, and location quotients. *Crime Patterns and Analysis*, 2(1), 31–46.

Anselin, L. (1995). Local indicators of spatial association—LISA. *Geographical Analysis*, 27(2), 93–115.

Baller, R. D., Anselin, L., Messner, S. F., Deane, G., and Hawkins, D. F. (2001). Structural covariates of U.S. county homicide rates: Incorporating spatial effects. *Criminology*, 39(3), 561–90.

Baller, R. D. and Richardson, K. K. (2002). Social integration, imitation, and the geographic patterning of suicide. *American Sociological Review*, 67(6), 873–88.

Brunsdon, C. F., Fotheringham, A. S., and Charlton, M. E. (1996). Geographically weighted regression: A method for exploring spatial non-stationarity. *Geographical Analysis*, 28(4), 281–98.

Cahill, M. and Mulligan, G. (2007). Using geographically weighted regression to explore local crime patterns. *Social Science Computer Review*, 25(2), 174–93.

Cohen, J. and Tita, G. (1999). Diffusion in homicide: exploring a general method for detecting spatial diffusion processes. *Journal of Quantitative Criminology*, 15(4), 451–93.

Dent, B. D. (1998). *Cartography: Thematic map design*, 5th edition. Dubuque, IA: William C. Brown Publishers.

Fotheringham, A. S. (1997). Trends in quantitative methods I: Stressing the local. *Progress in Human Geography*, 21(1), 88–96.

Fotheringham, A. S. (1999). Trends in quantitative methods III: Stressing the visual. *Progress in Human Geography*, 23(4), 597–606.

Fotheringham, A. S. and Wong, D. W. S. (1991). The modifiable areal unit problem in multivariate statistical analysis. *Environment and Planning A*, 23(7), 1025–44.

Fotheringham, A. S., Brunsdon, F. C., and Charlton, M. E. (1997). Two techniques for exploring nonstationarity in geographical data. *Geographical Systems*, 4(1), 59–82.

Fotheringham, A. S., Brunsdon, C., and Charlton, M. (2002). *Geographically weighted regression: The analysis of spatially varying relationships*. Chichester, UK: John Wiley & Sons.

Gehlke, C. E. and Biehl, H. (1934). Certain effects of grouping upon the size of the correlation coefficient in census tract material. *Journal of the American Statistical Association, Supplement*, 29(185), 169–70.

Griffiths, E. and Chavez, J. M. (2004). Communities, street guns and homicide trajectories in Chicago, 1980–1995: Merging methods for examining trends across space and time. *Criminology*, 42(4), 941–78.

Harries, K. (1999). *Mapping crime: Principle and practice*. Washington, DC: U.S. Department of Justice, Office of Justice Programs, National Institute of Justice.

Hipp, J. R. (2007). Block, tract, and levels of aggregation: Neighborhood structure and crime and disorder as a case in point. *American Sociological Review*, 72(5), 659–80.

Lees, L., Slater, T., and Wyly, E. K. (2007). *Gentrification*. New York, NY: Routledge.

Messner, S. F., Anselin, L., Baller, R. D., Hawkins, D. F., Deane, G., and Tolnay, S. E. (1999). The spatial patterning of county homicide rates: An application of exploratory spatial data analysis. *Journal of Quantitative Criminology*, 15(4), 423–50.

Monmonier, M. (1996). *How to lie with maps,* 2nd edition. Chicago, IL: University of Chicago Press.

Morenoff, J. D., Sampson, R. J., and Raudenbush, S. W. (2001). Neighborhood inequality, collective efficacy, and the spatial dynamics of urban violence. *Criminology*, 39(3), 517–59.

Openshaw, S. (1984a). Ecological fallacies and the analysis of areal census data. *Environment and Planning A*, 16(1), 17–31.

Openshaw, S. (1984b). *The modifiable areal unit problem.* CATMOG (Concepts and Techniques in Modern Geography) 38. Norwich: Geo Books.

Robinson, W. S. (1950). Ecological correlations and the behavior of individuals. *American Sociological Review*, 15(3), 351–7.

Sampson, R. J., Morenoff, J. D., and Earls, F. (1999). Beyond social capital: Spatial dynamics of collective efficacy for children. *American Sociological Review*, 64(5), 633–60.

Sherman, L. W., Gartin, P., and Buerger, M. E. (1989). Hot spots of predatory crime: Routine activities and the criminology of place. *Criminology*, 27(1), 27–55.

Wooldredge, J. (2002). Examining the (ir)relevance of aggregation bias for multilevel studies of neighborhoods and crime with an example of comparing census tracts to official neighborhoods in Cincinnati. *Criminology*, 40(3), 681–709.

Chapter 10

Hot spots of crime

Introduction

It should be clear by now in this textbook that crime is neither randomly nor uniformly distributed across space. The theories within environmental criminology, more generally, and routine activity theory and the geometric theory of crime, specifically, predict that there will be places that have disproportionate volumes of criminal events, or hot spots. According to routine activity theory a criminal event occurs when a motivated offender and a suitable target converge in time and space without the presence of a capable guardian. Using this simple framework Lawrence Cohen and Marcus Felson were able to explain the rise in crime rates that occurred after the Second World War. This convergence, of course, occurs in particular places, so routine activity theory is at least implicitly a spatial theory of crime. As such, routine activity theory has been used in many spatial analyses of crime, as discussed in Chapter 3. And because our routine activities are neither randomly nor uniformly distributed across space, the spatial patterns of crime will not be either. In other words, routine activity theory predicts that there will be hot spots and cool spots of criminal events. In the context of the geometric theory of crime, criminal events occur at nodes, pathways, and edges. These three phenomena are also in particular places meaning that the geometric theory of crime predicts that criminal events are neither randomly nor uniformly distributed across space. As with routine activity theory, the geometric theory of crime predicts that there will be hot spots of criminal events and cool spots of criminal events. Because of these high concentrations of criminal activity, hot spots of crime tend to be hot topics in the news—pardon the pun—but people rarely think critically about them. As a consequence, I would argue that hot spots of crime, or hot spots in general, are often misunderstood.

So what is a hot spot? John Eck and colleagues state that there is no common definition of what a hot spot of crime is, but offer a common understanding: "[a] hot spot is an area that has a greater than average number of criminal or disorder events, or an area where people have a higher than average risk of victimization" (Eck et al., 2005, p. 2). However, it should be noted that when one thinks of an area for a hot spot that area could be conceived in a number of ways. John Eck and colleagues consider four different types of hot spots that allow us to consider different types of areas.

The first type of hot spot is the hot place or hot point. This is literally a hot *spot*. A hot place/point is a very specific location such as an address (representing a business/residence/park) or a street corner that generates a lot of criminal events. Examples of the hot place may be a (high) school or a drinking establishment. Considering the geometric theory of crime, a hot place/point will generally be within an activity node and not the entire node. As such, the hot area may even be a hot spot within a hot spot, a very localized convergence of motivated offenders and suitable targets that is often located within an edge. The second type of hot spot is the hot street/road/alley. This represents a pathway that is a set of locations bringing together many motivated offenders and suitable targets in time and space but along a vector. Examples of a hot street/road/alley may be a number of drinking establishments along one street or an alley that is common for drug users to frequent to ingest their illicit drugs. But this type of hot spot may not necessarily be so dubious. Because of our automobile culture in North America, we have strip malls that are designed for automobile access, not pedestrian access. There are many shopping and entertainment nodes that are located along major roadways. The third type of hot spot is the hot area. This is usually what people think of when they hear the term "hot spot." This type of hot spot may be thought of as a neighborhood that has high volumes of criminal events. A neighborhood in the zone in transition (social disorganization theory) would be a prime example of this type of hot spot. Most often a hot area will be an activity node for a number of motivated offenders, making the area either a crime generator or a crime attractor. And the fourth type of hot spot is the hot target. This target could be a person or a thing (house, automobile, etc.) that is repeatedly victimized. In the context of personal victimization a hot target will generally have routine activities that put them at risk, usually spending a lot of time on edges in primary activity nodes and pathways. Another term for the hot target is the phenomenon of "repeat victimization," discussed in Chapter 14. This type of hot spot is difficult to map, primarily because the map would not really make sense aside from understanding that target's victimization pattern across space.

The overall point here is that hot spots (and cool spots) of criminal events should be expected, especially within the context of environmental criminology. Consequently, it is important to have a critical understanding of what a hot spot is, how it can be measured/identified, and any measurement and/or conceptual issues with the identification of hot spots.

How are hot spots measured and identified?

There are numerous ways in which hot spots may be measured and identified, with distance-based methods and area-based methods being the two primary categories. We will not go into much detail here, but we will briefly discuss the distance-based method and then go over in detail the most common area-based method for identifying hot spots, kernel density estimation.

Distance-based methods for identifying hot spots typically use the cartographic distances between two events in the data set (event-event) or the cartographic distance between randomly selected coordinates within the study space and events in the data set (point-event) to determine if a spatial point pattern is random, clustered, or uniform (Bailey and Gatrell, 1995). Distance-based methods of hot spot detection have two primary limitations: one that can be addressed relatively easily and another that is more problematic. The first primary limitation is that distance-based hot spot methods typically use cartographic or Euclidean distance in the calculation of any statistics. However, very few (if any) human phenomena occur in pure cartographic or Euclidean space. Rather we move through our predefined networks such as highways, roads, and other pathways. Because of this, the use of cartographic or Euclidean distance may be inappropriate—see Okabe et al. (1995) and Yamada and Thill (2007), who review a number of methods that address this issue. The second primary limitation is that distance-based methods have to address edge, or boundary, effects. Edge or boundary effects occur because most study areas are part of a larger geographical region, and the underlying spatial process operates across the larger geographical region. The problem with edge/boundary effects emerges when any events outside of the study area but within the larger geographical region interact with the events in the study area (Diggle, 2003). The most common method used to address this issue is the use of a buffer zone (guard area) in order to create a distance within the outer edge of the study area. With this method, distances are only calculated for events in the primary study area, not the buffer zone, but events within the buffer zone are used for calculations involving events in the primary study area (Bailey and Gatrell, 1995; Yamada and Rogerson, 2003). The use of the buffer zone method does eliminate any bias that emerges from the edge effect, but there is the cost of increased variance because fewer data observations are being used in the analysis (Diggle, 2003).

The second type of method used to identify hot spots is area-based methods. These methods count the number of point events within a defined spatial area and measure the intensity of points within that defined spatial area. This spatial area is the spatial unit of analysis for the output of the hot spot method, hence such methods being area-based—think of a grid of square cells placed over the study area. The primary limitation of this form of identifying hot spots is its potential susceptibility to the modifiable areal unit problem (MAUP), discussed in Chapter 8. In this context, the aspect of the MAUP that most often matters is the scale effect because the researcher defines the spatial area.

The most common hot spot method used in spatial crime analysis is area-based kernel density estimation. Because it is an areal-based method, kernel density estimation uses the points on a map, but the output from the technique is an areal unit. The general method for doing this is shown in Figure 10.1. The parallelogram in Figure 10.1 represents the study area and the dots represent the (criminal)

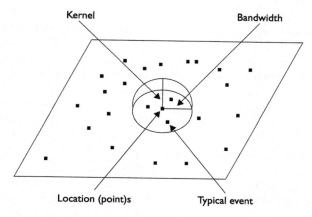

Figure 10.1 Kernel density.

events. For each location point in the study area, defined as the center point of each cell in the grid placed on top of the study area, a circle is "drawn," with the radius of that circle being called the bandwidth. The kernel is then the "height" for that location point calculated as some function of the number of points within the circle—there are a number of different ways to calculate this value. The greater the number of points, the greater the value of the kernel/height. This is repeated for each of the grids over the study area so that the output can be mapped to see where the hot spots emerge.

Measurement and conceptual issues for identifying hot spots

There are a number of measurement and conceptual issues with the calculation of these hot spot maps, particularly the area-based maps. First, in the case of kernel density estimation, the researcher must define the bandwidth, or radius of the circle. If the bandwidth is too big, then the resulting hot spot map will be too smooth (not showing any hot spots) because each grid uses criminal events from so many other grids around it; if the bandwidth is too small, then the resulting hot spot map will be too jagged and very difficult to interpret. Generating many kernel density hot spot maps with different bandwidths is a worthwhile exercise for someone in a (spatial) crime analysis class/lab. However, the point of discussing these issues here is simply to make the student of environmental criminology aware of the many data representations they may come across and the benefits and limitations of those data representations.

The choice of the bandwidth most certainly has an impact on the output of the kernel density estimation and any resulting interpretations. However, such a decision emerges only once the decision has been made to undertake kernel density estimation. There is a more fundamental issue that relates to all area-based hot spot methods—kriging is one of the other more common methods used. In essence, these methods take discrete point data and create a continuous surface. This is why the output of the kernel density estimation can be viewed for an entire municipality, showing where hot spots are located. The original use of such methods was to (randomly) sample a continuous variable across a study area and recreate that continuous surface with an interpolation technique. Consider the variable of temperature. Temperature is everywhere, so it is a continuous surface across the landscape—for any two points in a study area where temperature is measured, you can measure temperature in between those two points. But sampling can become very expensive both in terms of time and resources, so you will only want to sample as much as you need to in order to get the information you need. This is why the census samples 20 percent of the population for some of its variables—20 percent is what is necessary in order to make "good" inference regarding the whole population. For most circumstances, if the temperature at point A is 10 degrees and the temperature at point B is 12 degrees, the tempera-ture at the midpoint between points A and B will be 11 degrees—interpolation.

But does this make sense in the context of criminal events? Are criminal events parts of a continuous surface? Certainly not. We know that criminal events are only expected to be, or at least concentrate, in particular places. In fact, as discussed in Chapter 15 regarding the crime and place literature, there are many places within a municipality that have no criminal events. Consequently, area-based hot spot methods are turning a set of discrete criminal events into a continuous surface. At the very least, this must be recognized as potentially prob-lematic because the nature of these techniques will place intensity values at places that do not have any criminal events, possibly ever. It may be argued that, despite being methodologically incorrect, such area-based methods can still provide useful information and be instructive as an indication of the risk of criminal victimiza-tion. After all, we analyze and visualize census tracts and other spatial units of analysis and these could be subject to the same criticism. This is certainly true. The take-away lesson here, in Chapters 8 and 9, and below, is to be very critical of any information you are trying to interpret, because complicated (or even incomprehensible!) techniques are not always correct.

Another measurement issue relates to the ability of the researcher to even find a hot spot, of any kind. This is related to the discussion of the MAUP above, and may or may not impact a kernel density estimate in a significant manner. This measurement issue is represented in Figure 10.2 using points within a 2 × 2 grid system. In Figure 10.2a there is no hot spot. Each of the four cells simply has ten randomly placed (criminal) events. Figure 10.2b also only has ten events in each of four cells, but one of the cells (upper left) is clearly different from the other three. This is a visual representation of a hot street/road/alley. There are two things to note from this spatial pattern. First, if the researcher was only investigating the counts of criminal events in each of the cells, this hot spot would not even be

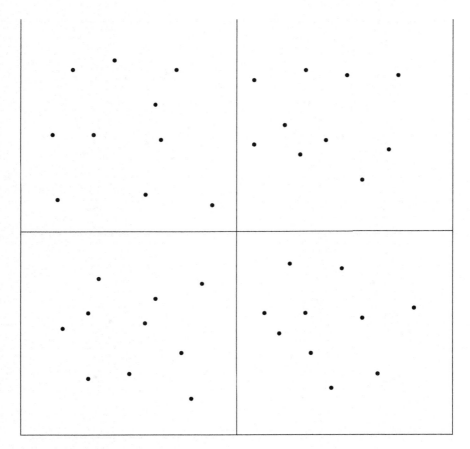

Figure 10.2a Hot spots.
a) No hot spot

noticed because the hot street has ten events. Second, the vast majority of the upper left cell has no events whatsoever. This means that any interpolation method will very likely place a positive intensity value in these areas when there should not be any. Figure 10.2c is similar to Figure 10.2b in the sense that it also only has 10 events in the upper left cell that would go unnoticed in an analysis of the cells as areal units. However, this is a clear example of a hot spot. Again similar to Figure 10.2b, the vast majority of the upper left cell has no events whatsoever and is problematic for interpolation. Lastly, Figure 10.2d represents an area hot spot that exhibits many more events in the upper left cell than the other cells—a total of fifty events in the upper left cell. This is the only situation of these four that would have a hot spot identified if only the counts within areas were considered. The point of this discussion is that when you read about hot spots in research or

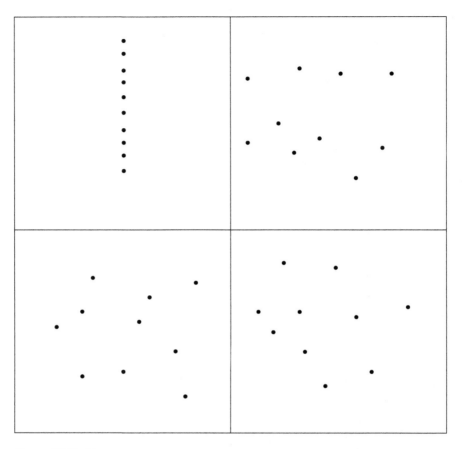

Figure 10.2b Hot spots.
b) Linear hot spot

in the media you will be aware of this measurement-related issue and be critical about what you are being asked to interpret.

Lastly, in terms of measurement and conceptual issues with regard to hot spots, is the way in which kernel density maps are most often presented. The specific type of kernel density estimation we have been discussing thus far is a single kernel. That simply means that we have only considered a single variable that is used to map the kernel density map—(criminal) events. However, we know from the theoretical and measurement issue chapters earlier in this textbook that only considering criminal events to measure crime risk is problematic. We have definitely known for at least fifty years that there are a greater number of criminal events where there are a lot of people, such as central business districts (Boggs, 1965;

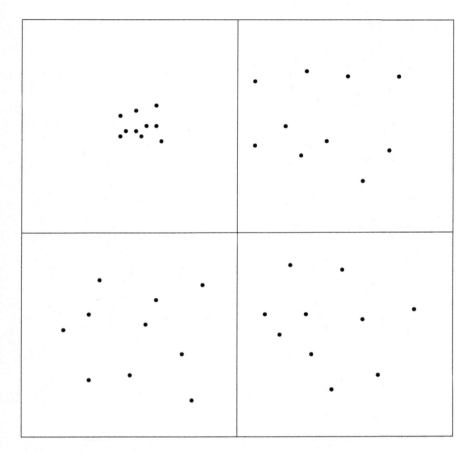

Figure 10.2c Hot spots.
c) Point hot spot

Schmid, 1960a, 1960b). This is why we calculate crime rates, or other crime statistics such as the location quotient, in order to obtain a better idea of how much criminal victimization risk is actually present. After all, if there are only more criminal events because there are more people and this increase is proportional, there is no actual change in the risk of criminal victimization. So, why would we pay any attention to a single kernel density map?

The simple answer is that most people do not know better. Single kernel density maps are very easy to generate and one only needs criminal event data available as points. It is worth stating at this point that single kernel density maps may be useful in situations in which criminal event counts are also useful, such as the deployment of policing resources. However, from a research perspective, single

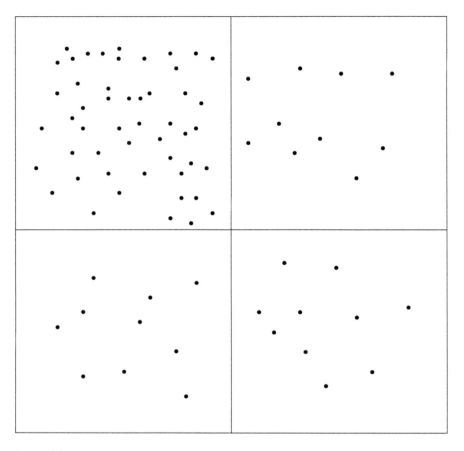

Figure 10.2d Hot spots.
d) Area hot spot

kernel density maps are of very limited utility. The alternative is a dual kernel density map. The difference between the two types of kernel density map is that the dual kernel density map incorporates new information from a second variable that represents the population at risk. As such, the dual kernel density map may be referred to as a risk-adjusted density. The reason for this is shown in Figure 10.3. Figure 10.3a is a single kernel map of violent crime in Vancouver. This map clearly shows the high-density cells being located in the central business district peninsula and radiating outward with a distance decay pattern. It should be noted that there are some moderate densities of violent crime on the west side of Vancouver, a relatively low crime area. Figure 10.3b is a dual kernel density map that uses the resident population as the population at risk and the same legend

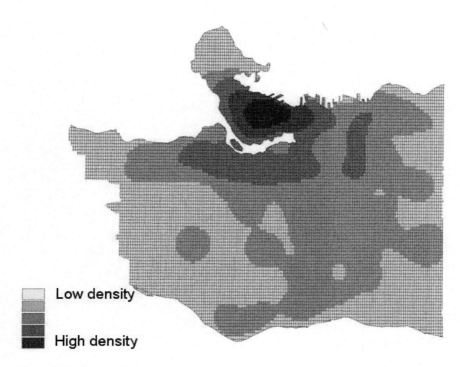

Low density

High density

Figure 10.3a Kernel density, single versus dual kernel.
a) Single kernel

categories as Figure 10.3a. This is quite clearly a very different representation of violent crime in Vancouver. The greatest density of violent crime risk is still in the central business district, but now on its edge closer to skid row. And, the rest of Vancouver is now shown as having a low density of violent crime risk.

Risk terrain modeling

Despite the limitations in hot spot identification discussed above, these methods are relatively commonplace. In fact, as noted by Rachel Boba Santos in her *Crime Analysis with Crime Mapping* textbook published in 2013, crime mapping has become an integrated part of the strategic and operational aspects of policing. However, because of limitations with data accessibility (not criminal event data, though!), technological limitations because of costs and training (some spatial analysis computer software is very expensive), and temporal constraints because of other job demands, most crime mapping applications are restricted to relatively simple techniques, such as the kernel density maps discussed above (Groff and La Vigne, 2002). Joel Caplan and colleagues (2011) refer to such crime mapping techniques

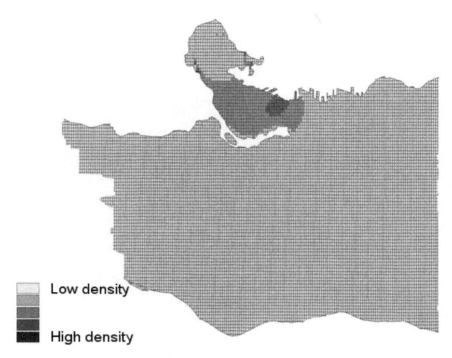

Low density

High density

Figure 10.3b Kernel density, single versus dual kernel.
b) Dual kernel

as retrospective crime analysis because historical criminal event data are used to predict future criminal event locations. Though past criminal events may be a good predictor of future criminal events, this practice is dependent upon the assumption of ecological stability. As shown in Chapter 8, ecological stability may not always be an appropriate assumption for relatively short time periods (even a few years), particular spatial units of analysis (the smaller the better), and specific crime types. And there are also environmental factors that we know are associated with specific crime types that could be used to forecast the probable locations of future criminal events.

A relatively new spatial analysis method developed by Joel Caplan and Leslie Kennedy (in collaboration with some other researchers) is a straightforward application of the theories within environmental criminology to spatial crime analysis—risk terrain modeling. Though the theories within environmental criminology often speak about the opportunities for crime—after all, "opportunity makes the thief" (Felson and Clarke, 1998)—Caplan and Kennedy chose to avoid opportunity, per se, because it is very difficult to measure (Caplan et al., 2011). As the name implies, risk terrain modeling assesses risk rather than opportunity. This also addresses one of the problems with hot spot methods such as kernel density estimation: criminal events are discrete, whereas the output from kernel density is a continuous surface. As stated above, risk may be interpreted as a continuous surface. This difference between methods such as kernel density estimation and risk terrain modeling is that risk terrain modeling does not only use historical criminal event data to predict future criminal event locations—historical criminal event data may or may not be a component in the generation of a risk surface. This is a critical distinction because, as mentioned above, the methodological purpose of methods such as kernel density estimation is to recreate an entire continuous surface from discrete sample points within that continuous surface, not turn discrete data into a continuous surface.

Risk terrain modeling is a spatial analysis method that is relatively straight-forward. Through the process of various forms of research (review the academic literature, speak with the appropriate professionals, etc.), the risk terrain modeling practitioner identifies the factors that are related to a specific crime type in order to identify the risk surface. This may appear to be a formidable task of its own, and difficult to do for those not in an academic institution with access to academic research through a library. However, in their *Risk Terrain Modeling Compendium* Joel Caplan and Leslie Kennedy have identified the risk factors for the following crime types: arson, sexual assault, aggravated assault, simple assault, automotive theft, residential burglary, drug dealing in open-air markets, larceny-theft, loitering, murder and non-negligent manslaughter, street prostitution, forcible rape, street robbery, and shootings. They have also provided case studies and applications of risk terrain modeling for street robberies, residential burglaries, aggravated assault, police resource allocation, and violent crime forecasting (Caplan and Kennedy, 2011). This compendium is available for free download from the web page at the Rutger's Center on Public Safety: http://www.rutgerscps.org/rtm/. Needless to say, risk terrain modeling is a method that is being developed in such a manner to allow for all interested parties to have access to the necessary resources for its implementation.

Once the risk factors for a particular crime type have been identified, they are all transformed, or operationalized, into a common spatial unit of analysis. This spatial unit of analysis is the grid, as discussed in the above discussion regarding kernel density estimation. Using this grid, each cell in the study area can be assigned a value for each risk factor: the presence, absence, or intensity of each risk factor. The end result will be a set of layers of risk factors and each has a value associated with each cell, common for each risk factor. Though multiple methods may be used, the researcher then uses map algebra to generate the final risk terrain map. The easiest way of thinking about this step is to add all the values in the cells representing an area, repeating this step for each area's cell. For example, suppose there are three risk factors: the presence of a drinking establishment, in or out of the central business district, and a mass public transit line. These are all dichoto-mous (dummy) variables, so if a cell representing an area has all three of them present its risk value is 3. Map algebra allows this calculation to be rather complicated to include not only addition, but also subtraction, division, multiplication, and weighting schemes, to allow the value for one risk factor to be more important than the value for another. The end result is a continuous surface of cells representing the risk of a specific crime type for an entire study area. If the geography of the risk factor changes, this updated layer of information simply replaces the old one, updating the risk terrain map.

We will now briefly turn to a few examples of risk terrain modeling. The first is an application of risk terrain modeling to shootings in the urban community of Irvington, New Jersey in order to test its predictive power—this urban community had a murder rate almost eight times that of the national average (Caplan et al., 2011). Joel Caplan and his colleagues considered the following three risk factors as variables to generate the risk terrain map: dwellings of known gang members, locations of retail business infrastructure, and the locations of drug arrests. Their data were divided into three mutually exclusive time periods to allow for different comparisons: using the risk terrain map from period 1 to predict period 2 shootings and the period 2 risk terrain map to predict period 3 shootings. In order to investigate the predictive power of the resulting risk terrain maps, Caplan and his colleagues used a number of techniques. The first was a method called logistic regression, that is used to predict the probability of an event occurring, a shooting in this case. They found that an increase in the unit of risk led to an increase in the probability of a shooting of 56–69 percent, depending on which model they used. Though the baseline probability of a shooting in any given cell may be relatively low, this is an impact that is not only statistically significant but of a meaningful magnitude. And in a comparison of risk terrain modeling to retrospective crime mapping, risk terrain modeling was able to predict as much as 21 percent more shootings.

Leslie Kennedy and colleagues (2011) applied risk terrain modeling to police resource allocation strategies in Newark, New Jersey. In this application, the authors identified five risk factors (out of fifty that were available) through conversations with various groups within the Newark Police Department that were supported by the empirical academic literature: open-air drug markets, gang members and other high-risk offenders, public housing and other large-scale complexes, risky facilities such as drinking establishments, and previous incidents of firearms-related crimes such as shootings and armed robbery. They found that risk terrain modeling can be useful to anticipate criminal event problems early, allowing the police to allocate their resources more effectively. Most notable is that these authors argue for risk terrain modeling to supplement the current practices in spatial crime analysis within police departments, not replace them.

Lastly, in 2013 Joel Caplan and his colleagues published an article that compared the utility of risk terrain modeling in the context of violent criminal events in Irvington, New Jersey against hot spot mapping, point pattern analysis, and near-repeat analysis. The purpose of this analysis was to investigate if the police in Irvington, New Jersey would benefit from spatial crime analysis methods that identified existing hot spots of crime and places at great risk of crime, even if no crime was taking place at those locations at the time of analysis. Not surprisingly, the authors found that the previous year's violent criminal event locations were a significant predictor of the violent criminal events occurring in the study year. However, including output from risk terrain modeling added significantly to those predictions. The most striking result of their study was the use of both near-repeat analysis and risk terrain modeling—near-repeat analysis will be discussed in Chapter 14. The near-repeat analysis identified a circular area surrounding a violent criminal event location within which another violent criminal event was expected to occur. And another violent criminal event did occur within that circular area, as predicted. However, the risk terrain model predicted that a little less than 45 degrees of that circle, or less than 12.5 percent of the area, were at the greatest risk of a violent criminal event. It was within this small area that the subsequent violent criminal event occurred. At the end of this article, Joel Caplan and his colleagues put forth the benefits of an integration of hot spot mapping, near-repeat analysis, and risk terrain modeling. Each of these methods adds to the other, generating a better understanding, and prediction, of criminal event locations. Again, as with the investigation of police resourcing, these authors argue for risk terrain modeling to supplement, rather than replace, existing spatial crime analysis methods.

Review questions

1 Why do environmental criminologists, among others, expect the presence of hot spots?
2 Why is it important to understand the nature of a hot spot for crime prevention activities?
3 List and define the four types of hot spots, providing an example for each.
4 What is the fundamental flaw for using area-based hot spot methods (kernel density estimation, for example) in spatial crime analysis?
5 Explain how a hot spot analysis using areal data may not be able to identify a hot spot. Provide two examples.
6 What is the difference between single and dual kernel density maps?
7 What makes risk terrain modeling predictive?
8 Briefly explain how risk terrain modeling measures risk at any location.

References

Bailey, T. C. and Gatrell, A. C. (1995). *Interactive spatial data analysis*. Harlow, UK: Prentice Hall.
Boggs, S. L. (1965). Urban crime patterns. *American Sociological Review*, 30(6), 899–908.
Caplan, J. M. and Kennedy, L. W. (eds.) (2011). *Risk terrain modeling compendium*. Newark, NJ: Rutgers Center on Public Security.
Caplan, J. M., Kennedy, L. W., and Miller, J. (2011). Risk terrain modeling: Brokering criminological theory and GIS methods for crime forecasting. *Justice Quarterly*, 28(2), 360–81.

Caplan, J. M., Kennedy, L. W., and Piza, E. L. (2013). Joint utility of event-dependent and environmental crime analysis techniques for violent crime forecasting. *Crime & Delinquency*, 59(2), 243–70.

Diggle, P. J. (2003). *Statistical analysis of spatial point patterns*, 2nd edition. London, UK: Arnold Publishers.

Eck, J. E., Chainey, S., Cameron, J. G., Leitner, M., and Wilson, R. E. (2005). *Mapping crime: Understanding hot spots*. Washington, DC: National Institute of Justice, Office of Justice Programs, United States Department of Justice.

Felson, M. and Clarke, R. V. (1998). *Opportunity makes the thief: Practical theory for crime prevention*. London, UK: Home Office, Policing and Reducing Crime Unit Research, Development and Statistics Directorate.

Groff, E. R. and La Vigne, N. G. (2002). Forecasting the future of predictive crime mapping. *Crime Prevention Studies*, 13, 29–57.

Kennedy, L. W., Caplan, J. M., and Piza, E. (2011). Risk clusters, hotspots, and spatial intelligence: Risk terrain modeling as an algorithm for police resource allocation strategies. *Journal of Quantitative Criminology*, 27(3), 339–62.

Okabe, A., Yomono, H., and Kitamura, M. (1995). Statistical analysis of the distribution of points on a network. *Geographical Analysis*, 27(2), 152–75.

Santos, R. B. (2013). *Crime analysis with crime mapping*, 3rd edition. Los Angeles, CA: Sage Publications.

Schmid, C. F. (1960a). Urban crime areas: Part I. *American Sociological Review*, 25(4), 527–42.

Schmid, C. F. (1960b). Urban crime areas: Part II. *American Sociological Review*, 25(5), 655–78.

Yamada, I. and Rogerson, P. A. (2003). An empirical comparison of edge effect correction methods applied to K-function analysis. *Geographical Analysis*, 35(2), 97–109.

Yamada, I. and Thill, J. C. (2007). Local indicators of network-constrained clusters in spatial point patterns. *Geographical Analysis*, 39(3), 268–92.

Chapter 11

The temporal dimension of crime

Introduction

In the introduction to Part II, the theories of environmental criminology were introduced as part of a theoretical movement within criminology that considered the importance of the spatial and temporal dimensions of crime. Up until this point, however, the temporal dimension has shown to be important but most often in an indirect manner. The most direct reference to the temporal dimension of crime was within routine activity theory and its original goal of explaining the increases in crime rates over a period of two decades; this resulted from a change in the routine activities of people at a societal scale. Routine activity theory is clearly a theory that considers the temporal dimension because human ecology is at its heart; understanding rhythm, tempo, and timing are critical to understanding routine activity theory. As such, it should come as no surprise that routine activity theory repeatedly emerges as the explanatory theory for temporal patterns of crime.

In this chapter, we will directly consider the temporal patterns of crime at a number of temporal scales. Daily, weekly, seasonal, and long-run patterns of crime are all discussed with explanations rooted in routine activity theory—other explanations for these temporal phenomena are present in the literature (and mentioned below) but do not perform as well as routine activity theory. However, before we turn to understanding these various temporal patterns of crime, we will cover two aspects of this literature. First, the addition of the temporal dimension adds yet another dimension of measurement issues; and second, a specifically temporal theory of crime that brings together both time and space.

Missing information for daily crime patterns: aoristic analysis

Some criminal justice databases include temporal information regarding the criminal event of interest—calls for service data from a police detachment are a prime example. Most often, this temporal information will include the date, month, and year of the criminal event. More detailed criminal event data, especially calls for service data, may include the time at which the criminal event occurred. However, there are some crimes such as (residential and commercial) burglary, theft from automobile, and theft of automobile for which the exact time is not known. In these cases, all that is known is a time range, or time window, within which the criminal event took place. As such, the temporal data for these crimes list a potential start and end time for the criminal event. The easiest example to consider this phenomenon is residential burglary. Unless the person living at the home has a burglar alarm that records the time it went off, the victim only knows when s/he left home and when s/he returned home, 8 a.m. and 6 p.m., for example. Without some method of estimating the time of these criminal events, a considerable amount of data would have to be ignored in any investigation of the daily rhythm of crime types, particularly residential burglary (Ratcliffe, 2000). Some of the methods used have included choosing the potential start time, the potential end time, or the midpoint (1 p.m. in the example above) as the time the criminal event took place. The difficulty with these methods is that there is no theoretical or empirical support for their implementation.

Jerry Ratcliffe and Michael McCullagh pioneered an alternative to these methods in a journal article published in 1998, aoristic analysis. The method of aoristic analysis is used when time windows exist that "can provide a temporal weight and give an indication of the probability that an event occurred within a defined period" (Ratcliffe, 2000, p. 669). The primary advantage of using aoristic analysis is that all raw police data, including exact times and range times, are incorporated into the analysis. As such, the researcher or crime analysis investigator does not have to ignore a potentially considerable amount of temporal range data. If aoristic analysis can resolve this time range issue, it would prove to be a crucial advancement for dealing with the temporal criminal event.

An example of an aoristic implementation is presented in Figure 11.1. The entire timeline represents a 24-hour day, with four time/search blocks that each represent 6 hours (12 a.m.–6 a.m., 6 a.m.–12 p.m., 12 p.m.–6 p.m., and 6 p.m.–12 a.m.)—a greater number of search blocks could be used. Four criminal events are listed vertically on the lefthand side of Figure 11.1, each having a start and end time. The first criminal event occurred between 1 a.m. and 10 p.m., a total duration of twenty-one hours. Because five of the twenty-one hours fall within the first search block, it is assigned a value of 5/21. The second and third search blocks are spanned completely, giving 6/21 for each. The four remaining hours in the event fall in the fourth search block, 4/21 (Andresen and Jenion, 2004). This process of assigning time ranges to search blocks is continued for all available data. When completed, the cells are added vertically for each of the search blocks in order to produce an aoristic sum. In order to calculate the aoristic probability, the aoristic sum is divided by the number of events.

The more frequently criminal events fall within a specific time range, the greater the aoristic value and probability. These statistics can then be used to assign criminal events with long periods between their start and end times to

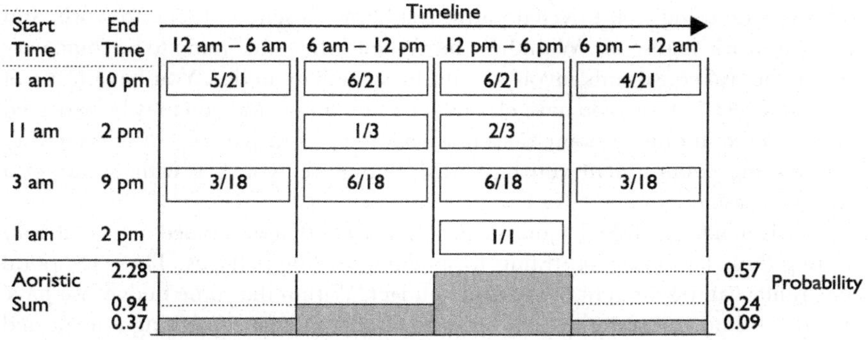

Start Time	End Time	Timeline 12 am – 6 am	6 am – 12 pm	12 pm – 6 pm	6 pm – 12 am
1 am	10 pm	5/21	6/21	6/21	4/21
11 am	2 pm		1/3	2/3	
3 am	9 pm	3/18	6/18	6/18	3/18
1 am	2 pm			1/1	
Aoristic Sum	2.28 / 0.94 / 0.37				Probability 0.57 / 0.24 / 0.09

Figure 11.1 Aoristic analysis.
Source: Adapted from Andresen and Jenion (2004) and Ratcliffe (2000, 2002).

specific search blocks allowing more data to be included in the analysis. Though not discussed by Jerry Ratcliffe and Michael McCullagh, an aoristic analysis could be done based on categories. For example, it may be the case that certain neighborhoods have specific temporal patterns such that it makes more sense to perform separate aoristic analyses for each neighborhood in order to obtain more precision in temporal estimates.

Though this is an instructive technique that allows for the inclusion of more data in a temporal pattern analysis of crime, it is not without its limitations. The primary limitation actually runs counter to environmental criminology: the assumption that the probability of criminal event occurrence is evenly distributed across the time range. Though a weighted assignment to search blocks could be implemented based on known temporal patterns, this may impose more bias than it is trying to solve. As such, there is little that can be done to avoid this limitation. However, if a residential burglary occurred between 4 p.m. and 8 p.m. more weight should be placed on the hours between 4 p.m. and 6 p.m. because those would be the hours in that time range when the home is most likely empty. That said, aoristic analysis is an instructive method that allows for the inclusion of more data in an analysis that should help to increase the precision of statistical inference.

A temporal constraint theory of crime: linking time and space

I have argued throughout this textbook that opportunity is the root of all crime. You can be as motivated as you want to commit a whole score of criminal events, but if there is no opportunity to do so, there will be nothing to report. Also, a lot of these opportunity-based criminal events are presented as opportunities that we encounter throughout the day while we undertake our non-criminal activities. In these travels throughout the day we are most often moving from activity node to activity node using well-traveled pathways: home to school, home to work, and school to work, and so on. With these movements there are going to be some very clear temporal constraints involved with these activity nodes. You have to be at work by a certain time, you have classes at certain times, and you may be expected home at certain times—home does not have to be your parents waiting for you; simply some commitment you have with whomever you live with or to get a particular task done.

Jerry Ratcliffe published a journal article in 2006 that developed a novel theory relating these temporal constraints to spatial offending patterns. These temporal constraints can be thought of as a time budget. Within that time budget we have our travel time and some reserve time, hopefully, in case something unexpected emerges—usually this reserve time is for dealing with excess traffic, missing a bus, and so on. This reserve time, however, may also be allocated for undertaking a criminal event: if it takes you 40 minutes to get to school, you leave an hour ahead of time just in case something comes up, so you have 20 minutes to deal with traffic and commit a criminal event.

This aspect of the time budget can be visualized using Figure 11.2. This figure is a stripped-down version of Figure 4.3. But rather than the search area being

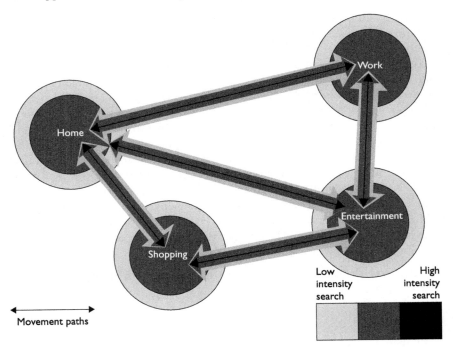

Figure 11.2 Temporal constraint theory.
Source: Adapted from Ratcliffe (2006).

considered only spatial, it is now spatial-temporal. What this figure represents is that there is a very distinct area that may be targeted for criminal events. An example of a youth on his or her way to school is a prime example. Given the origin (home) and destination (school), you cannot stray too far because you have to get back to the path that takes you to school. You must also remember that it takes time to commit a criminal event.

Consider the crime type of residential burglary. The intrusion time of the home has been found to typically be 3–5 minutes in duration (Rengert and Wasilchick, 1985, 2000). However, there is much more to a residential burglary than the time spent inside the home being burgled. Time must be taken to select the home to be burgled, make sure no one is home, getting into the home, and getting away with the stolen property. This process could take anywhere from 20 minutes to 4 hours depending on the methods used by the residential burglar. When you consider that travel has to be undertaken to and from the location being burgled, the time to prepare, commit, and escape from the burglary, most people would not be able to deviate from their movement paths by any great degree. Because of this, a lot of areas can be eliminated as being potential targets for any given individual burglar, particularly if that individual was known to be at two different places at specific times.

The most striking aspect of the temporal constraint theory of crime is its spatial component. Because we are constrained by time we are also constrained in space. This is because it takes *time* and effort to overcome distance. The figures that Jerry Ratcliffe produced for his 2006 journal article do differ from Figure 11.2 presented here, but they are fundamentally the same and very closely resemble the figures generated by Paul and Patricia Brantingham when they formulated the geometric theory of crime twenty-five years before. And this is why environmental criminology is about the spatial and the temporal dimension of crime—these two dimensions cannot easily be separated.

Daily crime patterns

We have already briefly discussed one aspect of daily crime patterns in the context of residential and commercial burglary research undertaken by Greg Jenion (2003). In his research, Jenion found that residential burglary peaked from 10 a.m. to 2 p.m., whereas commercial burglary peaked from 10 p.m. to 2 a.m. These are completely reversed temporal patterns that are rather intuitive. In both cases, most burglars will wish to minimize the probability of having someone present in order to minimize the probability of being caught, charged, prosecuted, convicted, and sent to prison. Because of our daily activity patterns, many residences are empty between 10 a.m. and 2 p.m. because the occupants are either at work or at school, and many commercial outlets are empty between 10 p.m. and 2 a.m. because they are closed for business. This research makes it clear, as indicated above in Chapter 8 on crime measurement, that specific crime types must be considered whenever possible because of the nuances of routine activity patterns for victims. Opportunity is at the root of all crime and the temporal pattern of opportunity for one crime type will not necessarily be the same as the temporal pattern of opportunity for another crime type.

Regardless of the need for specificity in most contexts, there are also some general considerations that are necessary for the study of daily crime patterns. Arguably, similar considerations are necessary for other temporal scales of analysis as well. Marcus Felson and Erika Poulsen published a journal article in 2003 that outlined these considerations as well as some suggested descriptive statistics that were for the purpose of understanding criminal events based on the time of day. Felson and Poulsen began their discussion of understanding daily crime patterns with a discussion of Amos Hawley's human ecology, that we covered in Chapter 3 on routine activity theory. They note that tempo, rhythm, and timing are all important for understanding temporal crime patterns in general. Tempo is the number of criminal events per unit time. Rhythm is the periodicity of those criminal events, such as the seasonality of crime that is discussed below. And timing refers to the coincidences of the rhythms of multiple people that allow for a criminal event to occur—the convergence in time and space of a motivated offender and a suitable target, for example.

Marcus Felson and Erika Poulsen then moved into a set of tasks that are necessary to undertake an analysis of daily crime patterns. The first task is to decide when the day begins. There is the trivial statement that it begins at 12 a.m. (midnight), but this is hardly satisfactory for a criminological context. For some individuals the night does not even begin until midnight and many criminal events that occur after midnight really had their beginnings in the late evening the official day before. Marcus Felson and Erika Poulsen suggested that 5 a.m. is the beginning of the criminological day because those who would have committed criminal events past midnight would be sleeping or at home by that time; also, most people do not begin their day before 5 a.m., getting ready for work, and so on. This may seem to be a rather trivial task and that 5 a.m. is a good choice—I agree with the latter—but there are some considerations that may have implications for understanding daily crime patterns. In a more recent journal article by Lisa Tompson and Michael Townsley, published in 2010, these authors started their criminological day at 7 a.m. in an investigation of street crime. Neither start to the criminological day is right or wrong, and no comparison was made to reveal any implications, but it is a choice that must be made nonetheless.

As discussed further below, the routine activities of people change with the seasons. Consequently, when the criminological day begins and ends may change throughout the year. This may be amplified in particular places. Consider places with the "midnight sun" such as Alaska, northern Canada, and Scandinavia. For a period of time in the summer, the sun never really sets and for a period of time in the winter it is only daylight for a few hours of the day. These seasonal patterns may have an impact on daily routine activity patterns and, subsequently, daily crime patterns.

The second task outlined by Marcus Felson and Erika Poulsen is to choose which crime types and which time period to analyze. We have already partially touched on the first choice: use crime types that are as specific as possible. However, Felson and Poulsen were also concerned with the choice of crime types to analyze with a particular concern regarding incompleteness in criminal event data. In fact, they discussed residential burglary as we have discussed in the context of aoristic analysis above. If many of the criminal events in the crime type of interest are missing detailed temporal information, making generalizations regarding any research results may be a dubious task. With regard to the second choice, I would argue to analyze as much data as possible. Though this may greatly increase the time necessary for analysis (pardon the pun!), it greatly reduces the possibility of analyzing an aberrant year of criminal event data. For example, something extraordinary may have occurred within a particular time frame, even something as pedestrian as an unusually dry spring, that may have an impact on the results. However, in many cases the provider of the criminal event data may make these decisions for the researcher. The criminal justice agency providing the data may only be willing to provide particular crime types for a specified period of time. In these cases, we must take what we can get (beggars cannot be choosers), but more data and more detailed data are almost always better, because a small number of crime types and a shorter period of time can always be chosen such that a subset of the entire data set is analyzed.

The next four tasks provided by Marcus Felson and Erika Poulsen relate to some descriptive statistics that we will not go into in detail, because there is no requirement that a statistics course will be taken before a course in environmental criminology. First, Marcus Felson and Erika Poulsen are interested in the "median minute of crime." This is the point in the day in which exactly one-half of all criminal events have occurred. Is this at the midpoint of the criminological day, 5 p.m.? Or is it earlier or later? This most definitely depends upon the crime type because of opportunity. I suspect that the median minute of crime will be earlier for residential burglary than simple assault, for example. Second, they wish to break the day into quartiles such that 25 percent of the criminal events fall within each of those quartiles. With that information, the third of these tasks is to see how these quartiles are spread across the day. This is potentially useful information because a crime type that has its criminal events evenly dispersed across the day will require very different research and practical attention than another crime type that has its criminal events very clustered in time. And last, Marcus Felson and Erika Poulsen put forth the "5-to-5 share of offenses" that is another summary indicator to reveal how criminal events are distributed across the day. This summary indicator simply reports the percentage of criminal events that occur within the first half of the criminological day, 5 a.m., to 4.59 p.m.

Marcus Felson and Erika Poulsen then proceeded to apply their descriptive indicators for the crime type of robbery in thirteen different cities in the United States. They found that the descriptive indicators varied across the cities, sometimes substantially. For example, the 5-to-5 share of offenses ranged from 25 to 35 percent. This provided an indication that robbery was indeed a crime type that primarily occurred later in the criminological day. Based on the other descriptive indicators, it would certainly be the case that if the calendar day, 12 a.m. to 11.59 p.m., were used, criminal events would appear to be much more uniformly distributed.

The results from their study are easily understood in the context of routine activity theory. As discussed in Chapter 3, in order for a criminal event to occur a motivated offender and a suitable target must converge in time and space with the absence of a capable guardian. For most of the day, most individuals are not susceptible to such a convergence because they are at home and/or at work. Consequently, most people do not converge with motivated offenders and even if they do there are capable guardians present, such as co-workers or family members. This is why the 5-to-5 share of offenses was so low, despite the fact that the temporal factor is one-half of the criminological day. Though it would be difficult to investigate because of a lack of temporal criminal event information, as discussed above, I suspect that residential burglary would have a very different 5-to-5 share of offenses because most homes will be burgled while the victims are out of the home (work, school, shopping, etc.) rather than in the evening, when most people are home.

As alluded to above, the implications of understanding daily crime patterns are for those in academic research and criminal justice practice, notably the police. If we are to better understand the criminal event we need to know where it happened and when it happened, because the environmental backcloth is something that changes throughout the day. And from a public policy perspective, Marcus Felson and Erika Poulsen pointed to a study undertaken by Jan Ahlberg and Johannes Knutsson, published in 1994, that showed there was a major disjuncture between the levels of police service by the hour of the day and the volume of criminal events by the hour of the day. Such a situation could result in a significant waste of policing resources.

Weekly crime patterns

Just as we can expect daily crime patterns to result from our changing routine activities, we can also expect weekly crime patterns from changing routine activities over the course of the week. Our routine activities not only change as to when we go out, but to where as well. Generally speaking, Monday through Friday afternoon consists of going from home to work, home to school, and work to school. Yes, there are times and places during those days in which we are relatively more vulnerable than at other times and places; most people will be safer from criminal victimization within their workplace than where they may go for lunch, for example. Younger populations, in particular, will be much more susceptible to criminal victimization on the weekend because they are more likely to frequent locations such as drinking establishments that are known for their criminogenic properties—clusters of alcohol establishments (places that sell and/or serve alcohol) tend to lead to clusters of violence (Grubesic and Pridemore, 2011).

A brief example of weekly crime patterns is shown in Table 11.1 and Figure 11.3, assaults in Vancouver, 2001. From the low on Tuesday to the high on Saturday, there is almost a 30 percent increase in the volume of these criminal events. Sunday still has a greater volume of assaults than during the week, but a lesser volume of assaults than Friday and Saturday—the dramatic changes in the count of assaults is far more evident in Figure 11.3. Again, this is an expected result based on routine activities because most people will not have activities out late at

Table 11.1 Count and percent of assaults by day of week, Vancouver, 2001

Day of week	Assaults (count)	Percent
Monday	684	13.1
Tuesday	660	12.7
Wednesday	709	13.6
Thursday	709	13.6
Friday	831	15.9
Saturday	852	16.3
Sunday	769	14.7

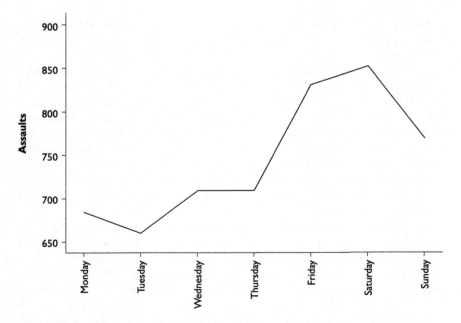

Figure 11.3 Count of assaults by day of week, Vancouver, 2001.

night frequenting drinking establishments, because of work and/or school the following day. This example involving alcohol will not apply to all individuals, but one does not need to drink at these establishments in order to be at a greater risk of criminal victimization and there also tend to be other venues of interest around these locations, because clusters of drinking establishments tend to be within or close to the central business district—many small-scale music concerts and other cultural festivals will be in these areas because of their centrality and accessibility through public transit.

Similar to the differences in daily crime patterns when different crime types are considered, weekly crime patterns are also expected to vary by crime type. Again, this harks back to the opportunity surface for criminal events. Where and when will these opportunities emerge? Once one considers the importance of opportunity, it is essentially self-evident that the spatial and temporal patterns of crime will vary by crime type. I would expect residential burglaries to occur more frequently during the week than the weekend because—assuming burglars do not wish to encounter the resident of the home during the commission of the criminal event—people tend to be home for more of the day on Saturday and Sunday. Yet again, routine activity theory provides a simple yet instructive explanation of this temporal crime pattern.

Seasonal crime patterns

Seasonal crime patterns are arguably the most common form of research explicitly investigating the temporal dimension of criminal events. Recalling that the concept of rhythm in human ecology applies to the temporal variations in crime patterns, it is simple to understand why this is the case. There are some routine activities that change very little throughout the year such that there is no change in their rhythm: home to work, home to school, school to work, and so on. Rather, our leisure activities change at different times of the year. In areas with a temperate climate, much of fall, winter, and spring are spent undertaking indoor activities because in these climates temperatures tend to be low and rainfall tends to be high, making outside activities less desirable. However, in late spring, summer, and early fall more time is spent outside, especially during the weekend and July and August, when children are out of school. These are societal level changes that may prove to impact the spatial and temporal (daily, weekly, and monthly) patterns of crime.

Though research on seasonal crime patterns predates routine activity theory by almost 140 years (see Quetelet 1842), much of the recent research on seasonal crime patterns invokes routine activity theory as a theoretical framework—there is a branch of this literature that considers temperature/aggression theory, but we will not cover that material here (see Hipp et al., 2004). But before we turn to the research that explicitly invokes routine activity theory, there was a research study by L. T. Lewis and J. J. Alford, published in 1975, that showed the importance of routine activities regardless of climatic conditions. In their research study, L. T. Lewis and J. J. Alford analyzed monthly assault data from fifty-six municipalities in the United States, some of which included municipalities that had warmer temperatures in all seasons—assault is the most common crime type investigated in this literature. They found that all municipalities, regardless of latitude, exhibited an increase in assaults during the summer months. Therefore, it was not absolute temperature that impacted the volume of criminal events (assaults), but relative temperature and that led people to undertake more of their activities outside of the relatively protective environment of the home. In other words, summer months are the time of the year when holidays from work and school are more common, leading to changes in routine activities.

Research investigating seasonal crime patterns have been undertaken in locations such as England (Farrell and Pease, 1994; Field, 1992), Israel (Landau and Fridman, 1993), the United States (Cohn and Rotton, 2000; Rotton and Cohn, 2003), Brazil (Ceccato, 2005), The Netherlands (van Koppen and Jansen, 1999), and Scotland (Semmens et al., 2002). Overall, these authors found that seasonal crime patterns varied based on crime type and geography: most crime types, violent and property crime types, exhibited a seasonal crime pattern, but some did not, and the lack of a seasonal crime pattern was at times based on geography—the seasonal crime pattern emerged in one location, but not another, for the same crime type.

In addition to this research is a subset of research on seasonal crime patterns that investigates the spatial variations of seasonal crime patterns. This research has found that the increases in assaults occur disproportionately in lower socio-economic neighborhoods; this is partially attributed to those who live in high socio-economic neighborhoods being better able to escape the summer heat through the use of air conditioning (Harries and Stadler, 1983; Harries et al., 1984)—similar results have been found in the context of homicide in Brazil (Ceccato, 2005) and assaults in South Africa (Breetzke and Cohn, 2012). In 2009, Chris Brunsdon and his colleagues published a journal article that found disorder and disturbances in calls for service data were more likely to occur outside of the city center during the summer months.

The most recent research on seasonal crime patterns, and its impact on spatial patterns of crime, is some work I undertook with Nicolas Malleson, published in 2013. In this journal article, we analyzed eight crime types for Vancouver, 2001: all crimes, assaults, burglaries, robberies, sexual assaults, thefts, thefts from vehicle, and thefts of vehicle. Output from this research is presented in Figures 11.4 and 11.5.

The crime type of all crimes (Figure 11.4a) shows a clear seasonal pattern peaking from July through to October and falling thereafter. Recall from Chapter 8 that such an aggregate crime type may, in fact, obscure more disaggregate crime type patterns, but there is clearly a seasonal crime pattern in Vancouver, on average. Assault, Figure 11.4b, is the most common crime type investigated in this literature and exhibits the most prominent seasonal pattern peaking in the summer months (the greatest being July), decreasing almost monotonically on either side.

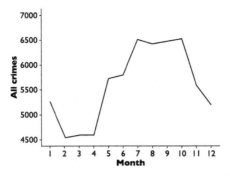

Figure 11.4a Monthly trends in crime, Vancouver, 2001.
a) All crimes
Source: Andresen and Malleson (2013a).

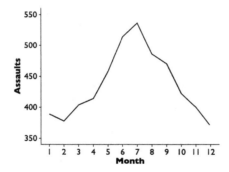

Figure 11.4b Monthly trends in crime, Vancouver, 2001.
b) Assaults
Source: Andresen and Malleson (2013a).

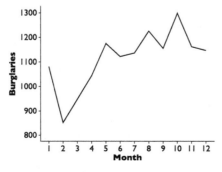

Figure 11.4c Monthly trends in crime, Vancouver, 2001.
c) Burglaries
Source: Andresen and Malleson (2013a).

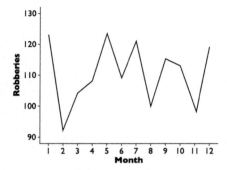

Figure 11.4d Monthly trends in crime, Vancouver, 2001.
d) Robberies
Source: Andresen and Malleson (2013a).

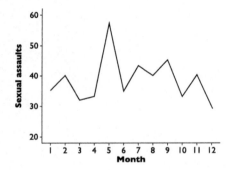

Figure 11.4e Monthly trends in crime, Vancouver, 2001
e) Sexual assaults
Source: Andresen and Malleson (2013a).

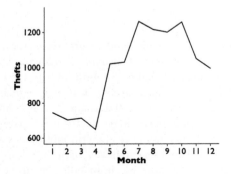

Figure 11.4f Monthly trends in crime, Vancouver, 2001.
f) Thefts
Source: Andresen and Malleson (2013a).

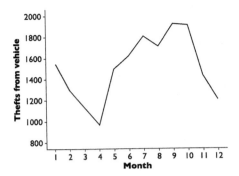

Figure 11.4g Monthly trends in crime, Vancouver, 2001.
g) Thefts from vehicle
Source: Andresen and Malleson (2013a).

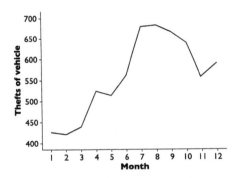

Figure 11.4h Monthly trends in crime, Vancouver, 2001.
h) Thefts of vehicle
Source: Andresen and Malleson (2013a).

Burglary is a category that includes both residential and commercial criminal events, shown in Figure 11.4c. Burglaries are lowest in February, increase until the beginning of the peak in late spring and remain relatively constant for the rest of the year. The seasonal crime pattern does not manifest itself that strongly here, but this is partially because of the way the data are presented. If the data were presented from February to January, a seasonal crime pattern would be much more apparent. This is a similar issue to the choice of the beginning to the criminological day, discussed above. How we choose to present our data can have a significant impact on its subsequent interpretation. Robbery, Figure 11.4d, shows little evidence of a seasonal crime pattern at first glance. However, the peaks in robbery are at expected times of the year. May and July typically have nice weather in Vancouver, leading to more people being outside of the relatively protective environment of the home; and December and January are months of the year when a lot of people are out shopping—once again, opportunity reveals itself to be an important factor for criminal events. Also worthy of note here is that if the start month for Figure 11.4d were February, not January, a seasonal crime pattern would be more apparent. Sexual assaults, Figure 11.4e, show no meaningful seasonal crime pattern. Theft, theft from vehicle, and theft of vehicle (Figures 11.4f, 11.4g, and 11.4h, respectively) also exhibit seasonal crime patterns that are similar to that of all crimes. These three crime types all peak through summer and fall.

Overall, these descriptive results are consistent with previous research. Seasonal crime patterns are present for most, but not all, crime types. This shows that seasonal crime patterns are important for understanding the temporal pattern of crime, but seasonality is clearly not monolithic.

Turning to the effect of seasonal crime patterns on the spatial patterns of crime, the most interesting result emerges when comparing the yearly aggregate of criminal events to criminal events occurring only in the summer (June 21 to September 20). This comparison was undertaken using the spatial point pattern test initially presented in Chapter 8, with the results shown in Figure 11.5. These

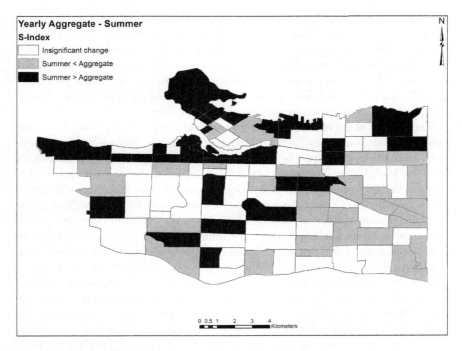

Figure 11.5 Spatial variations in seasonal crime patterns.
Source: Andresen and Malleson (2013a).

results show a definite increase in the concentration of criminal events during the summer months along the northern borders of Vancouver. Stanley Park, the most northern portion of the central business district peninsula, exhibits an increase in criminal events during the summer months, as does the northern border of Vancouver to the west of the central business district peninsula. Another set of areas that show an increase in the concentration of criminal events during the summer months is Spanish Banks, Kitsilano, English Bay, and False Creek. This is the strip of "Summer > Aggregate" along the northern coast of Vancouver, immediately south and then west of the central business district peninsula—and an area of popular beaches and water activity during the summer months. Other areas that include increases in the concentration of criminal events during the summer months include shopping centers, large parks, and the location of the summer fair, the Pacific National Exhibition, on the northeast corner of the map. Therefore, Vancouver's seasonal crime pattern reveals a strong spatial component that is simple to understand in the context of routine activity theory.

Long-run temporal crime patterns: the crime drop of the 1990s

We will now end this chapter on the temporal dimension of crime with a brief discussion of long-run trends. Just as there are crime patterns within the day, within the week, and across the seasons, there are also patterns, or trends, that emerge and persist for decades. Considering time series of crime data for Canada that spans 125 years in a number of different publications, there are a number of notable trends and local peaks in this series that are worthy of note here, some of which relate to the theoretical chapters discussed earlier.

The tail-end of the nineteenth century had the lowest level of recorded criminal activity in recent memory, with no notable trend. In the beginning of the twentieth century, the crime rate began to rise slowly with a peak at the beginning of the First World War. This peak subsided by the end of the war with no notable trend until the beginning of the Great Depression, when the crime rate rose rather quickly reaching a peak at the beginning of the Second World War. The crime rate then remained relatively constant from the early 1940s until the early 1960s. It is unfortunate that detailed crime type information is not consistently and reliably available for this time period. Because of the rationing of certain food items during the First and Second World Wars (sugar, meat, tires, gasoline, etc.), opportunities were created for theft and a subsequent underground market for these goods. Also, the Great Depression would have severely impacted the legitimate and illegitimate opportunities for many working-class people (decreasing the former and increasing the latter), leading to many more rational choices for illegitimate opportunities in order to feed themselves and their families. For these reasons, I would expect that much of the increase in the crime rate was driven by increases in the property crime rate.

The rapid increase in the crime rate from the early 1960s until 1990 has already been discussed in Chapter 3, on routine activity theory. This rapid increase in crime rates across the Western world at the national and subnational level for a variety of crime types is best understood as the result of changing routine activity patterns and the development of more criminal opportunities. The flipside of this rapid increase in crime rates is that it had set the stage for the equally dramatic decrease in crime rates since approximately 1990. As discussed in the following chapter, this rapid decrease in crime rates has caught the interest of many academics (not just criminologists), has generated a lot of debate regarding the explanations for this phenomenon, and is still largely misunderstood. However, the most robust explanations for this "crime drop" are rooted within environmental criminology and opportunity.

Review questions

1   What does aoristic analysis do and what is its purpose in crime analysis?
2   What is a time budget and why is it useful in crime analysis?
3   Why does a temporal constraint theory produce spatial patterns in crime?
4   Why does it matter when the criminological day begins? Our calendar practices say the day begins at midnight, so why not just use this point in time to mark the beginning of the criminological day?
5   Why would you expect a temporal crime pattern over the course of the week? Provide two examples, using different crime types with different weekly temporal crime patterns.
6   Why would we expect a seasonal pattern in crime?
7   Is the seasonal pattern of crime the same for all crime types? Why or why not?
8   Explain why the seasonal pattern of crime would affect the spatial patterns of crime.

References

Ahlberg, J. and Knutsson, J. (1994). More crimes while police resources remain constant: What will happen with the clearance rate in the future? *Studies on Crime and Crime Prevention*, 3, 132–45.
Andresen, M. A. and Jenion, G. W. (2004). The unspecified temporal criminal event: What is unknown is known with aoristic analysis and multinomial logistic regression. *Western Criminology Review*, 5(3), 1–11.
Andresen, M. A. and Malleson, N. (2013a). Crime seasonality and its variations across space. *Applied Geography*, 43, 25–35.
Breetzke, G. D. and Cohn, E. G. (2012). Seasonal assault and neighborhood deprivation in South Africa: Some preliminary findings. *Environment & Behavior*, 44(5), 641–67.
Brunsdon, C., Corcoran, J., Higgs, G. and Ware, A. (2009). The influence of weather on local geographical patterns of police calls for service. *Environment and Planning B: Planning and Design*, 36(5), 906–26.

Ceccato, V. (2005). Homicide in San Paulo, Brazil: Assessing spatial-temporal and weather variations. *Journal of Environmental Psychology*, 25(3), 307–21.

Cohn, E. G. and Rotton, J. (2000). Weather, seasonal trends and property crimes in Minneapolis, 1987–1988: A moderator-variable time-series analysis of routine activities. *Journal of Environmental Psychology*, 20(3), 257–72.

Farrell, G. and Pease, K. (1994). Crime seasonality: Domestic disputes and residential burglary in Merseyside 1988–90. *British Journal of Criminology*, 34(4), 487–98.

Felson, M. and Poulsen, E. (2003). Simple indicators of crime by time of day. *International Journal of Forecasting*, 19(4), 595–601.

Field, S. (1992). The effect of temperature on crime. *British Journal of Criminology*, 32(3), 340–51.

Grubesic, T. H. and Pridemore, W. A. (2011). Alcohol outlets and clusters of violence. *International Journal of Health Geographics*, 10(1), Article 30.

Harries, K. D. and Stadler, S. (1983). Determinism revisited: Assault and heat stress in Dallas. *Environment & Behavior*, 15(2), 235–56.

Harries, K. D., Stadler, S., and Zdorkowski, R. (1984). Seasonality and assault: Explorations in inter-neighborhood variation, Dallas 1980. *Annals of the Association of American Geographers*, 74(4), 590–604.

Hipp, J. R., Bauer, D. J., Curran, P. J., and Bollen, K. A. (2004). Crime of opportunity or crimes of emotion? Testing two explanations of season change in crime. *Social Forces*, 82(4), 1333–72.

Jenion, G. W. (2003). Analysis of the burglary phenomena: Problem solving unspecified temporal break and enters in the City of Burnaby. Unpublished MA thesis, School of Criminology, Simon Fraser University. Available online at http://summit.sfu.ca/item/8513 [accessed May 23, 2013].

Landau, S. F. and Fridman, D. (1993). The seasonality of violent crime: The case of robbery and homicide in Israel. *Journal of Research in Crime and Delinquency*, 30(2), 163–91.

Lewis, L. T. and Alford, J. J. (1975). The influence of season on assault. *Professional Geographer*, 27(2), 214–17.

Quetelet, L. A. J. (1842). *A Treatise on man and the development of his faculties*. Edinburgh: W. and R. Chambers.

Ratcliffe, J. H. (2000). Aoristic analysis: The spatial interpretation of unspecified temporal events. *International Journal of Geographic Information Science*, 14(7), 669–79.

Ratcliffe, J. H. (2002). Aoristic signatures and the spatio-temporal analysis of high volume crime patterns. *Journal of Quantitative Criminology*, 18(1), 23–43.

Ratcliffe, J. H. (2006). A temporal constraint theory to explain opportunity-based spatial offending patterns. *Journal of Research in Crime and Delinquency*, 43(3), 261–91.

Ratcliffe, J. H. and McCullagh, M. J. (1998). Aoristic crime analysis. *International Journal of Geographic Information Science*, 12(7), 751–64.

Rengert, G. F. and Wasilchick, J. (1985). *Suburban burglary: A time and place for everything*. Springfield, IL: Charles C. Thomas.

Rengert, G. F. and Wasilchick, J. (2000). *Suburban burglary: A tale of two suburbs*, 2nd edition. Springfield, IL: Charles C. Thomas.

Rotton, J. and Cohn, E. G. (2003). Global warming and U.S. crime rates: An application of routine activity theory. *Environment & Behavior*, 35(6), 802–25.

Semmens, N., Dillane, J., and Ditton, J. (2002). Preliminary findings on seasonality and the fear of crime: A research note. *British Journal of Criminology*, 42(4), 798–806.

Tompson, L. and Townsley, M. (2010). (Looking) back to the future: Using space-time patterns to better predict the location of street crime. *International Journal of Police Science & Management*, 12(1), 23–40.

van Koppen, P. J. and Jansen, R. W. J. (1999). The time to rob: Variations in time of number of commercial robberies. *Journal of Research in Crime and Delinquency*, 36(1), 7–29.

Chapter 12

Environmental criminology and the crime drop

Introduction

The crime drop of the 1990s was first mentioned in Chapter 3 when discussing crime rate trends and routine activity theory. Routine activity theory performed very well in explaining the increase in crime rates from 1960 through to the 1990s. But beginning around 1990 (the exact year varies by crime type and by location) crime rates began to decrease, most often drastically. Figure 12.1 provides an indication of these decreases in crime from 1990 up to 2011 in Canada and the United States. As noted in Chapter 3, in the years preceding 1990 property crime rates increased 300 percent in both Canada and the United States, while violent crime rates increased by 500 percent in Canada and by 400 percent in the United States. These are incredible increases in both property and violent crimes. The decreases since 1990 have not been as dramatic, but the downward trend does not seem to have reached bottom yet. The property crime rate, from its peak until 2011, has decreased by 58.7 percent and 43.4 percent for Canada and the United States, respectively; the violent crime rate has decreased by 20.1 percent and 49.1 percent in Canada and the United States, respectively, from its peak until 2011. Needless to say, this is a phenomenon that has attracted the attention of many criminologists, sociologists, and economists.

The first systematic research to address the crime drop of the 1990s was a journal article published by Gary LaFree in 1999. In this article Gary LaFree is quick to point out that the declines in violent crime in the United States (violent crime rate declines were the first crime rates to be investigated) caught many researchers and policy makers by surprise. In fact, there were those who were predicting a continued rise in violent crime rates because of a cohort effect of "superpredators" (Bennett et al., 1996; Fox and Pierce, 1994). Graham Farrell and colleagues, in a 2008 newsletter from the British Society of Criminology, went as far as stating that the inability of the criminology profession to come close to an explanation for the crime drop of the 1990s is embarrassing.

Gary LaFree put forth a number of potential explanations for this phenomenon: a decrease in economic stress, a greater degree of political legitimacy considering collective political action, the institutionalization of different family units,

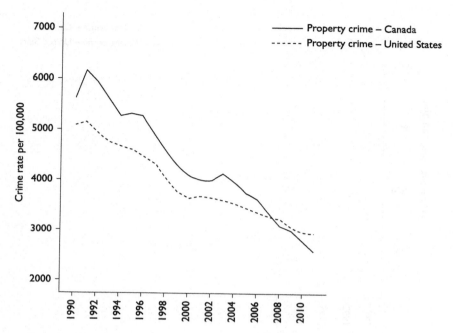

Figure 12.1a Property and violent crime rates for Canada and the United States, 1960–2011
a) Property crime
Source: Brennan (2012) and Federal Bureau of Investigation (2013).

demographics, drug markets, changes in routine activities, police initiatives, incarceration rates, education, and welfare. As discussed below, only one of these potential explanations holds any water with regard to empirical verification.

But the crime drop of the 1990s is far from a phenomenon occurring only in the United States. Consequently, any explanations for the decrease in crime rates, much like the increases in crime rates after the Second World War, must look beyond the borders of the United States. In fact, research undertaken by Andromachi Tseloni and colleagues, published in 2010, has found evidence for the crime drop of the 1990s in North America, Europe, Australia, Latin America, Africa, and Asia—also see van Dijk et al. (2012). This necessitates an attempt to explain the crime drop of the 1990s considering factors that are more international. As such, the crime drop of the 1990s should be referred to as the international crime drop of the 1990s because of the broad global scope of the decreases in crime rates.

In this chapter, we will briefly review the literature investigating the international crime drop of the 1990s. Following this review we will take a scientific view of how the international crime drop of the 1990s could be explained. What must we satisfy in order to turn a hypothesis into an explanation? The empirical literature

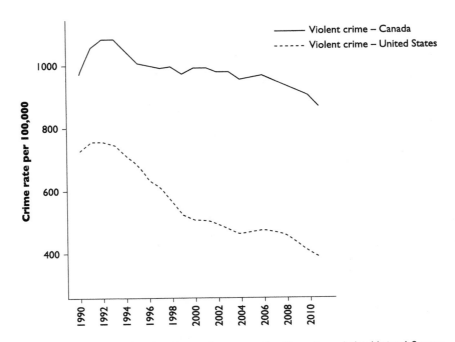

Figure 12.1b Property and violent crime rates for Canada and the United States, 1960–2011.
b) Violent crime
Source: Brennan (2012) and Federal Bureau of Investigation (2013).

is then held up to this standard. We will then discuss the implications of the international crime drop of the 1990s for academic research and public policy. And last, we will discuss the role of environmental criminology to explain further dimensions of the international crime drop of the 1990s.

The extensive and intensive nature of the crime drop

Though it is clearly evident in Figure 12.1 that Canada and the United States have had similar experiences with regard to the crime drop in the 1990s, particularly for property crime rates, looking at Canada is a natural first step for understanding the *international* crime drop of the 1990s. Internationally, Canada most resembles the United States and for good reason. Canada and the United States share a border that is almost 9,000 kilometers long with more than 90 percent of the Canadian population living within 160 kilometers of that border. Though the economic size of the United States is much greater than that of Canada, we are both developed nations with many commonalities with regard to socio-economic and socio-demographic indicators. And for Canada's recent history, the United States has been its most important trading partner, culminating in the Canada–United States Free Trade Agreement (January 1, 1989) and the North American Free Trade Agreement (January 1, 1994). With regard to crime, international comparisons have found that Canada and the United States are rather similar in terms of criminal victimization risk and the prevalence of most crime types, except for the most violent—homicide in the United States is a crime type that has historically been two to three times that of Canada, but the trends have been similar (Mayhew and van Dijk, 1997; Ouimet, 1999, 2002).

In 2002, Marc Ouimet published an article undertaking a comparison of Canada and the United States concerning the international crime drop of the 1990s. Ouimet investigated the crime types of homicide, sexual assault, assault, robbery, burglary, and motor vehicle theft—he cautioned regarding international comparison for sexual assault and assault because of differences in definitions. Ouimet found that Canada as a whole, as well as five regions of Canada (Atlantic Canada, Quebec, Ontario, Prairies, and British Columbia), exhibited large drops in the crime rates for almost all crime types. Canada exhibited crime drops similar in magnitude to those in the United States in all crime types except for motor vehicle theft; this result becomes particularly intriguing for understanding the causes of the international crime drop of the 1990s, below. Though not always of the same magnitude, all five regions in Canada also exhibited qualitatively similar crime drops as the United States, with motor vehicle theft being the exception—Quebec did experience a moderate decrease in motor vehicle theft in the 1990s. Needless to say, the similarities between Canada (and its regions) and the United States are much greater than the differences.

Richard Rosenfeld and Steven Messner published a journal article in 2009 that compared the crime drop of the 1990s phenomenon between the United States and nine European countries (Denmark, France, Germany, Greece, Hungary, Ireland, Italy, Netherlands, and Portugal), focusing on burglary because of general definitional consistency across the ten countries under study. When pooled together, these nine European countries did not exhibit the crime drop in burglary until the late 1990s. However, from 1995 to 2005 the burglary rate in these countries decreased approximately 25 percent. On average, Denmark, France, Greece, Ireland, Netherlands, and Portugal all exhibited decreases less than the United States, but Italy and Germany had decreases in burglary that were greater than in the United States. Considering data from the *International Crime Victim Survey*, Jan van Dijk and colleagues published a report in 2007 that found average criminal victimization rates within Europe peaked later than the United States (mid-1990s), but average criminal victimization rates had been declining, on average, ever since. Jan van Dijk and colleagues considered this finding to be practically universal and a challenge to theory within criminology. No longer can we focus on theoretical constructs that only work within a particular (set of) nation(s).

The *International Crime Victim Survey* was also used in another study published by Andromachi Tseloni and colleagues in 2010. In their journal article, these authors investigated crime trends from 1988 to 2004 for twenty-six countries and five crime types. They found that the beginning of the crime drop varied from country to country, ranging from the very early 1990s to the mid-1990s. On average, these authors found the following crime rate drops: theft from cars (77.1 percent), theft from person (60.3 percent), burglary (26.0 percent), assault (20.6 percent), and car theft (16.8 percent). Moreover, they found that aside from burglary all the crime types the authors examined decreased at approximately the same rate for all countries. Because these authors considered countries in North America, Europe, Australia, Latin America, Africa, and Asia, their analyses confirm and extend those of Jan van Dijk and colleagues in 2007, who compared the United States to European countries.

At this point there should be no doubt that the crime drop of the 1990s is indeed international. The strength of this statement manifested itself in one of Andromachi Tseloni and colleagues' final statements that there is little support for the use of country-specific explanations to understand and explain the international crime drop of the 1990s, particularly those rooted in the United States. But before these explanations are discarded here, they deserve our attention to see how many (if any) of the explanations for the crime drop in the United States are generalizable.

Explanations for the crime drop

Because of the similarities between Canada and the United States, outlined above, the first place to search for commonalities in explanations for the international crime drop of the 1990s is Canada. Ouimet (2002) performed such a comparison, considering some of the explanations put forth at the time: the number of police officers per 1,000 population, the incarceration rate per 100,000, the unemployment rate, and the proportion of the population aged 20 to 34, all in 1991 and 1999—1990 for the demographic variable. The results were generally not favorable for an international explanation. The unemployment rate did drop substantially in both Canada and the United States, 27 and 36 percent, respectively. Lower unemployment rates are often attributed to lower crime rates, supporting the generalizability of this factor at least to Canada. However, research on the relationship between unemployment and crime shows that the relationship can either be positive or negative, depending upon the time frame being analyzed (Andresen, 2012, 2013b; Cantor and Land, 1985; Phillips and Land, 2012). Additionally, and more importantly from a theoretical perspective, unemployment rates were quite low during the 1950s and 1960s when the crime rate was increasing substantially. Correlations must be viewed with caution here because they do not imply causation. The proportion of the population aged 20 to 34 is supported by the empirical research, particularly for young males (Boyd, 2000), so this is promising. But, as discussed below, other researchers have not found that demographic indicators can explain much of the international crime drop of the 1990s. And the number of police officers per 1,000 population and the incarceration rate per 100,000 are going in opposite directions in Canada and the United

States. This is especially true for the number of police officers per 1,000 population that exhibited an 11 percent change in both Canada and the United States, but negatively and positively, respectively. This brief discussion regarding the generalizability of any explanations for the international crime drop of the 1990s highlights the need for a set of criteria that must be met in order for an explanation to be considered.

Graham Farrell published a journal article in 2013 that provided a set of five tests for the evaluations of a theory of the international crime drop of the 1990s. The five tests Graham Farrell puts forth are as follows:

1   the preliminary empirical test,
2   the cross-national test,
3   the prior crime increase test,
4   the phone theft and e-crimes test, and
5   the varying trajectories test.

As we discuss each of these five tests, it will become apparent that any hypothesis for explaining the international crime drop of the 1990s must at least marginally pass each of these tests. Otherwise, the hypothesis simply fails to correspond with the known facts regarding international crime rate trends. Graham Farrell uses these five tests to assess the usefulness of fifteen hypotheses that have been put forth to explain the international crime drop of the 1990s: lead poisoning, the legalization of abortion, drug markets (the decline of crack-cocaine), demographics (relatively fewer young males), policing numbers, policing strategies, incarceration rates, healthy economies, the death penalty, (increased) gun control, right-to-carry handgun laws, immigration, consumer confidence, the decrease in political unrest, and crime opportunities/security.

The preliminary empirical test simply states that there must be some empirical justification to investigate a hypothesis. Moreover, this empirical justification should be based on solid theoretical grounds to justify any empirical justification such that spurious relationships are not used as a meaningful hypothesis. Many of the competing hypotheses for explaining the international crime drop of the 1990s fail this first test. Based on evidence put forth by a few scholars, the following hypotheses do not require any further attention: demographics, policing strategies, healthy economies, the death penalty, (increased) gun control, right-to-carry handgun laws, and immigration (Blumstein and Rosenfeld, 2008; Levitt, 2004; Stowell et al., 2009). It is actually surprising that some of these hypotheses made it into the academic literature because many of them would have been discarded simply by a cursory look at the statistics. A few examples are as follows: aside from a few economic downturns, Western economies have been exhibiting strong aggregate growth (some years better than others!) since the end of the Second World War; right-to-carry handgun laws were not extensive enough to have had an impact on aggregate crime rate statistics in the early 1990s, let alone today; and aside from a few "blips" in the late 1980s and early 1990s immigration in the

United States has only been increasing and the current academic literature (and some of the earliest academic literature) on this relationship does not support a positive relationship between immigration and crime (Andresen, 2013c).

The cross-national test has already been alluded to above. The work of Marc Ouimet stated that the number of police officers per capita and the incarceration rate fail the cross-national test. Other hypotheses that fail this test are (increased) gun control, right-to-carry handgun laws, the death penalty, better policing strategies, the legalization of abortion, and the decline of the crack-cocaine drug market. These are definitely factors that have impacted aspects of society in the United States. Some of them may even be able to partially explain the crime drop of the 1990s in the United States. But because these explanations are United States specific, they can only attempt to explain why the crime drop of the 1990s is *greater* in the United States. Of course, if the crime drop of the 1990s is not greater in the United States, these explanations can, therefore, not hold any water. The impact of legalization of abortion on crime is of particular interest with this test. John Donohue and Steven Levitt published a journal article in 2001 that stated legalized abortion appeared to account for as much as 50 percent of the crime drop of the 1990s. They supported their argument with a barrage of data and statistical tests and found states that legalized abortion earlier experienced crime drops earlier and states that had higher rates of abortion had greater crime drops. Their hypothesis was that the legalization of abortion led to fewer unwanted children who would grow up to be offenders because the timing of the changes in the law would have led to fewer high-risk young people around the time the crime drop began to occur. This hypothesis is based on two assumptions that I consider questionable: 1) the number of abortions (legal and illegal) actually increased enough to impact crime rates after the laws changed, and 2) these children would be disproportionately born into "high-risk" families more likely to have children who are criminal offenders because of socio-economic status. And, of course, this hypothesis is not supported with cross-national evidence. The only hypotheses that did pass this test were lead poisoning and the crime opportunity/security hypothesis. Lead poisoning most easily occurs through leaded paint and gasoline exposure causing brain damage to children. Lead exposure was drastically reduced in North America, Europe, Australia, and New Zealand in the early 1970s, that may have led to a reduction in the criminogenic population around the time of the international crime drop of the 1990s (Nevin, 2000, 2007).

The prior crime increase test is, I believe, one of the two tests that are the most significant and the most difficult to surpass. In essence, if a hypothesis is to explain the international crime drop of the 1990s, it should also be able to explain the crime increase from the 1950s to 1990. This test is failed by the following hypotheses: consumer confidence, incarceration rates, immigration, demographics, and policing numbers. Speaking in the context of the incarceration rate, the number of police officers, abortion, and the crack-cocaine market, Steven Levitt (2004) wondered why crime rates did not fall before 1990. I would argue that any hypothesis that failed this test did so for one of two reasons: 1) the researcher only investigated time series data that began at the point of the crime drop, or 2) pre-1990 data were not available at the time (or to the particular researcher) in order to properly assess the hypothesis.

The phone theft and e-crimes test is based on the fact that some crime types increased during the international crime drop of the 1990s. Similar to the rapid increase in crime rates that began in the 1950s, the increases in certain crime types after 1990 emerged because of the availability of new lightweight, valuable, electronic goods such as laptops, mobile phones, global positioning systems (GPS), and tablets, to name a few. In fact, in an article published in 2012, Allan Brimicombe attributed the proliferation of GPS units (satellite navigation systems, Sat Navs, in the United Kingdom) to the beginning of a crime wave in a borough of London, England. Because of these known facts, any hypothesis that stakes its claim on leading to universal increases or decreases in crime rates will fail this test. Only the crime opportunities/security hypothesis passes this test.

And lastly, the varying trajectories test relates to the differences in the timing of the international crime drops and the degree to which crime rates decline. Most hypotheses, all but one actually, fail this test because they predict that all crime types should decrease at the same time: incarceration of offenders, reductions in the population of offenders, less brain damage from lead poisoning, and so on. But we know from the empirical literature that the international crime drop of the 1990s began at different times for different crime types and in different countries. There is little that can be done to salvage any hypothesis that fails this test within a country (different crime types dropping at different times), but the timing of the crime drops in different countries can be explained if demographic shifts—in Europe, for example—occurred later than in the United States. There is little support for these attempts to salvage various hypotheses. In fact, the only hypothesis to pass this test is crime opportunities/security.

Overall, Graham Farrell found that one hypothesis failed all five of the tests, five hypotheses failed four of the tests, six hypotheses failed three of the tests, and two hypotheses failed two of the tests. The crime opportunity/security hypothesis was the only hypothesis to pass all five tests. Not surprisingly, given the context of this textbook, this hypothesis is rooted in environmental criminology.

The crime opportunity/security hypothesis (hereafter just referred to as the security hypothesis) asserts that changes in the quantity and quality of security were an important factor in the international crime drop of the 1990s. Specifically, with regard to automotive theft, the advent of electronic mobilizers and central locking were crucial for understanding decreases in this crime type. Moreover, Graham Farrell and his colleagues argued, in a journal article published in 2011, that reduced levels in automotive theft may have led to reductions in other crime types, including violent crime. With respect to the five tests, listed above, the security hypothesis has empirical evidence to support it, is relevant across many nations, is consistent with the prior crime increase, is consistent with other crime types increasing over the same time period, and can explain varying trajectories across different crime types and countries.

The support for the security hypothesis is gathered using automotive theft data from the United States, England and Wales, and Australia. The United States and England and Wales both had decreases in automotive theft of approximately 60 percent, but their respective crime drops occurred two years apart; Australia experienced a 55 percent drop in automotive theft, but their crime drop occurred ten years later than the crime drop in the United States, 2001. Graham Farrell and his colleagues explained these changes in automotive theft by considering immobilizers (expected to affect theft of vehicle, not theft from vehicle), alarms (expected to affect theft from vehicle, not theft of vehicle), and central locking (expected to affect theft of vehicle and theft from vehicle).

In England and Wales, automobile security increased substantially from 1991 to 2006. Central locking and alarms increased from 35 to almost 90 percent and approximately 22 to 62 percent, respectively. Immobilizers became available in 1999, increasing substantially to 2006. In Australia, automotive security focused on immobilizers and provided a natural experiment for the security hypothesis. In the state of Western Australia, the government provided subsidies in 1997 to encourage automobile owners to install electronic immobilizers, but they became mandatory in 1999; in the other states and territories of Australia electronic immobilizers became mandatory in 2001. In Western Australia automotive theft began to decrease in 1998, whereas automobile theft in the other states and territories continued to increase until 2001, followed by a steady decrease until 2007. Moreover, there was an increase in the average age of vehicles indicating a substitution effect resulting from offenders no longer attempting to steal the newer vehicles with the electronic immobilizers.

With regard to central locking, Graham Farrell and colleagues expected that better locks on newer vehicles would lead to the entry method switching from door forcing to window smashing. Though they found all forms of entry decreased, the majority of the measured decline in automotive theft in England and Wales could be attributed to the decrease in door forcing. They found similar results in Australia.

These authors then investigated their hypothesis regarding immobilizers having a greater impact on automotive theft than theft from automobile. Overall, fewer automobiles with central locking, electronic immobilizers, and tracking devices were stolen than falling victim to theft from automobile; automobile alarms and mechanical immobilizers exhibited no differential effect. Moreover, only 3.4 percent of vehicles had tracking devices, but this security device reduced the risk of automotive theft by 77.3 percent—only a 0.1 percent reduction in the risk of theft from automobile; automobiles with an electronic immobilizer had their risk of automotive theft reduced by almost 50 percent, while the same security device had a much lower impact on theft from automobile.

The evidence provided to support the security hypothesis is very strong indeed. Graham Farrell and colleagues have provided such evidence for multiple countries using multiple data sets and different crime types. Though it is always possible they have found a spurious relationship, it is rather unlikely. Because of this success, the authors put forth potential extensions of the security hypothesis that are testable in the context of burglary, robbery, theft, and violence. They identify automotive theft and theft from automobile as "debut crimes" committed by novice offenders. Consequently, if they are turned off automobile-based crime types, they may be deterred from committing more serious property crime and violent crime. Homes have also benefited from increases in security similar to those in automobiles. Of course, homes cannot have immobilizer devices installed, but burglar alarms are becoming increasingly complex with direct calling to the local police as well as live communications between the home and the alarm company to confirm or deny the legitimacy of the alarm. There have also been increases in the strength of windows, window locks, doors, and door locks. The improvements will be most apparent in newer residential developments that can be identified in a census with the expectation that these homes will have lower burglary victimization rates after controlling for other factors. Based on research within situational crime prevention, target hardening (increased security) has been found to reduce robberies in post offices (Ekblom, 1988), convenience stores (Hunter and Jeffery, 1997), and banks (Clarke et al., 1991; Grandjean, 1990). Specifically, it was found that having two store clerks on duty, particularly for night shifts, having clear sightlines to the inside of the convenience store from the outside, and reduced cash on hand reduced robberies (Bellamy, 1996; Hunter and Jeffery, 1997). These are all potentially related to the security hypothesis and deserve systematic investigation.

All of these security aspects for automobiles, homes, and convenience stores have, at least for some offenders, turned *suitable* targets into *unsuitable* targets. Hence, with the empirical evidence reviewed here, and the conjectures with regard to burglary and robbery, the security hypothesis has proven to be most instructive for understanding the international crime drop of the 1990s. Most notably, routine activity theory is at the forefront of explanations for the international crime drop of the 1990s.

Implications of the crime drop

There are a number of implications from the international crime drop of the 1990s. First, it is still ongoing, so some researchers simply refer to it now as the international crime drop. However, the international crime drop began in the 1990s, so its "original" name is used in this textbook.

Second, the international crime drop of the 1990s has a huge implication for theoretical testing. Much, if not all, of theoretical testing in the criminological literature, including environmental criminology, has taken place during a period of crime rates increasing or remaining relatively constant—no notable crime declines aside from after the world wars, but those declines were very short-lived. Social disorganization theory, routine activity theory, the geometric theory of crime, rational choice theory, and all of the other theoretical frameworks invoked within criminological research in the twentieth century have been formulated and tested in the context of increasing or stable crime rates. Putting all of these theories to the test using post-1990 criminal event data should prove to be most instructive. It is possible that many of the theories that we criminologists hold dear will fail to survive this test. I expect this to be the case because I am confident the five tests of the international crime drop put forth by Graham Farrell extend far beyond the scope of explanations for the international crime drop of the 1990s. Any criminological theory worth its weight in salt must be able to explain: criminal activity beyond the borders of its original formulation, criminal activity when it is increasing and decreasing, why some crime types have been decreasing drastically while others have risen, and why any changes in the trajectories of crime may vary from crime type to crime type and place to place. I realize that this is a tall order that may take many years (decades!) to investigate, but this drop in (most) crime rates over the past twenty or so years is a natural experiment so rare in the social sciences and a prime opportunity (pardon the pun) to see if our criminological theories can pass muster or fall into the dust heaps of theoretical history.

Third, the international crime drop of the 1990s and beyond has huge implications for policing. Anecdotally I have heard that many government offices are asking why police department budgets continue to rise when crime rates are, in some cases, half of what they were twenty years ago. Why do we still need so many police? Such questions and concerns are often born out of ignorance of policing. First and foremost, it assumes that all the police do is fight crime. Though this is obviously an important aspect of their job, police officers are often the front line when it comes to the provision of social services, more generally. For some time because of the deinstitutionalization of mental health patients across North America, the police have been spending ever more time dealing with mental health issues. Also because of the litigious nature of Western society, the police and other members within the criminal justice system must now undertake more (unnecessary?) tasks to close a police file. For example, if the time it takes to fill out a report of a criminal event has doubled because of the complexity of information required, a 50 percent decrease in criminal events becomes a wash—this is actually the case, again anecdotally, with some police records management systems versus the older paper reports, 30 minutes versus 15 minutes to fill out the "paperwork." Of course, this plethora of information regarding criminal events is a treasure for those criminologists who analyze official police data, but it means that the police are no less busy now than they were twenty years ago. Additionally, and related to the police being the front-line provider of social services, twenty years of calls for service data for one of my local police detachments indicate that there has been no significant decrease in the demand for police services. Add to this the increased complexity of policing over the past twenty-five years (Malm et al., 2005), and the workload of the police has actually increased during the international crime drop of the 1990s.

And fourth, there are potentially significant public policy implications that emerge from the international crime drop of the 1990s. Because of the lack of support for the effect of incarceration rates on the decreases in the crime rates, increasing the severity of sentences and building more prisons to be "tough on crime" is likely an inefficient approach to crime reduction—we have also known for decades that prisons do very little, if anything, to reduce recidivism (Jeffery, 1971). We must also be careful not to spend significant resources on initiatives such as gun control, the number of police officers per capita, various police strategies, and the war on drugs if further reductions in crime are the goal. There may or may not be good political/social/cultural reasons for supporting public policies such as these, but there is no evidence to support the idea that they have played a significant role in the international crime drop of the 1990s.

Environmental criminology and the crime drop

Though the majority of the early research in the international crime drop of the 1990s did not consider the role of environmental criminology, the explanation for the international crime drop of the 1990s that has thus far passed muster is a part of environmental criminology. The most obvious connection is to routine activity theory because the security hypothesis has impacted the suitability of targets and, potentially, guardianship; the definition of a capable guardian may have to be revised because it now appears to include tracking devices and electronic immobilizers. However, rational choice theory is also front and center in this explanation. Motivated offenders are choosing not to target particular automobiles because the cost is too great relative to the payoff. Additionally, they are substituting from one set of criminal events to another because the opportunities are better. Consequently, according to the security hypothesis, opportunity does indeed make the thief. If the conjectures regarding the implications for the security hypothesis put forth here and by Graham Farrell and colleagues prove to be correct, the opportunities for environmental criminology to explain this phenomenon will only increase.

Review questions

1 Why have some criminologists stated that it is embarrassing that the criminology profession has been unable to come close to an explanation for the crime drop of the 1990s?
2 What does the international nature of the crime drop of the 1990s mean for any explanations of this phenomenon?
3 List and briefly explain the five tests any hypothesis of the international crime drop of the 1990s must pass.
4 Briefly explain, with examples, the security hypothesis with regard to the crime drop.
5 Briefly state how the security hypothesis passes all five of the tests for a hypothesis to explain the international crime drop of the 1990s.
6 Briefly explain how the security hypothesis could apply to the crime drop for residential/commercial burglary and commercial robberies.
7 What are the implications of the international crime drop of the 1990s?

References

Andresen, M. A. (2012). Unemployment and crime: A neighborhood level panel data approach. *Social Science Research*, 41(6), 1615–28.

Andresen, M. A. (2013b). Unemployment, business cycles, crime, and the Canadian provinces. *Journal of Criminal Justice*, 41(4), 220–27.

Andresen, M. A. (2013c). International immigration, internal migration, and homicide in Canadian provinces. *International Journal of Offender Therapy and Comparative Criminology*, 57(5), 632–57.

Bellamy, L. (1996). Situational crime prevention and convenience store robbery. *Security Journal*, 7(1), 41–52.

Bennett, W., DiIulio, J., and Walters, J. (1996). *Body count*. New York, NY: Simon & Schuster.

Blumstein, A. and Rosenfeld, R. (2008). Factors contributing to US crime trends. In A. Goldberger and R. Rosenfeld (eds.), *Understanding crime trends: Workshop report* (pp. 13–44). Washington, DC: National Academies Press.

Boyd, N. (2000). *The beast within: Why men are violent*. Vancouver, BC: Greystone Books.

Brennan, S. (2012). *Police-reported crime statistics in Canada, 2011*. Ottawa, ON: Statistics Canada.

Brimicombe, A. (2012). Did GIS start a crime wave? SatNav theft and its implications for geo-information engineering. *Professional Geographer*, 64(3), 430–45.

Cantor, D. and Land, K. C. (1985). Unemployment and crime rates in the post World War II United States: A theoretical and empirical analysis. *American Sociological Review*, 50(3), 317–32.

Clarke, R. V., Field, S., and McGarth, G. (1991). Target hardening of banks in Australia and displacement of robberies. *Security Journal*, 2(2), 84–90.

Donohue, J. J. III, and Levitt, S. D. (2001). The impact of legalized abortion on crime. *Quarterly Journal of Economics*, 116(2), 379–420.

Eckblom, P. (1988). Preventing post office robberies in London: effects and side effects. *Journal of Security Administration*, 11(2), 36–43.

Farrell, G. (2013). Five tests for a theory of the crime drop. *Crime Science*, 2(1), Article 5.

Farrell, G., Tilley, N., Tseloni, A., and Mailley, J. (2008). The crime drop and the security hypothesis. *British Society of Criminology Newsletter*, 62(2), 17–21.

Farrell, G., Tseloni, A., Mailley, J., and Tilley, N. (2011). The crime drop and the security hypothesis. *Journal of Research in Crime and Delinquency*, 48(2), 147–75.

Federal Bureau of Investigation. (2013). Uniform Crime Reporting Statistics. Available online at http://bjs.gov/ucrdata/ [accessed 08 May 2013].

Fox, J. A. and Pierce, G. (1994). American killers are getting younger. *USA Today*, January 24–6.

Grandjean, C. (1990). Bank robberies and physical security in Switzerland: A case study of the escalation and displacement phenomena. *Security Journal*, 1(3), 155–9.

Hunter, R. D. and Jeffery, C. R. (1997). Preventing convenience store robbery through environmental design. In R. V. Clarke (ed.), *Situational crime prevention: Successful case studies*, 2nd edition (pp. 191–9). Monsey, NY: Criminal Justice Press.

Jeffery, C. R. (1971) *Crime prevention through environmental design*. Beverly Hills, CA: Sage Publications.

LaFree, G. (1999). Declining violent crime rates in the 1990s: Predicting crime booms and busts. *Annual Review of Sociology*, 25, 145–68.

Levitt, S. D. (2004). Understanding why crime fell in the 1990s: Four factors that explain the decline and six that do not. *Journal of Economic Perspectives*, 18(1), 163–90.

Malm, A., Pollard, N., Brantingham, P. J., Tinsley, P., Plecas, D., Brantingham, P. L., Cohen, I., and Kinney, B. (2005). *A 30 year analysis of police service delivery and costing: "E" Division*. Abbotsford, BC: University College of the Fraser Valley.

Mayhew, P. and van Dijk, J. J. M. (1997). *Criminal victimization in eleven industrialized countries: Key findings from the 1996 International Crime Victims Survey*. The Hague, Netherlands: Ministry of Justice, WODC.

Nevin, R. (2000). How lead exposure relates to temporal changes in IQ, violent crime, and unwed pregnancy. *Environmental Research*, 83(1), 1–22.

Nevin, R. (2007). Understanding international crime trends: The legacy of preschool lead exposure. *Environmental Research*, 104(3), 315–36.

Ouimet, M. (1999). Crime in Canada and the United States: A comparative analysis. *Canadian Review of Sociology and Anthropology*, 36(3), 389–408.

Ouimet, M. (2002). Explaining the American and Canadian crime "drop" in the 1990s. *Canadian Journal of Criminology*, 44(1), 33–50.

Phillips, J. A. and Land, K. C. (2012). The link between unemployment and crime rate fluctuations: An analysis at the county, state, and national levels. *Social Science Research*, 41(3), 681–94.

Rosenfeld, R. and Messner, S. F. (2009). The crime drop in comparative perspective: The impact of the economy and imprisonment on American and European burglary rates. *British Journal of Sociology*, 60(3), 445–71.

Stowell, J. I., Messner, S. F., McGeever, K. F., and Raffalovich, L. E. (2009). Immigration and the recent violent crime drop in the United States: A pooled, cross-sectional time-series analysis of metropolitan areas. *Criminology*, 47(3), 889–929.

Tseloni, A., Mailley, J., Farrell, G., and Tilley, N. (2010). Exploring the international decline in crime rates. *European Journal of Criminology*, 7(5), 375–94.

van Dijk, J., van Kesteren, J., and Smit, P. (2007). *Criminal victimisation in international perspective: Key findings from the 2004–2005 ICVS and EU ICS*. The Hague: Boom Juridische Uitgevers.

van Dijk, J., Tseloni, A., and Farrell, G. (eds.) (2012). *The international crime drop*. London, UK: Palgrave Macmillan.

Chapter 13

Geographic profiling

Introduction

Geographic profiling was pioneered by Professor D. Kim Rossmo, currently at Texas State University, San Marcos, and is a technique used by police to prioritize suspect lists in a criminal investigation. Geographic profiling uses the locations of a connected series of criminal events to determine the offender's "anchor point"— most often offender's residence, but it may also be a workplace, school, hangout, or friend's residence. Because this technique uses a connected series of criminal events, the most common uses of geographic profiling are in the investigation of serial murder, rape, arson, burglary, or robbery. Though the discussion below will focus on serial offending for simplicity, it should be noted that geographic profiling can also be used for non-serial criminal events that involve multiple locations. For example, the series of criminal events may be connected as the locations of where an offender stole a vehicle, robbed a convenience store, robbed a liquor store, and then abandoned the vehicle. Geographic profiling has proven, and continues, to be a useful method for understanding the nature of serial offenders from an academic perspective, partially because it allows for the classification of different offender types. But geographic profiling has also proven to be an instructive tool for the practice of investigative policing.

From a theoretical perspective geographic profiling is rooted in the geometric theory of crime (see Chapter 4). However, geographic profiling also takes routine activities and rational choice into account because it considers where an offender may travel to and assumes that offenders are rational because otherwise their actions could not be predicted. Probably the most critical aspects of the geometric theory of crime necessary to understand geographic profiling are the concepts of the buffer offenders will "place" around their home and distance decay. Both of these concepts are represented in Figure 4.2 and show how offenders are expected to travel some distance from their residence (anchor point), but not too far; they only travel as far as necessary. As discussed in Chapter 4, the buffer zone around the home is an attempt by the offender to hide the location of their residence or other anchor point, but is also a product of the geometry of space such that there are fewer criminal event opportunities close to any offender's home (or any single point in space).

In this chapter, geographic profiling will be explained in the context of what it is and how it is done. This is important to understand, because geographic profiling has a specific function within investigative policing—most notably, it does not solve crimes. Once we have covered geographic profiling in the context of criminology, we will move into how geographic profiling has been applied in the fields of counterinsurgency, counterterrorism, biology/zoology, and epidemiology. This is a fascinating literature that shows how good research in the social sciences can inform research in the so-called hard sciences. These new applications of geographic profiling show the strength of this method for understanding predatory species, more generally than human predators, but will also have a feedback effect to criminological research. A better understanding of the predatory behaviors of other species may help us to better understand the predatory behaviors of humans. We conclude with a brief discussion of the future of geographic profiling along these lines, and others.

Geographic profiling: what it is and how it is done

As stated above, geographic profiling is a criminal investigation technique with the purpose of trying to determine where the offender lives (Rossmo, 2000). Geographic profiling, on its own, cannot solve crimes, but it can aid in this process because it is able to help sort through the (often) massive amount of information that police must sort through in major investigations. One of the best analogies I have come across to describe geographic profiling comes from the television show *Numb3rs*. In the pilot episode, geographic profiling was used to help identify a serial criminal. The FBI were trying to figure out who the serial offender was and a mathematician (a brother of an FBI agent) said he could help them figure out where the serial offender lived. Because of the nature of television shows, the FBI agent was very puzzled and did not see how they could figure out where the serial offender lived when they could not even figure out where the next target was going to be victimized. The mathematician used the analogy of a water sprinkler that operated in a circle. He stated that it would be impossible to predict the next location where a drop of water would land because there were too many variables to consider: the order of the droplets leaving the sprinkler, wind direction and velocity, evaporation rates, and so on. However, if you know the pattern of where previous water droplets have landed, you will be able to make a very precise estimate of where the sprinkler is located. This is what geographic profiling does. But this is not a simple task. There are a number of steps that must be undertaken when geographic profiling is used as an investigative technique.

The first and extremely important step is to determine that a serial offender is behind the crimes of interest. This step is extremely important, because geographic profiling is useful in identifying the most probable location of the offender's residence. Consequently, there can only be one offender to identify; if there are multiple offenders involved, geographic profiling will focus on the most prominent offender's residence under the assumption that location decisions for the crimes are based on his/her awareness space. Needless to say, geographic profiling begins at the original investigation stage that determines which offences, if any, are connected. This is called a linkage analysis or a comparative case analysis and must be done before a geographic profiling case can be considered. As outlined by D. Kim Rossmo (2006, 2014), this process involves identifying the similarities and differences between the different criminal events with the need to have more of the former than the latter. This is done through the use of physical evidence, offender descriptions, or crime scene behavior (Rossmo, 2000).

Once it has been determined that a serial offender is at work, geographic profiling may be brought in as a criminal investigation tool. This involves a mathematical representation of the spatial pattern of the crime sites. The locations of the linked crimes are entered into software that uses the Criminal Geographic Targeting (CGT) computer algorithm. This CGT computer algorithm is then used to generate jeopardy surfaces that are three-dimensional probability surfaces identifying the most probable locations of the offender's residence. This is done using several different considerations, a number of which we have discussed in the previous theoretical chapters (namely Chapters 3 and 4, on routine activity theory and the geometric theory of crime, respectively), that may be classified as activity nodes, pathways, crime generators, and crime attractors. These considerations may include: crime locations, offender type, the target backcloth, the street network, bus stops and transit stations, physical and psychological boundaries (edges), zoning and land use, neighborhood demographics, the routine activities of the victims, displacement (media coverage and/or uniformed police presence can cause spatial displacement of subsequent criminal events in the crime series that the CGT computer algorithm can account for because our behavior is predictable), and the hunting style/pattern of offenders.

The hunting style of serial offenders is based on research published by D. Kim Rossmo in 1997, based on serial murder cases. The hunting style is a typology that describes the methods by which the serial offender searches for and attacks his/her victims. Rossmo identified four methods that serial offenders use to search for victims: hunter, poacher, troller, and trapper. Hunters leave their home residence and search for victims within their awareness space; poachers begin their victim search from an anchor point other than their home residence, sometimes traveling outside of their home municipality; trollers are opportunistic serial offenders who simply encounter victims throughout the course of their routine activities; and trappers lure victims into their home or some other location in order to better control the victim. There are three methods of attack identified by D. Kim Rossmo: raptor, stalker, and ambusher. Raptors attack their victims very shortly after the first encounter, stalkers will wait for the best opportunity to attack, and the ambusher attacks in locations where the serial offender has a high degree of control. There are various combinations of these victim identification and attack methods that lead to even more combinations of when, how, and where the serial offender will encounter/identify the victim, attack the victim, commit the primary criminal event (rape, murder, sexual murder, etc.), and release the victim or dispose of the body. Each one of these steps could have a different location (Rossmo, 2000).

From all this information, the CGT computer algorithm generates the geographic profile (jeopardy surface). The output of the CGT computer algorithm is a 40,000-pixel grid as shown in Figure 10.3 that represents the output. Figure 13.1 shows two geographic profile images, one two-dimensional (geoprofile) and one three-dimensional (jeopardy surface)—white shows a high degree of probability for finding the serial offender's home residence in Figure 13.1a and the peaks in Figure 13.1b show the same information in three dimensions. D. Kim Rossmo has described this output as representing a volcano with a caldera (Rossmo, 2014).

This geographic profile can then be used within the criminal investigation process through a number of strategies, generally classified as suspect-based and

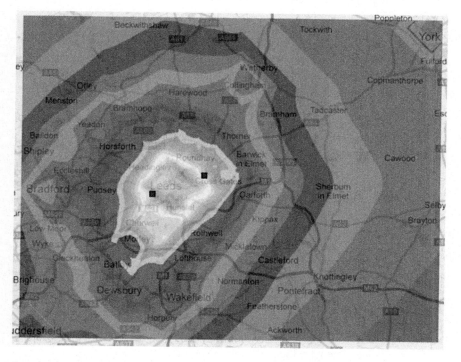

Figure 13.1a Geographic profile.
a) Two-dimensional representation (geoprofile)
Source: Images courtesy of Professor D. Kim Rossmo.

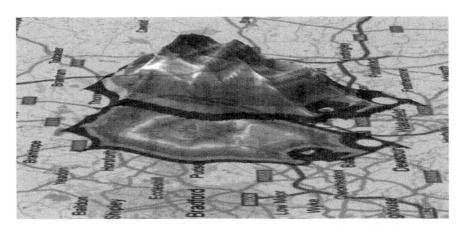

Figure 13.1b Geographic profile.
b) Three dimensional representation (jeopardy surface)
Source: Images courtesy of Professor D. Kim Rossmo.

area-based. Suspect-based strategies include, but are not limited to searching or prioritizing: police records; court records; sex offender registers; and government databases regarding parole, probation, mental health, schools, current and past property ownership, various vehicle registrations, and credit information. Area-based strategies can include directing police patrols or surveillance to particular areas, or prioritizing individuals based on particular locations (Rossmo, 2006, 2014).

It should be clear from this brief discussion of the process of geographic profiling that it is no simple task. Performing geographic profiling requires a geographic information system because of the spatial data used in the calculation of the jeopardy surface, a database management system, and visualization capabilities to view the resulting jeopardy surface and potentially have it interact with other spatial information. The first commercial application for performing geographic profiling was *Rigel*, developed in 1995 by D. Kim Rossmo while he was studying at Simon Fraser University—D. Kim Rossmo developed the original software himself in 1991. *Rigel* is the most widely used geographic profiling software in law enforcement, and common in academic circles, with two other software packages available (*CrimeStat* and *Dragnet*) that are primarily used for academic research. Needless to say, in order to be proficient in this application of geographic profiling, and its related software, training in both the theory of environmental criminology and the practice of geographic profiling is necessary.

One final consideration on the technical side of geographic profiling is worthy of discussion at this point: How well does geographic profiling perform? There are two methods that have been used to determine how well a geographic profile performs: error distance and the hit score percentage. The error distance is a measurement of the distance between the absolute peak of the jeopardy surface and the actual location of the serial offender's home residence; the greater the distance, the greater the error. Though this may initially appear to be a reasonable method of assessing geographic profiling, it is not particularly instructive because it does not evaluate geographic profiling based on what it is supposed to do. Recall from above that geographic profiling does not directly solve serial crimes. Geographic profiling is a criminal investigation tool to help in the process of filtering through the potentially huge amount of information law enforcement officials have to process. Fundamentally, error distance assumes that the primary goal of geographic profiling is to solve the serial criminal events because the criterion it uses is the distance between the peak of the jeopardy profile (the greatest probability of the offender's home residence location) and the actual location of the serial offender's home residence. This is a problematic evaluation criterion because geographic profiling is not used to simply investigate a single address located within the entire jeopardy surface. D. Kim Rossmo (2011) puts forth a much more appropriate evaluative measure for geographic profiling, the hit score percentage. The hit score percentage is the ratio of the geographic size of the area that must be searched (from the highest probability grid cell to the lowest probability grid cell) before the serial offender's home residence is located relative to the entire hunting area. For example, if all of the serial criminal events occurred within a 10 square kilometer area and the serial criminal offender is located within the first square kilometer of the jeopardy surface, the hit score percentage would be 10 percent. However, in research on the evaluation of geographic profiles based on actual police operational performance in various police agencies, D. Kim Rossmo (2011) reported an average hit score percentage of 5 percent and a median hit score percentage of 3 percent. In other words, 95–97 percent of the total hunting areas did not have to be searched, a considerable time and resources saving for law enforcement agencies.

New applications of geographic profiling

The use of geographic profiling in criminal investigations is indeed an important endeavor that must continue. However, there have also been some very interesting recent geographic profiling applications that have included: cellular telephone switch tower sites in kidnapping cases, the stores in which bomb components have been purchased, and an historical analysis of the locations of anti-Nazi propaganda postcards left in the streets of Berlin, Germany in the early 1940s (Rossmo, 2014). Additionally, there have been new applications of geographic profiling that have proven to be very instructive, but for different reasons: counterinsurgency, counterterrorism, biology/zoology, and epidemiology (Rossmo, 2012). As argued below, understanding these more recent applications of geographic profiling may be able to help develop new knowledge for the application of geographic profiling to criminal investigations.

Counterterrorism and geographic profiling

The Central Intelligence Agency (2003, p. 1) in the United States defines terrorists as "[t]hose who employ terrorism, regardless of their specific secular or religious objectives, strive to subvert the rule of law and effect change through violence and fear. These terrorists also share the misguided belief that killing, kidnapping, extorting, robbing, and wreaking havoc to terrorize people are legitimate forms of political action." This is a serious threat to populations around the globe because these acts of terrorism occur in many countries, rich and poor alike. Despite the political economy issues surrounding the presence of terrorists and terrorism, any efforts to reduce these acts contribute to the betterment of society. Of course part of this effort should be removing, or at least reducing, the reasons for why terrorists exist in the first place, but this effort should also include addressing the problem we have today. As has been shown in some recent research, geographic profiling has proven to be instructive in this area. At this time, geographic profiling has been applied to: help military analysts identify the location of enemy military bases (Brown et al., 2005), identify the location of terrorist hideouts based on their attack locations (Bennell and Corey, 2007), and identify the targets of terrorist attacks (Rossmo and Harries, 2011).

Craig Bennell and Shevaun Corey published a book chapter in 2007 that investigated the possibility of applying geographic profiling to terrorists. In their research, they wished to know if geographic profiling could be instructive to locate the hideout of the primary terrorist orchestrating a set of terrorist attacks. In this sense, this application of geographic profiling is similar to the situation, mentioned above, that if there are multiple terrorists involved as is often the case, geographic profiling will focus on the most prominent terrorist's hideout under the assumption that location decisions for the terrorist attacks are based on his/her awareness space. Craig Bennell and Shevaun Corey noted that the assumptions for geographic profiling may not always be met in the context of terrorists and their attacks. Though terrorists do typically have multiple crime sites that can be linked to the same group (because they tend to take responsibility for the terrorist attacks for political reasons), it cannot be assumed that the terrorists are not commuting into the area where the attack is to take place or that the terrorists cannot move their anchor point—these authors also refer to an assumption regarding the uniform distribution of suitable targets, but this is not a concern for geographic profiling (Rossmo and Velarde, 2008). Despite the inability to always maintain that assumptions hold true, Craig Bennell and Shevaun Corey undertook their analysis (using *Dragnet*) to analyze the terrorist attacks of two groups, one in France and one in Greece. They found that geographic profiling did not work well for the terrorist attacks undertaken by the French group, Action directe. For this terrorist group, the primary terrorist of concern had his anchor point (hideout) location in Portugal and committed the terrorist acts in France. Needless to say, the hit score percentage for this case study was 100 percent. The second terrorist group, Epanastatikos Laikos Agonas (ELA), was based in Greece and committed the analyzed terrorist attacks in Greece. In this particular case, the geographic profile proved to be useful.

The lesson to learn from this research was that geographic profiling is instructive for the application of identifying terrorist hideouts, but only if the hunting style is hunter—this hunting style is also referred to as a marauder. This is true for geographic profiling, in general. If the hunting style is poacher, also referred to as a commuter, geographic profiling will not prove to be instructive for identifying the location of a terrorist hideout. Again, the same applies to geographic profiling, in general. The difficulty in this context, or any context involving geographic profiling, is that it is very difficult to know if the principal person in the terrorist group is behaving like a marauder or a commuter. Though this is possible if there is *some* intelligence on the terrorist group, this may not be able to be known, *a priori*. Consequently, geographic profiling can be useful in the context of counterterrorism to help find the location of terrorist hideouts but it must be remembered that the resulting geographic profile would only be applicable if the principal/planning terrorist in the terrorist group is committing the terrorist attacks "close" to his or her hideout.

In another application of geographic profiling to counterterrorism, D. Kim Rossmo and Keith Harries (2011) took a different approach. The study of terrorist activities has identified the existence of "terrorist cell sites." These terrorist cell sites may be meeting places, rented apartments, telephone calls, storage, cell houses, safe houses, and so on, that are used as part of the planning of a terrorist attack. As would be expected because of the spatial constraints we operate within through our everyday routine activities, there is a strong spatial component to these terrorist cell sites as well. Rossmo and Harries performed a geospatial analysis on terrorism data from Turkey (terrorist cell sites and their corresponding target sites) in order to obtain a better understanding of the spatial character of terrorist activities.

In an example of an assassination of a Turkish government minister, Rossmo and Harries showed that most of the terrorist cell site locations were approximately 1.5–5.5 kilometers (average distance approximately 4 kilometers) from the assassination site. This clearly showed that the terrorist cell sites were close, but not too close, to the terrorist target sites. In their analysis of a total of thirty-eight terrorist attacks they found that there was a definite geospatial structure to the terrorist activities. For example, Rossmo and Harries found that terrorist cell sites were clustered and that the two distance distribution characteristics put forth in the geometric theory of crime (and the pattern theory of crime) were definitely present: a buffer zone and distance decay. This information could then be used to help identify, through prioritizing information, other related intelligence information: police reports, intelligence assessments, cellular telephone intercepts, suspects, suspicious purchases, and so on.

Overall, Rossmo and Harries found that "minor terrorism incidents" such as theft and graffiti could be explained using the pattern theory of crime, whereas "major terrorism incidents" such as assassinations and bombings could be explained using an inverted version of the pattern theory of crime. These terrorist cell sites could be used as crime locations in the creation of a standard geographic profile to then predict the most probable location of the terrorist attack itself. Essentially, these authors proposed an extremely novel approach to geographic profiling to "flip it on its head" and use geographic profiling as a target identification technique. This is an area of future research in geographic profiling.

Biology and epidemiology

The application of geographic profiling to the various phenomena of terrorism is an important and an interesting extension of this criminal investigation technique. However, such an extension is still within the criminological realm. In another set of research, D. Kim Rossmo has teamed up with a group of biologists to study the applicability of geographic profiling to predatory behavior, more generally. This extension has been used to study the predatory behavior of bats, bumblebees, and sharks; it has also proven to be instructive in the context of infectious disease control and the control of invasive species.

Steven Le Comber and colleagues published a journal article in 2006 that investigated the applicability of geographic profiling to the foraging behavior of two species of bats in Scotland. Thirteen bats from each species (a total of twenty-six bats) were captured and tagged with a radio transmitter to track their movements. Based on the foraging activities of these tagged bats, Steven Le Comber and colleagues were able to locate the roosts for the bats much more efficiently than just performing a random search. One species of bat had a hit score percentage of 27 percent and the other species of bat had a hit score percentage of 7 percent, a significant improvement over a 50 percent hit score percentage for a random search. This analysis showed the utility of geographic profiling in analyzing the foraging patterns of the different species, specifically being able to show that the two different species of bats exhibited different patterns of foraging. The fact that the foraging patterns of two species of bats can be modeled in the same manner as serial criminals is interesting in and of itself, but this also means that geographic profiling can be used for ecological purposes. For example, if a species is protected or endangered, geographic profiling could be used to identify the roost, or nest, of the species and, potentially, identify its foraging grounds for the purposes of conservation and restricting various forms of development.

In a laboratory study of bumblebee foraging behavior Nigel Raine and colleagues (2009) were able to show that geographic profiling could be used to identify the likely locations for the nests of bumblebees, including the consideration of flower (target) densities. This is a particularly useful application because these authors note that it tends to be very difficult to locate the nesting sites of wild bees. And because of the declines in bumblebee populations across Europe and North America (Carvell et al., 2006), knowledge of these nesting sites may prove to be helpful. As such, the use of geographic profiling in this context is similar to the discussion above, conservation.

In an extremely interesting application of geographic profiling, R. A. Martin and colleagues (2009) were able to use geographic profiling in order to discover that the spatial patterns of shark predation were not random. These authors were able to identify the search base (anchor point) for these sharks at Seal Island, False Bay, South Africa and to understand the predatory strategies of these sharks considering factors such as prey detection, capture rates, and competition from other sharks. Perhaps most interesting, Martin and colleagues (2009) found that smaller (younger) sharks exhibited significantly greater areas for their prey search patterns than larger (older) sharks. There may be other factors at play that these authors recognize, but this does suggest that as sharks age they learn, or at least refine, their hunting strategies. Though on the surface this may not appear to be particularly interesting in the context of criminal investigations, some recent research I have undertaken with Richard Frank and Marcus Felson indicates that this reduction in the area covered in search patterns may be a common pattern (Andresen et al., 2013). In our research, we investigated the distance traveled to crime based on the age of the offender. We found that for most crime types there was an initial increase in the distance traveled to crime as offenders aged but this distance subsequently decreased, substantially in some cases. In the case of humans this is partially because younger offenders need to avoid the watchful eyes of their parents and/or guardians, but this will also occur because the younger offenders need to investigate bigger areas to see what is actually available. If this is the case, what may be occurring is that once the offenders learn about the opportunity surface and that they do not have to travel as far as they initially did when they were younger, distance is minimized in order to be efficient. This is conjecture at this stage, and based on calculating the distance traveled to criminal events, not the awareness spaces of offenders, but it is intriguing that the predatory behavior of the great white shark appears to be similar.

Geographic profiling has also proven to be very instructive in the field of public health. Steven Le Comber and colleagues published a journal article in 2011 that investigated the application of geographic profiling to infectious disease control. They began their research with a reanalysis of the classic epidemiological study of the 1854 London cholera outbreak. This outbreak was first analyzed by Dr. John Snow, who identified the Broad Street pump as the source of the cholera outbreak, drawing water downstream from a sewage out-pipe. The handle for this water pump was removed and the outbreak stopped. Steven Le Comber and colleagues analyzed the 321 disease sites and the 13 neighborhood water pumps using geographic profiling and found that the Broad Street pump ranked first, with a hit score percentage of 0.2 percent! Subsequently, the authors analyzed 139 disease case locations and 59 mosquitogenic water sources in Cairo, Egypt for malaria. Of the 59 mosquitogenic water sources, 7 tested positive for being sources of malaria. In the application of geographic profiling, the geoprofile ranked all of the mosquitogenic water sources according to their probability of being contaminated. The geoprofile ranked 6 of the 7 contaminated water sources in positions 1 through 6, and all of the 7 contaminated water sources had a hit score percentage of 2 percent. In a comparative analysis these authors found that geographic profiling outperformed other spatial analytic techniques commonly used in this research area. Needless to say, geographic profiling, at this early stage of application, has proven to be a useful tool in public health.

And lastly, geographic profiling has been applied to identifying the source locations for invasive species (Stevenson et al., 2012). These authors analyzed 53 invasive species in Great Britain (flora and fauna) in a variety of habitats (man-made and natural). They found that in 52 of the 53 invasive species cases, geographic profiling outperformed more traditional spatial analytic techniques in this research area to identify the source populations of the invasive species, with an average hit score percentage of 2.6 percent. Moreover, the authors found that geographic profiling was able to identify the sources of the invasive species in the early stages of the invasions when controlling the invasion would be more likely to be effective.

Criminology to biology/epidemiology and back again

Despite the general interest of the newer applications of geographic profiling, and their direct implications for the safety and security of different human and animal populations, there is another significant implication of this more recent research. Though there are many serial criminal investigations that allow for more data to be available to refine the practice of geographic profiling, waiting for another set of serial homicides, for example, is not the most pleasant way of thinking of future data. If, and it does appear to be the case, the predatory behaviors of other animal species are similar to those of humans, this new research can be used to better understand the predatory behavior of humans. For example, if humans, similar to sharks off the South African coast, also reduce the size of their search area as they age, this information may be useful for the ranking of potential offenders in a criminal investigation; in such a situation, it may be possible to solve a serial criminal investigation sooner because of a better understanding of spatial predatory behavior, more generally. These, of course, are empirical questions that may be able to be answered with future research.

This is a very clear application of (environmental) criminological research that has been able to have an impact in fields outside of its original application. The very nature of environmental criminology is that ideas were "borrowed" from other disciplines such as geography and economics in order to provide a better understanding of criminological phenomena. The status of the field of environmental criminology is a testament to the success of this borrowing of ideas from other disciplines. Because of this success, these theories have developed within criminology such that the ideas are now more our own rather than simply co-opted ideas from elsewhere. But, as this chapter on geographic profiling has made perfectly clear, the borrowing of ideas is now in the other direction.

Geographic profiling is not only proving to be a useful tool in a number of applications, which will likely continue to grow, but helping to develop models within those respective disciplines because of new and valuable information. And, because of this new insight into predatory behavior in a wide variety of species ranging from marine invertebrates to bumblebees to bats to trees to sharks, we may be in a better position to understand ourselves.

Review questions

1   Does geographic profiling solve criminal cases? Why or why not?
2   List and briefly describe the four methods serial offenders use to search for their victims.
3   List and briefly describe the three methods serial offenders use to attack their victims.
4   What is the difference between a geoprofile and a jeopardy surface?
5   How did Rossmo and Harries "flip geographic profiling on its head" in the context of counterterrorism?
6   List and briefly discuss the usefulness (not just the uses) of geographic profiling in biology.
7   How can geographic profiling be useful in the field of public health? Provide an example.

References

Andresen, M. A., Frank, R., and Felson, M. (2013). Age and the distance to crime. *Criminology & Criminal Justice*, in press.
Bennell, C. and Corey, S. (2007). Geographic profiling of terrorist attacks. In R. N. Kocsis (ed.), *Criminal profiling: International theory, research, and practice* (pp. 189–203). Totowa, NJ: Humana Press.
Brown, R. O., Rossmo, D. K., Sisak, T., Trahern, R., Jarret, J., and Hanson, J. (2005). *Geographic profiling military capabilities*. Final report submitted to the Topographic Engineering Center, Department of the Army, Fort Belvoir, VA.
Carvell, C., Roy, D. B., Smart, S. M., Pywell, R. F., Preston, C. D., and Goulson, D. (2006). Declines in forage availability for bumblebees at a national scale. *Biological Conservation*, 132(4), 481–9.
Central Intelligence Agency (2003). *National strategy for combating terrorism*. Washington, DC: Central Intelligence Agency. Available online at https://www.cia.gov/news-information/cia-the-war-on-terrorism/Counter_Terrorism_Strategy.pdf [accessed July 22, 2013].
Le Comber, S. C., Nicholls, B., Rossmo, D. K., and Racey, P. A. (2006). Geographic profiling and animal foraging. *Journal of Theoretical Biology*, 240(2), 233–40.
Le Comber, S. C., Rossmo, D. K., Hassan, A. N., Fuller, D. O., and Beier, J. C. (2011). Geographic profiling as a novel spatial tool for targeting infectious disease control. *International Journal of Health Geographics*, 10(1), Article 35.
Martin, R. A., Rossmo, D. K., and Hammerschlag, N. (2009). Hunting patterns and geographic profiling of white shark predation. *Journal of Zoology*, 279(2), 111–18.

Raine, N. E., Rossmo, D. K., and Le Comber, S. C. (2009). Geographic profiling applied to testing models of bumble-bee foraging. *Journal of the Royal Society Interface*, 6(32), 307–19.

Rossmo, D. K. (1997). Geographic profiling. In J. L. Jackson and D. A. Bekerian (eds.), *Offender profiling: Theory, research and practice* (pp. 159–75). Chichester: John Wiley & Sons.

Rossmo, D. K. (2000). *Geographic profiling*. Boca Raton, FL: CRC Press.

Rossmo, D. K. (2006). Geographic profiling in cold case investigations. In R. Walton (ed.), *Cold case homicides: Practical investigative techniques* (pp. 537–60). Boca Raton, FL: CRC Press.

Rossmo, D. K. (2011). Evaluating geographic profiling. *Crime Mapping: A Journal of Research and Practice*, 3(1), 42–65.

Rossmo, D. K. (2012). Recent developments in geographic profiling. *Policing: A Journal of Policy and Practice*, 6(2), 144–50.

Rossmo, D. K. (2014). Geographic profiling. In D. Weisburd and G. J. N. Bruinsma (eds.), *Encyclopedia of criminology and criminal justice*. New York, NY: Springer-Verlag, 1934–42.

Rossmo, D. K. and Harries, K. D. (2011). The geospatial structure of terrorist cells. *Justice Quarterly*, 28(2), 221–48.

Rossmo, D. K. and Velarde, L. (2008). Geographic profiling analysis: Principles, methods, and applications. In S. Chainey and L. Tompson (eds.), *Crime mapping case studies: Practice and research* (pp. 35–43). Chichester: John Wiley & Sons.

Stevenson, M. D., Rossmo, D. K., Knell, R. J., and Le Comber, S. C. (2012). Geographic profiling as a novel spatial tool for targeting the control of invasive species. *Ecography*, 35(8), 704–15.

Chapter 14

(Near-)repeat victimization

Introduction

The Pareto principle, commonly known as the 80-20 rule, states that for a number of phenomena 80 percent of the events or outcomes are the result of 20 percent of the causes. Most often, the Pareto principle is heard in the context of economics and business: 80 percent of the wealth is held by 20 percent of the population, 80 percent of the profit comes from 20 percent of your products, 80 percent of your profit comes from 20 percent of your customers, and so on. Of course, the Pareto principle applies in a number of criminological contexts as well.

Almost by definition, because of the discussion of hot spots in Chapter 10, some form of the Pareto principle must apply to (environmental) criminology. For example, in a study of delinquency within a 1945 birth cohort of nearly 10,000 juveniles in Philadelphia, Pennsylvania, Marvin Wolfgang and his colleagues (1972) found that 6 percent of the birth cohort accounted for 52 percent of the criminal events and approximately two-thirds of all violent criminal events. Considering that one-third of the birth cohort committed at least one criminal offence, 18 percent of the offenders within that cohort committed approximately 67 percent of the violent criminal events. This is not an 80-20 ratio, but it is close enough to warrant the attention of (environmental) criminologists.

If a Pareto-type principle is present in the context of offenders, it is also expected to be present in a number of other criminological contexts. The discussion of hot spots in Chapter 10 tells us that a relatively large percentage of criminal events are occurring within a relatively small percentage of neighborhoods or areas—this is further explored in the following chapter on crime and place. We would also expect that a relatively large percentage of criminal victimizations would be inflicted upon a relatively small percentage of targets. This is precisely what occurs, a phenomenon referred to as repeat victimization in the criminological literature. In this chapter we will cover the topic of repeat victimization with its implications, most notably for (situational) crime prevention. We will also cover a similar phenomenon called near-repeat victimization. This is most often discussed in the context of residential burglary victimization such that neighboring homes of a recently burgled home are at an elevated risk of victimization for a short period of time. This is an interesting phenomenon within environmental criminology because it incorporates space into the repeat victimization concept.

Repeat victimization

Repeat victimization, formerly referred to as multiple victimization, is the phenomenon of repeatedly being a target of criminal victimization. This repeated nature of criminal victimization can take two general forms: repeatedly a victim of the same crime type, and repeatedly a victim of more than one crime type. Though there are accounts of measuring repeat victimization prior, Michael Gottfredson's 1984 Home Office Report is often considered the beginning of the repeat victimization literature because of its data source: the 1982 British Crime Survey. The British Crime Survey, similar to the National Crime Victimization Survey in the United States and the criminal victimization component of the General Social Survey in Canada, is widely regarded as the premier criminal victimization survey in the world. As discussed in Chapter 8, victimization survey data, when conducted properly, gets around the primary limitation of official crime data regarding criminal event reporting to the police. The British Crime Survey began in 1982 covering England, Wales, and Scotland, allowing for a comprehensive account of the phenomenon of repeat victimization.

Michael Gottfredson found that out of the sample of almost 11,000 individuals 14 percent were repeatedly victimized by any criminal event, 10.8 percent were repeatedly victimized by a household criminal event (residential burglary, for example), and 2.3 percent were repeatedly victimized by a personal criminal event (assault, for example). These percentages do appear to be low in magnitude, but there is another way of considering these numbers. Considering those who were victims of a personal criminal event, 72 percent were victims once, whereas 28 percent were repeatedly victimized, 39 percent of victims of household criminal events were repeatedly victimized, and 44 percent of victims of any criminal event were repeatedly victimized. Moreover, individuals who reported being the victim of one or more personal criminal events had twice the probability of being a victim of a household criminal event: 42 percent versus 20 percent, in the general population; and those individuals who were a victim of a personal criminal event had a probability of 16 percent of being a victim of a personal criminal event compared to 6 percent for those who were not victims of personal criminal events. These relative levels of repeat victimization are important to consider because criminal victimization is a relatively rare event: considering all offences in the 1982 British Crime Survey, more than two-thirds of those sampled were never victimized.

Though instructive for one country and one year, one of the criticisms of presenting such data is that the data are an artifact of that particular time and place (Farrell and Bouloukos, 2001). In an effort to address such a criticism, Jan van Dijk and Graham Farrell and Adam Bouloukos reported on data from the International Crime Victims Survey for the years 1988, 1992, and 1996. Selections of the data representing aggregate patterns presented by van Dijk (2001) are shown in Table 14.1, but more detailed data are available from Farrell and Bouloukos (2001). The first row of Table 14.1 shows the repeat victimization percentages for all of the countries involved in the International Crime Victims Survey. These percentages are calculated in the same manner as the latter percentages presented by Michael Gottfredson, the percentage of victims of criminal events who are victimized again. It is immediately clear that repeat victimization varies significantly across the crime types. The percentage of those re-victimized for any crime was 41.5 percent, very similar to the percentage found by Michael Gottfredson in the 1982 British Crime Survey. The percentages of repeat victimization ranged from a low of 12.2 percent (car theft) to a high of 34.3 percent (sex offences). There is also almost as much variation across the regions of the world. Generally speaking, repeat victimization is more prevalent in Latin America, sometimes substantially, and less prevalent in Asia. However, there are exceptions to this generality. Motorcycle theft (not shown in Table 14.1) had an extremely low rate of repeat victimization in Latin America, 0.4 percent, and Asia had a greater than average rate of repeat victimization for burglary, 23.2 percent. Also worthy of note is that the United States and Canada are substantially overrepresented in the repeat victimization rates for sex offences, assaults and threats, and violence against women.

One cannot argue over the existence of repeat victimization or its magnitude based on the data available. Though it is not always a large component of criminal events, it is almost always of sufficient magnitude for consideration in understanding criminal events. Based on the statistics above, it appears as though some

Table 14.1 International repeat victimization, International Crime Victims Survey, 1988–1996

	Any crime	Car theft	Theft from car	Burglary	Robbery	Personal theft	Sex offences	Assaults and threats	Violence against women
Total	41.5	12.2	27.4	20.4	20.1	20.7	34.3	29.9	33.3
Western Europe	37.3	9.3	19.1	12.8	14.7	12.7	35.8	28.8	36.6
United States and Canada	45.3	14.3	21.9	20.2	28.0	21.5	41.9	33.6	44.0
Eastern and Central Europe	41.6	13.8	35.5	19.7	19.6	21.0	29.3	29.8	24.8
Asia	30.9	5.1	12.1	23.2	15.1	20.7	26.2	26.6	33.9
Africa	44.0	16.7	27.7	28.2	15.7	22.1	38.1	25.7	36.5
Latin America	53.9	12.5	34.7	32.6	37.5	37.6	43.1	36.5	42.7

Source: van Dijk (2001).

targets are more suitable than others, leading them to be subject to repeat victimization. But are those targets always more suitable? Or just for a period of time? In other words, if repeat victimization is going to occur, will it occur within some prescribed time frame? Shane Johnson and his colleagues published a journal article in 1997 that investigated this aspect of repeat victimization for residential burglary. Specifically, they were interested in the following: Are the levels of repeat victimization greater than expected based on statistical likelihood? How (spatially) concentrated is repeat victimization? Is repeat victimization more prevalent in particular areas or neighborhoods? and Does the probability of repeat victimization decrease over time in a predictable manner?

Shane Johnson and his colleagues analyzed residential burglary data from Merseyside (county) in northwest England for the 12-month period of July 1, 1994 to June 30, 1995. During this time period there were a total of 19,649 residential burglary events, with 18,279 households victimized, and a total of 1,370 repeat victimizations. Of the 535,638 households in Merseyside, 96.7 percent were not victims of a residential burglary for the time period under study. This means that 3.3 percent of the households accounted for almost 20,000 residential burglaries. Of these 3.3 percent, 3.1 percent (17,153) were victimized once, 0.17 percent (959) were victimized twice, and 0.02 percent (167) were victimized three times or more. Residential burglary is quite clearly a very concentrated phenomenon.

In a spatial analysis of their data, Johnson and his colleagues found that there was a high degree of concentration of repeat victimizations within the residential burglary hot spots in Merseyside. As such, repeat victimization contributed to the identification of residential burglary hot spots. This overlap between repeat victimization and residential burglary hot spots was so strong that the proportion of households that suffered from repeat victimization within the residential burglary hot spots was fifteen times more densely packed than the number of victimized households for the entire study area. Further to this analysis of the concentration of repeat victimization, Johnson and his colleagues also found that repeat residential burglary victimization disproportionately occurred in areas of lower social class—Alan Trickett and colleagues, in a journal article published in 1992, found similar results for a broader range of property and violent crime types in the British Crime Survey. In a ranking of social class from 1 to 10, with 1 being the highest social class and 10 being the lowest social class, these authors found that the social classes of 1 to 4 had a lesser proportion of repeat victimization relative to Merseyside as a whole, the social classes of 5 to 7 were not significantly different from Merseyside as a whole, and the social classes of 8 to 10 had a greater proportion of repeat victimization relative to Merseyside as a whole. Therefore, not only was the phenomenon of repeat residential burglary victimization spatially concentrated, but spatially concentrated within the socially disadvantaged areas of Merseyside. With regard to the temporal aspect of repeat victimization, Johnson and his colleagues found that approximately one-third (32.5 percent) of all residential burglary repeat victimizations occurred within four weeks, with

11.34 percent of the repeat victimizations occurring within one week and most occurring within six months.

An obvious question at this stage of the discussion is: Why do repeat victimizations occur? In 1995, Graham Farrell and colleagues published a journal article that sought to answer this question in the context of a number of crime types. Their explanations are in the context of the three fundamental components of a criminal event: a motivated offender, a suitable target, and the lack of a capable guardian. In domestic violence, the suitable target is a person (this could be the male or the female in a heterosexual or homosexual relationship, but most often the female in a heterosexual relationship) who does not report the criminal event to the authorities. Aside from this risk, domestic violence will be repeated when or if the risk of a capable guardian appearing is low. Consequently, if the motivated offender is not turned over to the authorities after the first victimization, there is a low probability that s/he will be turned over to the authorities in subsequent victimizations; this is similar for the repeated abuse of children. In fact, the crime prevention literature has identified one initiative that works for domestic violence (on-scene arrest of the offender) and one initiative that works for child/infant abuse (frequent home visits by trained nurses) (Sherman et al., 1997). Ethnic-based attacks suffer from repeat victimizations for two reasons. First, if the ethnic group in question is a significant minority, simple arithmetic leads to repeated victimization: the population to draw from for ethnically based attacks (violent or otherwise) is small, so the probability of repeat victimization is far greater than in the majority population; second, if the ethnic minority is also a political minority, the motivated offenders may not be concerned about *capable* guardians—people may be present but do not intervene. There are a few reasons for such repeat victimization in the context of residential burglary. First, the offender, or an acquaintance of the offender, may return to obtain items that had to be left behind the first (or second) time because of a lack of resources to remove them from the property; this would occur in the context of an almost immediate repeat victimization. Second, in the context of a repeat victimization that occurred after a longer period of time, the offender may be returning to the household to steal the goods replaced from the initial burglary, from insurance or otherwise. And third, the home may just be a sufficiently suitable target that it attracts multiple *different* offenders—see also Polvi et al. (1990, 1991) for a discussion regarding the residential burglary repeat victimization. And theft of automobile will suffer from repeat victimization based on its target suitability: the demand for a particular type of automobile, where it is parked (Clarke and Mayhew [1994] found that theft of automobile increased as one parked further from the home, garage versus driveway versus street), the presence of target-hardening, and so on. Graham Farrell and colleagues continued with explanations for other crime types, but the story should be clear at this point: the targets of repeat victimizations are more suitable than other comparable targets and/or lack capable guardianship.

There are two general explanations discussed above that are instructive to explain the phenomenon of repeat victimization, particularly easy to understand in the context of residential burglary. First, there is the boost explanation: the risk of repeat victimization is *boosted* because offenders will return to exploit known opportunities such as items not stolen or items that may have been replaced since the first victimization. Second, there is the flag explanation: multiple offenders *flag* the same target as being particularly suitable for the offence—this has also been referred to as risk heterogeneity. As noted by Ken Pease in his 1998 report for the Home Office in the United Kingdom, the first offence boosts the probability of subsequent victimization. As such, the boost effect is expected to decay over time. Support for the boost effect from the original offender has been found in multiple countries, particularly if the repeat victimization occurred quickly (Bernasco, 2008; Everson and Pease, 2001; Kleemans, 2001). The risk heterogeneity, or flag, effect also has a lot of empirical support that we have already discussed in the context of social disorganization theory (Chapter 2), the geometric theory of crime (Chapter 4), and hot spots of crime (Chapter 10). Understanding which of these two explanations is more important, and for which crime types, is critical for understanding repeat victimization as well as (potentially) preventing it (Pease, 1998).

In an effort to disentangle these two effects to explain repeat victimization, Andromachi Tseloni and Ken Pease, in two journal articles published in 2003 and 2004, used data from the United States' 1994 National Crime Victimization Survey considering personal crimes: an aggregate of assault, larceny, pocket-picking, rape, robbery, sexual assault, and threats. In their analysis, they found support for the presence of both the boost and the flag effect—similar results were found in a journal article they published the following year. In a computer simulation of the spatial crime patterns of residential burglaries published in 2008, Shane Johnson was able to show that risk heterogeneity (flags) can generate spatial concentrations of crime, but the boost effect was necessary in order to generate the temporal pattern of repeat victimization found in actual criminal event data. Moreover, the boost effect on its own was not enough to generate the repeat victimization pattern either. Consequently, it is important to consider both the boost and flag explanations of repeat victimization. The results of these studies are important in the context of implications of repeat victimization, primarily its prevention.

Implications of repeat victimization

Aside from academic curiosity, the primary implication of repeat victimization is crime prevention. In the context of explanations for repeat victimization, there are temporal differences in how crime prevention would be applied for the boost explanation versus the flag (risk heterogeneity) explanations. In the context of risk heterogeneity, crime prevention initiatives are effectively time invariant. Particular places are at greater risk of criminal victimization so there are crime prevention techniques that should be implemented: target hardening, better security, burglar/automobile alarms, and so on. In the context of the boost explanation, however, crime prevention initiatives are going to be time dependent. As discussed above, the risk of subsequent victimization decreases rather quickly after the initial victimization. Because of this, crime prevention initiatives such as temporarily altered routine activities and increased police patrols may prove to be effective.

In 1993, Graham Farrell and Ken Pease published a report for the Home Office in the United Kingdom regarding the prevention of repeat victimization. In fact, these authors suggested that crime prevention should be targeted at those who were already victims of crime. They put forth this strategy for crime prevention, as opposed to advocating for everyone to simply perform some general target-hardening techniques, for a number of reasons. First, research has shown that once a place or person has been victimized they have a much higher probability of being victimized again versus a place or person not previously victimized. Therefore, targeting crime prevention on the previously victimized has a greater probability of being an efficient use of resources. Second, research has shown that repeat victimization most often occurs against the most vulnerable social groups. Using previous victimization as the criterion for targeting crime prevention initiatives avoids the potentially socially divisive act of identifying those populations and then giving them crime prevention attention. Third, research has shown that repeat victimization occurs in the crime hot spots that already tend to have the most serious crime types as well. Consequently, any crime prevention initiatives would be applied in the areas of greatest crime density anyway. Fourth, because repeat victimization is time sensitive, it does not always necessitate a prolonged response to crime. Because of this facet of repeat victimization, crime prevention tends to be less labor intensive and more sustainable in the long run. And fifth, even if the criminal events prevented are displaced (as discussed in Chapter 5, there is no empirical support for this claim), preventing repeat victimization "shares the agony" such that a small percentage of our society does not suffer the lion's share of criminal victimization.

Needless to say, the argument put forth by Graham Farrell and Ken Pease to focus crime prevention initiatives on repeat victimization is just based on the evidence. Though we must consider all members of our various societies when we allocate public resources, because these resources are scarce, they must be applied in a manner that will provide the greatest benefit. Armed with the reasons *why* repeat victimization should be the focus of crime prevention initiatives, there is the question of *how* to do it. Before we turn to the various steps outlined by these authors, it is important to recognize that because of the highly specific nature of repeat victimization (so few targets suffer from repeat victimization), the approach to addressing repeat victimization is highly situational. As such, a situational crime prevention perspective (see Chapter 7) is appropriate here rather than a more general crime prevention approach.

The first step is to gather as much local data as possible. What are the patterns of repeat victimization? Which type of targets? For example, in the case of residential burglary, which type of housing is more susceptible to repeat victimization? This information would allow for a swifter reaction to victimization because those responsible for crime prevention initiatives will have an idea of what to expect and, therefore, what to implement. Second, using the information from the first step, policy can be developed regarding how to address victimization. For example, because of the more serious nature of residential burglary, scarce resources may be better applied to prevent repeat victimization there instead of theft from automobile, despite the fact that theft from automobile may have a greater probability of repeat victimization. This is not necessarily the case, but is a consideration that must be made. Third, a set of crime prevention initiatives should be developed locally and be made available locally. Again, this is for the ability of a swift reaction to initial victimization. Fourth, the local police need to establish an internal communication network such that the officer who has the task of (hopefully) preventing repeat victimization can get the necessary information quickly. Fifth, a systemized plan must be put in place for the crime prevention initiative to be put in place. This would involve a chain of command with appropriate contact people within the police agency and the neighborhood such that the crime prevention initiative is carried out swiftly and with minimal interference to the victim, particularly in the case of a violent criminal event. Sixth, it must be recognized that the volume of crime is not the only performance measure for the police. Police agencies that proactively prevent (repeat) criminal victimization cannot be punished through a reduced budget because crime has decreased. As stated by Graham Farrell and Ken Pease, this would be like punishing health agencies for the prevention of disease. And lastly, this whole process could be continually evaluated. The purpose of this evaluation would be to test the impact of a repeat victimization crime prevention plan, more generally, but also the specific crime prevention initiatives implemented within the said repeat victimization crime prevention plan.

In 2005, Graham Farrell reviewed the literature investigating the prevention of repeat victimization. Generally speaking, what works in preventing repeat victimization harks back to situational crime prevention. First, the prevention initiatives need to be tailored to the specific context of the original victimization. As found in the situational crime prevention literature, more generally, the nature of repeat victimization varies from place to place. Second, multiple tactics work. This harks back to the discussions in Chapter 7 regarding the need to impact the decision-making processes of offenders. Having multiple initiatives to prevent the same repeat victimization will help in the situations of both the boost and risk heterogeneity effects: multiple crime prevention initiatives are more likely to have a greater effect on the decision-making process of an individual offender and more likely to have a greater effect on different offenders because what may work on the decision-making process of one offender may not work on another. Third, the implementation of the crime prevention initiative must be carried out to the end. This seems like a redundant point to make, but this lack of a strong implementation was found to impact the success of preventing repeat victimization. This is why step five, above, is so important; if a systemized plan to execution is not in place, a process is more likely to flounder. And fourth, there is a need to focus on the situations in which repeat victimization is greatest. Any repeat victimization crime prevention initiatives put in place must consider the crime types, places, and times of repeat victimization risk because those are the most appropriate applications of these crime prevention initiatives.

In a more recent systematic review of the prevention of repeat victimization published in 2012, Louise Grove and colleagues reiterated the importance of a strong situational crime prevention perspective when implementing crime prevention initiatives for repeat victimization. Additionally, advice and education on the prevention of repeat victimization did little good without *actual* implementation of crime prevention initiatives, however well intentioned the advice and education may have been. And, as stated above, these crime prevention initiatives must have a strong implementation process, because if they are not implemented properly they simply do not work. Overall, Louise Grove and colleagues found that repeat victimization crime prevention initiatives reduced repeat victimization by 15.5 percent, relative to areas without such crime prevention initiatives. This gives strong support for the further development of crime prevention initiatives that are specifically developed for repeat victimization.

Near-repeat victimization

The near-repeat hypothesis states that proximity to a recently victimized person or property item temporarily increases the risk of victimization for spatially near and similar targets in the same manner that repeat victimization operates. In essence, near-repeat victimization is an explicitly spatial variety of repeat victimization. The beginning of the near-repeat literature was a paper published in 2001 by Frank Morgan—Ken Pease identified the "virtual repeat" in 1998 as criminal events that have similar targets, but this was not based on spatial proximity. Frank Morgan coined the term "near-repeat" in an investigation of residential burglary repeat victimization in Perth, Australia. He found that a particular suburb had such a high concentration and volume of residential burglaries in one month that must have been committed by one or a group of very active offenders—he calculated that the probability of this set of events randomly occurring was approximately one in a billion. The identification of this phenomenon has become a keen interest to a number of environmental criminologists and, much like repeat victimization, is an active research area within environmental criminology.

In 2003 Michael Townsley and colleagues published the first journal article completely dedicated to the study of near-repeat victimization in the context of residential burglary in Brisbane, Australia. Though conceptually very similar to repeat victimization, near-repeat victimization is more methodologically complex to analyze because of the addition of the spatial dimension to the analysis. Additionally, it is not *just* that there are spatial and temporal dimensions in the analysis that matter, but they must be recognized simultaneously: near-repeat victimization occurs when another target (person or property) is victimized spatially close to the "original" criminal event *and* temporally close to when that original criminal event took place. In order to identify near-repeat victimizations, the authors used a statistical technique that identified space-time clusters, the Knox test. The details of this test are not important here, but it tests the significance of clusters in space and time relative to what would be expected by chance. This is a common method of space-time cluster detection in epidemiology. If space-time clusters are identified that are statistically significant from what would be expected by random chance, "disease transmission" has a contagious component—the epidemiological equivalent to near-repeat victimization. In order to implement the Knox test, the researcher chooses the distance that defines near and the number of days/weeks, and so on, that define close in time. These values are used as intervals for the output of the test, similar to the example shown in Table 14.2.

In Table 14.2, the "Distance apart" columns would probably be considered exhaustive, in terms of up to 1 kilometer to be considered near, but aggregating everything greater than five weeks would not be satisfactory. So remember that this table is just used as an example. Regardless, if near-repeat victimization is present we would expect to find significant differences from random chance in the upper left cells of this table. This would indicate that there are more residential burglaries spatially and temporally near the original victimized target than would be expected by chance. The exact pattern of near-repeat victimization may vary slightly from neighborhood to neighborhood and from offender to offender. For example, one burglar may wish to commit near-repeats immediately, striking the iron while it is hot, whereas another burglar may wish to commit near-repeats a short while later, waiting for the spatially immediate neighborhood to settle down and reduce their vigilance in some form of neighborhood watch.

Michael Townsley and his colleagues found strong evidence for the presence of near-repeat victimization, but only in particular areas. They originally hypothesized, and subsequently confirmed, two factors that would lead to a greater prevalence of near-repeat victimization. The first was homogeneity in residential developments. These authors expected that a lack of variation in housing would lead to greater rates of near-repeat victimization because these

Table 14.2 An example of Knox test output

Time apart (weeks)	Distance apart				
	0–250m	251–500m	501–750m	751–1,000m	> 1km
0–1					
1–2					
2–3					
4–5					
> 5					

Source: Adapted from Townsley et al. (2003).

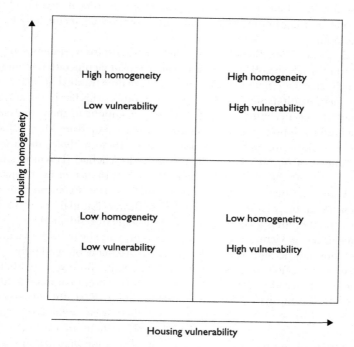

Figure 14.1. Housing homogeneity and vulnerability for near-repeat victimization.

Source: Adapted from Townsley et al. (2003).

areas would make it easier to identify *suitable* targets. The second was vulnerability, defined as the number of active offenders in an area that could be measured as the volume of residential burglaries in the area. This is represented graphically in Figure 14.1.

Near-repeat victimization is expected to be low in the lower left cell of Figure 14.1. This is because there is a low level of offender activity in the first place (a low level of infection, in epidemiological terms) and more diverse areas make it more difficult to identify good targets based on previous burglaries (the disease transmission rate is low). In the upper right cell of Figure 14.1, there is a high degree of housing homogeneity and vulnerability, meaning that it is easier to identify good targets based on previous burglaries and there is a high level of offender activity to take advantage of this situation. This is precisely what Michael Townsley and his colleagues found. The strongest indication of near-repeat victimization occurred in an area that was identified as having a high degree of housing homogeneity and high vulnerability, with another area that had a high degree of homogeneity and low vulnerability also showing statistically significant evidence for near-repeat victimization. This led these authors to claim that housing homogeneity and vulnerability were both important for near-repeat victimization to occur, but that housing homogeneity was a more important factor for near-repeat victimization.

Shane Johnson and Kate Bowers, also using methods from epidemiology, published a journal article in 2004 investigating near-repeat victimization in more detail. Specifically, they investigated the distance and the time frame that mattered for near-repeat victimization. Similar to repeat victimization, this has implications for those in the area of a criminal event for crime prevention. In their analysis, Shane Johnson and Kate Bowers used residential burglary data from Merseyside, England; these are the same data previously used by these authors, discussed above in the context of repeat victimization. Similar to Michael Townsley and colleagues, these authors found strong evidence for the existence of near-repeat victimization. Using months as the time apart variable and 100-meter intervals as the distance apart variable, Shane Johnson and Kate Bowers found that a residential burglary criminal event is a good predictor of subsequent residential burglary criminal events for repeat victimization within one month and near-repeat victimization for 1–2 months and 300–400 meters from the originally burgled home.

In a journal article published the following year, Kate Bowers and Shane Johnson found a number of characteristics for homes that were common in the presence of residential burglary near-repeat victimization. First, though repeat victimization tended to occur in relatively impoverished areas of the city, near-repeat victimization was more evident in the relatively affluent areas of the city. Second, houses immediately next to the originally burgled home were at a substantially greater risk of near-repeat victimization relative to those homes further away, especially within the first week of the original burglary. Third, homes that were on the same side of the street as the originally burgled home were at a greater risk of near-repeat victimization relative to those homes on the other side of the street even after controlling for the distance necessary to cross the street. And fourth, homes that are likely to have similar floor plans (a common feature in more recent large scale residential developments and, therefore, likely close to one another) were at a slightly greater risk of near-repeat victimization.

Despite the strong evidence Michael Townsley and his colleagues and Shane Johnson and Kate Bowers found for near-repeat victimization, this phenomenon may fall victim to the same criticism as repeat victimization did when it was first identified: this "near-repeat victimization" is an artifact found in a couple of locations that has no implications elsewhere and for (environmental) criminology, specifically—there are no grounds for generalizing about near-repeat victimization. This would be a difficult claim to make in the presence of *some* cross-national evidence and the fact near-repeat victimizations have specific characteristics. Nevertheless, in 2007 Shane Johnson and colleagues published a journal article that investigated residential near-repeat victimization in ten areas located in five different countries: Australia, Netherlands, New Zealand, United Kingdom, and United States. Not only did this analysis have a variety of areas and countries, the ten areas also substantially differed in criminal event volumes, the area covered (and, correspondingly, the number of targets at risk), and the target density. As such, this particular analysis sets the bar high for the generalization of the near-repeat victimization phenomenon. Overall, these authors found that for all ten datasets analyzed more residential burglaries occurred near an "original" residential burglary in both space and time than would be expected by chance. This was particularly the case in Netherlands, United States, and United Kingdom. Moreover, similar to the work of Shane Johnson and Kate Bowers discussed above, residential burglary near-repeat victimizations occurred very shortly after the original residential burglary and quite near in terms of distance, 200 meters and fourteen days.

Though the near-repeat victimization literature overwhelmingly focuses on residential burglary, there is some literature that investigates the near-repeat victimization phenomenon regarding other crime types. In 2008, Jerry Ratcliffe and George Rengert published a journal article investigating the near-repeat victimization of shootings in Philadelphia, Pennsylvania. These authors hypothesized the existence of near-repeat victimization in the context of shootings because of retaliation behavior that protects/reinforces drug-related activities, for example. They found that there was an elevated level of risk of shootings in the area of the original shooting of 33 percent, for a period of two weeks and one city block of the original incident. Another near-repeat victimization analysis using data from Philadelphia, Pennsylvania, published in 2012, was undertaken by Cory Haberman and Jerry Ratcliffe. In this research, the authors found that near-repeat victimization of armed street robberies was very tightly constrained by time. They found that armed street robberies in Philadelphia, Pennsylvania always took place within seven days and as far away as 366 meters (1,200 feet).

In 2008, a particularly interesting journal article was published regarding near-repeat victimization. Michael Townsley and colleagues investigated near-repeat victimization in the context of insurgent activity in Iraq. The authors were able to obtain three months of data regarding these activities in Iraq during the time period of February 4, 2004 to April 30, 2004. Though only a short time frame was available for analysis, the authors' data set contained almost 2,200 records and the time frame for near-repeat victimization in the existing literature tends to be rather short, less than or equal to four weeks. Of these nearly 2,200 records, the authors chose to focus on "improvised explosive devices" that comprised just over 42 percent of the data, 916 incidents. Michael Townsley and colleagues found that the time frame of insurgent near-repeat victimization in Iraq was even tighter than shootings: a period of two days and a distance up to 1 kilometer. Consequently, as with the case of geographic profiling (Chapter 13), near-repeat victimization is an interesting and useful concept and technique to address concerns regarding terrorist activity.

An obvious question to ask at this stage is: Why does near-repeat victimization occur, particularly in the case of residential burglary? The short answer is: For the same reason repeat victimization occurs—the boost effect and risk heterogeneity. However, the research that has investigated this aspect of near-repeat victimization does tend to focus on the boost effect, emerging from the same offender. In a journal article published in 2004, Kate Bowers and Shane Johnson compared the modus operandi of residential burglary near-repeat victimizations and unrelated residential burglary events. They found that for residential burglaries that occurred more than 400 meters away from the original burglary, the modus operandi did not significantly differ from what would be expected by chance. However, for residential burglaries that occurred within 400 meters of the original burglary the rate of similarity was significantly greater from what would be expected by chance—similar results were also found for the point of entry used during the residential burglary. Wim Bernasco, in 2008, also found that residential burglary near-repeat victimizations were committed by the same offender in a substantial portion of criminal events. And in an investigation of near-repeat victimization for both residential burglary and theft from automobile published in 2009, Shane Johnson and colleagues found evidence for "optimal foraging strategies" playing (at least) a partial role in explaining near-repeat victimization. Optimal foraging strategies, a concept borrowed from ecology, are a set of strategies used to increase resources (more residential burglaries and thefts from automobiles) while limiting expended energy and the risks associated with the criminal events. This is a more theoretically grounded and thorough explanation for the boost effect, discussed above.

Implications of near-repeat victimization

The primary implications with near-repeat victimization are very similar to those of repeat victimization. The main differences between the two relate to which people and properties are targeted for crime prevention and the time frame of the crime prevention initiative itself. Based on the definition of near-repeat victimization, the potential victims are "neighboring" people and places. As such, in addition to any crime prevention initiatives implemented for the original victim, in an effort to reduce the probability of repeat victimization, they must also be implemented for neighboring victims. However, because the time frame for a near-repeat victimization tends to be very short, the lack of a need to maintain the crime prevention initiatives for long periods of time can help to maintain the longevity of crime prevention programs.

Shane Johnson and Kate Bowers also recommend the publicity of a criminal victimization, particularly in the case of a residential burglary that is not too much of a personal criminal event—this does not mean that there are no psychological impacts from a residential burglary, however. The hope from the publicity of the criminal event is to impact the decision-making processes of the offender such that risks are perceived greater than before because people are (potentially) more vigilant and the police are obviously aware of the criminal activity in the area. Shane Johnson and Kate Bowers also argue for the use of prospective, or anticipatory, hot spot mapping. The hot spot mapping techniques discussed in Chapter 10 all use historical crime data to make maps of crime hot spots. Prospective hot spot mapping would use today's criminal events and the known propensities of repeat and near-repeat victimizations to anticipate where tomorrow's criminal events will take place.

In addition to these more general and applicable crime prevention activities, Kate Bowers and Shane Johnson also put forth some specific recommendations in regard to residential burglary. First, a residential burglary should trigger crime prevention initiatives: the primary crime prevention initiatives in relatively poor areas should be to prevent repeat victimization, whereas the primary crime prevention initiatives in relatively affluent areas should be to prevent near-repeat victimization. Second, in all areas (poor, affluent, and everything in between), the crime prevention initiatives must be implemented swiftly, particularly in the case of near-repeat victimization. Third, the houses of greatest increased risk of victimization after an initial victimization are those homes that are very close to the initial victimization (immediate neighbors are at the greatest risk), on the same side of the street, have similar floor plans, on straight streets, and have relatively homogeneous housing.

And lastly, in the context of armed street robberies, Cory Haberman and Jerry Ratcliffe state that, despite the fact that the near-repeat victimization pattern could be useful to forecast future armed street robberies, the short time frame for this particular crime type does make it somewhat difficult. For example, if Compstat meetings within police departments (meetings in which police officers are updated with the latest data on crime in their area) are held weekly or biweekly it may simply be too late to address the potential for near-repeat victimization. Consequently, Cory Haberman and Jerry Ratcliffe advocate for the "rapid assessment of crime patterns conducted at the local level." This rapid assessment would require analysis in "real time" such that these near-repeat patterns can be identified, potentially with automated systems that could alert the appropriate people within police departments.

Is it all connected?

The similarity between repeat victimization and near-repeat victimization is completely obvious. The only real difference between the two is the spatial component for subsequent victimization. In the context of residential burglary, the distance between targets is zero for repeat victimization and greater than zero (though not large) for near-repeat victimization. But these concepts of (near-)repeat victimization are also related to hot spots (Chapter 10). It was stated above that repeat victimization and near-repeat victimization tend to occur in crime hot spots; moreover, repeat victimization and near-repeat victimization contribute to the establishment of hot spots. Recall the concepts of crime generators and crime attractors from Chapter 4, the geometric theory of crime; crime generators are places that generate a lot of criminal events simply because of the volume of people present; crime attractors attract motivated offenders to the area because of (well-)known criminal opportunities (Brantingham and Brantingham, 1995a). Also recall that, by definition, a hot spot is either a crime generator or a crime attractor. The facts that repeat victimization occurs when an offender re-victimizes the original target and near-repeat victimization occurs when an offender victimizes a target in the original area also suggest that repeat victimizations and near-repeat victimizations are a form of crime attractor. This is because at least one offender is attracted to the target because of its known criminal opportunities, at least for a short period of time—in the case of risk heterogeneity, there would be multiple offenders knowing about the criminal opportunities. Lastly, risk heterogeneity has been identified as one of the contributors to repeat victimization and near-repeat victimization, but is also, practically by definition, the cause of hot spots of criminal events. Needless to say, the overlap between hot spots, repeat victimization, and near-repeat victimization is not only empirical, but theoretical.

Graham Farrell and Ken Pease published an essay in 2014 that considered the connections between hot spots, repeat victimization, and near-repeat victimization and proposed a method for synthesizing these phenomena to consider a theory of crime concentration. They considered their work to be in progress, but it is very instructive to understand the similarities between these three phenomena—we will only consider one component of their synthesis. They argued that the term "near-repeat victimization" needs to be broadened to consider various dimensions of "near," not just the spatial dimension in the "near-repeat victimization" literature. With this broader consideration, "near" can mean spatially near (the same or a close target), temporally near (short time periods between criminal events, however defined), crime type near (the same or similar crime type, robbery and armed robbery, for example), and tactically near (the modus operandi used in different offences is the same or similar). The degree of similarity can be measured by how many "degrees of nearness" are satisfied. For example, repeat victimization satisfies all the different considerations of near, as does near-repeat victimization—all of these similarities are discussed above. Consequently, we would expect there to be a lot of commonality between these two phenomena, and there is. Hot spots satisfy spatially near, temporally near, and crime type near. The spatially near component of the hot spot is obvious, as is the crime type near component, but temporally near must be thought of differently than in the discussion regarding repeat victimization and near-repeat victimization. In the case of hot spots, the respective criminal events must be considered temporally near because they must occur frequently enough to be noticed. In other words, not much time will pass before another residential burglary will occur in an area if a residential burglary hot spot is present. Consequently, temporally near in this case does not necessarily mean that there is a pattern to the temporal sequence as with repeat victimization and near-repeat victimization. There may be a temporal sequence because repeat victimization and near-repeat victimization are components of hot spots, but it is not necessary.

Though we have not yet arrived at a unified theory of crime concentration, considering the similarities of these various criminological phenomena is moving us in the right direction. What we must remember to do is to keep Occam's razor in mind: the principle of parsimony, the simplest explanation is most likely the correct explanation. But simple does not mean simple-minded. The three primary theories of environmental criminology (routine activity theory, geometric theory of crime, rational choice theory) are all simple (and related) explanations of criminal events, but they are far from simple-minded. In the end, a unified theory of crime concentration will consider the interconnected nature of space, time, crime types, and modus operandi, when they coincide, when they do not, and why. And the end goal of such a unified theory is to better understand the phenomena of crime in order to prevent it.

Review questions

1 Why would we expect repeat victimization based on the theories of environmental criminology?
2 State and briefly discuss the two general explanations for (near-)repeat victimization.
3 Which of the two general explanations for (near-)repeat victimization is more important?
4 In the context of repeat victimization, who should be targeted for crime prevention initiatives? Why and for how long?
5 State and briefly discuss the five reasons why previously victimized people and/or places should receive more crime prevention attention.
6 Why is situational crime prevention appropriate for repeat victimization?
7 What is near-repeat victimization and why do we expect it to occur in the context of environmental criminology?
8 What are the two factors that are expected to result in the general presence of near-repeat victimization? Which factor is more important?
9 What are the four factors common for near-repeat victimization in the context of residential burglary? Provide any relevant context.
10 In what ways are near-repeat victimizations different from repeat victimizations in terms of crime prevention?

References

Bernasco, W. (2008). Them again? Same offender involvement in repeat and near repeat burglaries. *European Journal of Criminology*, 5(4), 411–31.
Bowers, K. J. and Johnson, S. D. (2004). Who commits near repeats? A test of the boost explanation. *Western Criminology Review*, 5(3), 12–24.
Bowers, K. J. and Johnson, S. D. (2005). Domestic burglary repeats and space-time clusters: The dimensions of risk. *European Journal of Criminology*, 2(1), 67–92.
Brantingham, P. L. and Brantingham, P. J. (1995a). The criminality of place: Crime generators and crime attractors. *European Journal on Criminal Policy and Research*, 3(3), 5–26.
Clarke, R. V. and Mayhew, P. (1994). Parking patterns and car theft risks: Policy relevant findings from the British Crime Survey. *Crime Prevention Studies*, 3, 91–107.

Everson, S. and Pease, K. (2001). Crime against the same person and place: detection opportunity and offender targeting. *Crime Prevention Studies*, 12, 199–220.

Farrell, G. (2005). Progress and prospects in the prevention of repeat victimisation. In N. Tilley (ed.), *The handbook of crime prevention and community safety* (pp. 145–72). Cullompton, Devon: Willan Publishing.

Farrell, G. and Bouloukos, A. C. (2001). International overview: a cross-national comparison of rates of repeat victimization. *Crime Prevention Studies*, 12, 5–25.

Farrell, G. and Pease, K. (1993). *Once bitten, twice bitten: Repeat victimization and its implications for crime prevention*. London, UK: Police Research Group, Home Office.

Farrell, G. and Pease, K. (2014). The near future: prediction and crime clusters. In D. Weisburd and G. Bruinsma (eds.), *Encyclopedia of criminology and criminal justice*. New York, NY: Springer-Verlag, 3862–71.

Farrell, G., Phillips, C., and Pease, K. (1995). Like taking candy: Why does repeat victimization occur? *British Journal of Criminology*, 35(3), 384–99.

Gottfredson, M. R. (1984). Victims of crime: The dimensions of risk. Home Office Research Study, no. 81. London, UK: HMSO.

Grove, L. E., Farrell, G., Farrington, D. P., and Johnson, S. D. (2012). *Preventing repeat victimization: A systematic review*. Stockholm, Sweden: Swedish National Council for Crime Prevention.

Haberman, C. P. and Ratcliffe, J. H. (2012). The predictive policing challenges of near repeat armed street robberies. *Policing: A Journal of Policy and Practice*, 6(2), 151–66.

Johnson, S. D. (2008). Repeat burglary victimization: A tale of two theories. *Journal of Experimental Criminology*, 4(3), 215–40.

Johnson, S. D. and Bowers, K. J. (2004). The burglary as clue to the future: The beginnings of prospective hot-spotting. *European Journal of Criminology*, 1(2), 237–55.

Johnson, S. D., Bernasco, W., Bowers, K. J., Elffers, H., Ratcliffe, J., Rengert, G., and Townsley, M. (2007). Space-time patterns of risk: A cross national assessment of residential burglary victimization. *Journal of Quantitative Criminology*, 23(3), 201–19.

Johnson, S. D., Bowers, K., and Hirschfield, A. (1997). New insights in the spatial and temporal distribution of repeat victimisation. *British Journal of Criminology*, 37(2), 224–41.

Johnson, S. D., Summers, L., and Pease, K. (2009). Offender as forager? A direct test of the boost account of victimization. *Journal of Quantitative Criminology*, 25(2), 181–200.

Kleemans, E. R. (2001). Repeat burglary victimization: Results of empirical research in the Netherlands. *Crime Prevention Studies*, 12, 53–68.

Morgan, F. (2001). Repeat burglary in a Perth suburb: Indicator of short-term or long-term risk? *Crime Prevention Studies*, 12, 83–118.

Pease, K. (1998). *Repeat victimisation: Taking stock*. London, UK: Police Research Group, Home Office.

Polvi, N., Looman, T., Humphries, C., and Pease, K. (1990). Repeat break-and-enter victimization: Time-course and crime prevention opportunity. *Journal of Police Science and Administration*, 17(1), 8–11.

Polvi, N., Looman, T., Humphries, C., and Pease, K. (1991). The time-course of repeat burglary victimization. *British Journal of Criminology*, 31(4), 411–14.

Ratcliffe, J. H. and Rengert, G. F. (2008). Near repeat patterns in Philadelphia shootings. *Security Journal*, 21(1/2), 58–76.

Sherman, L. W., Gottfredson, D., MacKenzie, D., Eck, J., Reuter, P., and Bushway, S. (1997). *Preventing crime: What works, what doesn't, what's promising*. Washington, DC: U.S. Department of Justice, Office of Justice Programs.

Townsley, M., Homel, R., and Chaseling, J. (2003). Infectious burglaries: a test of the near repeat hypothesis. *British Journal of Criminology*, 43(3), 615–33.

Townsley, M., Johnson, S. D., and Ratcliffe, J. H. (2008). Space time dynamics of insurgent activity in Iraq. *Security Journal*, 21(3), 139–46.

Trickett, A., Osborn, D., Seymour, J., and Pease, K. (1992). What is different about high crime areas? *British Journal of Criminology*, 32(1), 81–90.

Tseloni, A. and Pease, K. (2003). Repeat personal victimization: "boosts" or "flags"? *British Journal of Criminology*, 43(1), 196–212.

Tseloni, A. and Pease, K. (2004). Repeat personal victimization: random effects, event dependence and unexplained heterogeneity. *British Journal of Criminology*, 44(6), 931–45.

van Dijk, J. J. M. (2001). Attitudes of victims and repeat victims toward the police: Results of the International Crime Victims Survey. *Crime Prevention Studies*, 12, 27–52.

Wolfgang, M. E., Figlio, R. M., and Sellin, T. (1972). *Delinquency in a birth cohort*. Chicago, IL: University of Chicago Press.

Chapter 15

Crime and place

Introduction

This textbook began in Chapter 1 stating that spatial criminology was not new, beginning almost 200 years ago, and that the trajectory of this research has been continually moving towards smaller spatial units of analysis. In this last chapter, on crime and place, we will focus on the smallest spatial unit of analysis that has been used in citywide analyses of crime. This smallest spatial unit of analysis can be the discrete address, the street intersection, or street segments, sometimes referred to as micro-places or the micro-spatial unit of analysis. However, the street segment is the most common spatial unit of analysis in the crime and place literature.

As discussed above in the theoretical chapters, criminal events are highly patterned and predictable when considering a spatial perspective (Brantingham and Brantingham 1978, 1981b). And, also discussed above, particularly within the context of spatial heterogeneity within larger spatial units of analysis, when the "cone of resolution" changes—more terminology for changing the spatial scale— many of the observed spatial patterns of crime also change (Brantingham et al., 1976). This is why the trajectory of spatial criminology has been to ever smaller spatial units of analysis (Weisburd et al., 2009a). As stated in previous chapters, research in spatial criminology has shown that studies focusing on larger spatial units of analysis mask important spatial heterogeneity in criminal activity (Groff et al., 2010), potentially leading to inaccurate inferences about criminal activity at the individual level, the ecological fallacy (Robinson, 1950). In an even stronger argument put forth for the use of the street segment, in a book published in 2012 David Weisburd and colleagues stressed the accuracy of the street segment when assessing criminal event volumes because it is a "social unit that has been recognized as important in the rhythms of everyday living in cities" (p. 27).

In this chapter we will review the crime and place literature (sometimes referred to as the criminology of place). This will begin with why we would expect the micro-place to be the appropriate spatial unit of analysis. This is followed by a review of the key research that has been undertaken in the crime and place literature. And we will conclude with policy implications and theoretical considerations that have emerged because of the crime and place literature.

Why crime at places?

The spatial unit of analysis in spatial criminology had moved from counties to towns to wards and to neighborhoods over the course of approximately one hundred years. The neighborhood has been the spatial unit of analysis of choice since the early twentieth century and even to this day. Moreover, there is still a substantial literature (within the spatial criminology perspective) that considers larger spatial units of analysis. But is the neighborhood the appropriate spatial unit of analysis, particularly when we know that spatial heterogeneity may be present? In the case of social disorganization theory, it is generally assumed that the entire neighborhood is more alike than it is different, socially organized, socially disorganized, or somewhere in between. However, because we are a social *science*, these claims cannot simply be assumed. Rather, we must test them as previous generations of spatial criminologists have done so and arrived at the neighborhood level of analysis. It may be the case that a small percentage of places within entire neighborhoods are a significant source of the whole neighborhood's reputation, much like how research has found that a small percentage of offenders are responsible for a relatively large percentage of crime (Wolfgang et al. 1972). Consequently, it is important that policy makers, crime analysts, and theoreticians alike are aware of the risks associated with spatial heterogeneity within their spatial units of analysis. Otherwise it is possible that criminal justice policy, crime reduction strategies, and theories of crime will not be effectively focused and fail to prove their full benefit or usefulness. As we will see below, the crime at places literature began in 1989 with the publication of a journal article by Lawrence Sherman and colleagues. However, the term "crime at places" was coined by John Eck and David Weisburd in their 1995 edited collection dedicated to the study of the micro-spatial unit of analysis. This has led to the development of a new, albeit still small, branch of literature on "crime at places."

But why would we expect criminal events to occur at micro-places? Invoking the concept of behavior settings (Barker, 1968), Taylor (1997) used street segments in a theoretical framework for understanding the variation in social disorder within the community/neighborhood from an informal social control perspective. Though Taylor's (1997) framework was instructive, the importance of micro-spatial analysis predates this work by ten to twenty years.

Routine activity theory (Chapter 3) posits that criminal events occur when a motivated offender and a suitable target converge in space and time without the presence of a capable guardian. An important aspect of this convergence to note is that it occurs at a discrete location: an address, an intersection, a place. Convergence in a neighborhood or a community is far too imprecise to lead to a criminal event, especially when neighborhoods/communities can be one or two square kilometers in area. Therefore, routine activity theory can be thought of as an investigation into the criminology of places (Sherman et al. 1989).

The geometric theory of crime (Chapter 4) is based on understanding the activity nodes (places) of offenders and victims, as well as the pathways between them. According to the geometric theory of crime, criminal events do not occur uniformly within these areas (usually activity nodes) but at particular places within these activity nodes; crime generators and crime attractors are located within these activity nodes. As such, not all the area of an activity node—that is, most often geographically smaller than a neighborhood/community—is equally likely to experience criminal events. Rather, criminal events occur when the available/ suitable targets coincide with the crime template of a motivated offender. For example, not many thefts from automobiles occur immediately in front of the entrance to a shopping mall; more often, such criminal events occur in the more isolated places of the parking lot.

Lastly, rational choice theory (Chapter 5) states that criminal events are the result of context specific choices. Not only must the analysis within a rational choice framework be specific in terms of the crime type, but specific in terms of each criminal choice being made. The literature in situational crime prevention is a prime example of this approach (Clarke, 1980, 1983) that focuses on reducing rewards and increasing effort for very specific criminal incident types—see Chapter 7. For example, as shown by Rengert and Wasilchick (1985, 2000) in the context of suburban residential burglary, burglars did choose neighborhoods within which to commit their criminal events, but they also selected particular homes—not all homes within a neighborhood were at the same risk of being burgled. Consequently, the place, not the neighborhood/community, is critical within the rational choice perspective.

In addition to the spatial theories of crime, research that utilizes modern crime-mapping techniques is revealing the importance of local-level spatial crime analysis. For example, Chainey and Ratcliffe (2005), among others, clearly illustrated that analyzing crime at typical "community" levels of analysis hides important spatial heterogeneity at geographically smaller spatial units of analysis. Despite this, and despite seminal spatial theories being in practice for thirty-five years, very little research on crime at places has emerged, particularly for citywide investigations of spatial crime patterns.

Crime and place: a review

In 1989, Lawrence Sherman and colleagues published a study to systematically analyze crime at places in the context of predatory crime in Minneapolis, Minnesota. Perhaps one of the significant findings to emerge from this study was that 50 percent of all calls for service to the police were generated from 3 percent of street segments. This is a phenomenal concentration of criminal events, similar to the concentration of repeat victimization discussed in Chapter 14. Consequently, even within the neighborhoods that had the highest crime rates, criminal events tended to cluster at only a few locations within those neighborhoods. This meant that the majority of any given neighborhood was (relatively) criminal event free— this is similar to some of the clustering of criminal events shown in Figure 10.1. A proper understanding of this phenomenon is critical because there is now evidence that any spatial analysis of crime at the neighborhood level is at a great risk of committing the ecological fallacy (Robinson, 1950). Additionally, because these micro-places of criminal activity were discrete locations within neighborhoods that often consisted of non-resident populations (Sherman et al., 1989), any and all census-based information regarding these neighborhoods may not represent the population at risk at these crime places; this relates back to some of the issues in the context of crime measurement discussed in Chapter 8. Additionally, because only a few of these discrete locations really mattered for criminal activity, using census-based information for the entire neighborhood would necessarily misrepresent those few discrete locations. As such, any inference that is based on neighborhood level census data information may not be an accurate representation of the nature of criminal activity.

Just over a decade would pass before another journal article, published in 2000, would study the citywide spatial crime patterns at a micro-spatial unit of analysis. Using data from a medium-sized southeastern city in the United States, William Smith and colleagues investigated the integration of routine activity theory and social disorganization theory at the micro-spatial unit of analysis. William Smith and colleagues noted that the empirical support for integrating routine activity theory and social disorganization theory has not been strong. However, these authors argued that the reason for this was not because these two theories should not be integrated, but because the spatial units of analysis have not been appropriate—previous attempts of theoretical integration have used spatial units of analysis that were too coarse. Considering the street segment as the spatial unit of analysis, William Smith and colleagues were far more successful with this integration than previous research. It was argued that this success was because of the inherent heterogeneity within neighborhoods that may help explain where criminal events occurred.

In what is arguably the most well-known crime and places study, published in 2004, David Weisburd and colleagues undertook a set of "trajectory analyses" of crime at places in Seattle, Washington—trajectory analysis will explained shortly, below. Similar to the results of Lawrence Sherman and colleagues, David Weisburd and colleagues found that approximately 5 percent of street segments accounted for 50 percent of all criminal events, over a fourteen-year period—this research study considered the crime type of "all crime." Additionally, they found that the concentration of criminal events at micro-spatial units of analysis remained remarkably stable over time. And through the use of kernel density estimation and mapping, discussed in Chapter 10, these authors found some evidence that the spatial patterns of criminal event trajectories were clustered. In a more explicit spatial analysis of the trajectories in Seattle, Elizabeth Groff and colleagues, in a book chapter published in 2009, confirmed that indeed street segments with the same trajectory clustered together. Elizabeth Groff and colleagues also found significant variation within the trajectory patterns of street segments, meaning that any spatial aggregation, even aggregating to a spatial unit of analysis as small as United States census blocks, would have resulted in the loss of a tremendous amount of information.

The research study published by David Weisburd and colleagues in 2004 is definitely worthy of further discussion. The fouteen-year study period for this research was 1989–2002, analyzing over 1.4 million incident reports from the Seattle Police Department. Overall, these authors found that criminal events in Seattle experienced a 24 percent decline for these years, relating to the crime drop of the 1990s (Chapter 12). In addition to the finding that 5 percent of street segments accounted for 50 percent of all criminal events, they also found that all criminal events were found in between 48 and 53 percent of street segments. Moreover, only 1 percent of the street segments had more than fifty crimes per year within each of the fourteen years under study.

The trajectory analysis was a statistical analysis that investigated if each street segment was experiencing a stable, increasing or decreasing trajectory over the fourteen-year period. The details of this statistical technique are not important for our purposes here, but are available in great detail in the original journal article. However, it is important to note the general results. The statistical technique identified eighteen different trajectories. Of those eighteen trajectories, eight were considered stable, meaning that they exhibited no statistically significant change over time. These street segments represented 84 percent of all street segments in Seattle and evidenced low levels of criminal events. Only 3 of the 18 trajectories were identified as increasing, accounting for approximately 2 percent of all street segments in Seattle—one trajectory evidenced an increase in its average crime rate of more than fourfold during the study period. The remaining seven trajectories had a decreasing trajectory and accounted for approximately 14 percent of all street segments. Consequently, 14 percent of the street segments in Seattle accounted for the 24 percent drop in crime over the fourteen-year study period. This means that the crime drop of the 1990s in Seattle should not be seen as a phenomenon occurring uniformly across the city's landscape. Rather, the crime drop of the 1990s was driven by changes in the number of criminal events in a small percentage of Seattle's street segments. It will prove to be most instructive if this pattern is true for other cities that have experienced the crime drop in recent years.

In 2009, David Weisburd and his colleagues published another journal article investigating the trajectories of street segments in Seattle, but specifically for criminal events committed by juveniles. The analyses of the criminal events committed by juveniles were even more striking than the aggregate of all criminal events in Seattle. From 1989 to 2002, juvenile criminal events exhibited a 41 percent decline, all juvenile criminal events occurred within approximately 3 to 5 percent of street segments, and less than 1 percent of street segments accounted for 50 percent of all criminal events. In their trajectory analysis, the authors found that the vast majority of street segments experienced little or no juvenile criminal events: one trajectory consisted of 85 percent of all street segments that only included 12 percent of all criminal events over the fourteen-year study period. David Weisburd and his colleagues also found that there was a high degree of stability in the spatial crime patterns in Seattle: three trajectories accounted for approximately one-third of all juvenile criminal events, but only included eighty-six (or 0.29 percent) of all street segments in Seattle.

The following year, Elizabeth Groff and her colleagues analyzed the same criminal event data to investigate whether street segment trajectories of the same classification were clustered in space and whether street segments of different trajectories were more likely to be found spatially near or far from each other than one would expect by chance. These authors found that "chronic street segments," defined as street segments with high counts of criminal events, exhibited the greatest degree of local clustering. Additionally, street segments with low criminal event volumes but slightly increasing over the study period were also more likely to be spatially close to one another, followed by the low decreasing street segments. Curiously, the street segments categorized as either having zero criminal events or low criminal event volumes and stable over time were the least likely to be clustered. This suggested that these trajectories had a more random distribution across Seattle—further statistical analysis showed that street segments with zero criminal events, street segments with low criminal event volumes and a stable trajectory, and street segments with low criminal event volumes and decreasing trajectories, were statistically independent of one another. This research by Elizabeth Groff and her colleagues highlights the spatial variability of micro-places. Because of this spatial variability, within any given neighborhood there may be crime free zones, next to street segments with consistently high crime, next to street segments with consistently low crime, and so on. Consequently, the importance of understanding criminal events at the micro-spatial level is critical, calling into question the labeling of larger areal units of a city (such as neighborhoods or census tracts) as either "good" or "bad" in nature. As stated by Lawrence Sherman and colleagues, there may be unsafe places in safe neighborhoods and safe places in unsafe neighborhoods.

The most recent and comprehensive examination of crime and places was undertaken in the book published in 2012 by David Weisburd and his colleagues. In this book, these authors extended the Seattle, Washington dataset to sixteen years, 1989 to 2004. Not only did they undertake a trajectory analysis that confirmed their previous analyses—this could have proven to be important because trends can change in two years, altering overall results—but they also undertook a spatial analysis of the respective trajectory patterns and examined the characteristics of the chronic street segments. This led David Weisburd and colleagues to develop a model to explain the trajectories of street segments over time. The authors were able to find that street segments with a lot of criminal events were located in the northern section of Seattle concentrated along main or arterial roadways. The downtown area of Seattle exhibited a strong degree of clustering for these street segments as well as a considerable amount of street-by-street segment variation. Overall, David Weisburd and colleagues found that hot spot street segments were interspersed throughout Seattle, and that street segments with a lot of criminal events were often interspersed amongst street segments with very few criminal events.

In addition to this descriptive account of what the various street segments in Seattle were doing and where the street segments were doing it, David Weisburd and colleagues also wanted to understand the characteristics of the various trajectories. These authors began this analysis using a multivariate statistical model (logistic regression), and variables representing routine activity theory and social disorganization theory. In the context of routine activity theory, David Weisburd and colleagues found that the presence of high-risk juveniles (motivated offenders) increased the probability of street segments with a lot of criminal events by twofold; for every additional employee on a street segment (representing an industrial/business area), the probability of that street segment being chronic increased by 8 percent; the presence of a public facility (community center or high school, for example) within 400 meters of any given street segment increased the probability of a chronic street segment by 25 percent; and the larger the resident population, the greater the probability of there being a chronic street segment. In the context of the convergence of motivated offenders and suitable targets, every additional bus stop doubled the probability of a street segment with a lot of criminal events. Any street segment that was part of an arterial road had a greater probability of being a chronic street segment. And one of the most significant predictors of chronic street segments was the presence of vacant land: a 1 percent increase in the area of vacant land increased the probability of a chronic street segment by almost 50 percent. The results for the social disorganization variables showed that a unit increase in the residential property value on a street segment was associated with a 30 percent decrease in the probability of a chronic street segment, whereas the increased presence of subsidized housing was associated with a 10 percent increase in the probability of a chronic street segment. Statistically significant effects were also found for the presence of physical disorder and the presence of truant juveniles to increase the probability of a chronic street segment. And lastly, the authors found that street segments with residents involved in public affairs had far lower levels of criminal events, generally speaking.

Overall, the research on Seattle and its street segments by David Weisburd and his various colleagues not only contributed significantly to showing the instructive nature of examining criminal events at the micro-spatial unit of analysis, but also attempted to explain why these various development patterns exist. Their research found that both routine activity theory and social disorganization theory characteristics were statistically significant. Moreover, this was the first attempt within spatial criminology to develop an explanatory model for micro-spatial units of analysis and their trajectories over time. This seminal work conducted by David Weisburd and his colleagues has offered the field of crime and places tremendous insight into understanding the disproportionate distribution of criminal event activity.

Despite the intensive nature of the analysis on the street segments of Seattle, Washington, and the analysis of micro-spatial units of analysis in Minneapolis, Minnesota, there is still the question of generalizability in terms of the degree of concentration with criminal events. However, there have been some other analyses of criminal event concentration I have undertaken for Ottawa, Ontario and

Vancouver, British Columbia, undertaken with Nicolas Malleson in 2011 and Shannon Linning in 2012. As shown in Table 15.1, a very small percentage of street segments in Ottawa and Vancouver account for 50 percent of the various crime types. For example, in the example of Ottawa, less than 2 percent of all street segments account for 50 percent of crimes. This incredibly high concentration of criminal events even occurs for total crimes in this particular data set. The concentration of criminal events in Vancouver is also quite high, with less than 8 percent of street segments accounting for 50 percent of the various crime types. But most often, less than 5 percent of street segments account for 50 percent of criminal events.

Perhaps one of the more interesting results in Table 15.1 is the percentage of street segments than have *any* crime. The Ottawa data only have a small number of crime types available, but a very low percentage of street segments accounts for all of its crime; more than 90 percent of Ottawa was free from these reported

Table 15.1 Crime concentration at the street segment, Ottawa and Vancouver, Canada

	Percentage of street segments accounting for 50 percent of crime	Percentage of street segments that have any crime	Percentage of street segments with crime that account for 50 percent of crime
Ottawa, 2006			
Commercial break and enter	0.55	2.31	23.78
Residential break and enter	1.36	4.86	27.95
Total break and enter (aggregate)	1.67	6.61	25.30
Commercial robbery	0.01*	0.30	27.84
Individual robbery	0.31	0.65	47.66
Other robbery	0.30	0.82	35.93
Total robbery (aggregate)	0.38	1.46	26.10
Theft of vehicle	0.99	4.50	22.02
Total (without double counting)	1.70	9.52	17.87
Vancouver, 2001			
Assault	1.62	18.75	8.64
Burglary	7.61	39.43	19.31
Robbery	0.84	5.32	15.87
Sexual assault	1.12	2.99	37.32
Theft	2.58	26.79	9.64
Theft of vehicle	5.97	27.11	22.01
Theft from vehicle	2.64	18.75	8.64
Total (without double counting)	5.02	61.42	8.18

Note: *actual value: 0.000823.

Source: Adapted from Andresen and Malleson (2011) and Andresen and Linning (2012).

crimes in 2006. Vancouver had a lesser degree of concentration than Ottawa, but Vancouver's criminal event concentration is still noteworthy for certain crime types. Overall, just over 60 percent of Vancouver's street segments accounted for all of Vancouver's reported criminal events for these crime types during 2001. Of particular interest are the examples of robbery and sexual assault: only 5 and 3 percent of street segments, respectively, account for all of these reported criminal events in Vancouver. This percentage is greater than its counterpart in Ottawa, but it is a similar result for both cities that robbery has (one of) the greatest concentrations of criminal events. Further, within these street segments that have any crime, there were even greater concentrations evident in the last column of Table 15.1. In all cases, less than 50 percent of street segments within any crime type accounted for 50 percent of all criminal events. This result clearly indicates that there were concentrations of crime within concentrations of crime, or hot spots within hot spots.

Implications for criminal justice policy, practice, and theory

The implications for public policy and practice stem from the fact that the spatial patterns of crime are relatively stable at the street segment level. In other words, there is strong evidence for ecological stability when the micro-spatial unit of analysis is being used. Though ecological stability is not necessary for the applications of crime prevention through environmental design (CPTED) (Jeffery, 1969, 1971, 1976, 1977), there is a particular interpretation through theory with CPTED that is instructive. In the crime prevention literature, the victims of crime are often informed how their routine activities put them at greater risk of criminal victimization. This is not a form of victim blaming, but victim empowering, in order to help them understand how they can control their exposure to risk: change your routine activities, change your pathways, and, perhaps, your activity nodes and your risk of criminal victimization can decrease. However, as discussed in Chapter 4, our awareness and activity spaces are slow to change over time and in many ways we are quite constrained. For example, an alternative public transit route home that greatly decreases the risk of criminal victimization may add a lot of time to the commute interfering with other routine activities. This is why Lawrence Sherman and his colleagues advocated for changing or regulating the routine activities of places rather than individuals. Because of the highly specific nature of micro-places, highly specific crime prevention initiatives are necessary, along the lines of situational crime prevention. Recall from Chapter 7 that situational crime prevention should be used in the context of the micro-place because situational crime prevention works best when applied to crime- and place-specific crime problems. Consider, for example, the crime types of robbery and sexual assault. As noted above, these two crime types have a high degree of ecological stability such that the very few micro-places that support these two crime types should be able to be disrupted such that the choice-structuring properties of these crime types no longer facilitate the criminal events. But this disruption should not only be considered for crime types that have a concentration of criminal events as high as robbery and sexual assault, in the case of Vancouver. In their most recent work, accepted for publication in 2013, David Weisburd and colleagues found that over a sixteen-year time period 1 percent of street segments in Seattle represented 23 percent of all criminal event activity across the city. This is a relatively small number of street segments to target for situational crime prevention that may lead to significantly high returns on investment through crime reduction across the spectrum of crime types. Consequently, the practice of situational crime prevention, much like the theories within environmental criminology, is based on micro-spatial units of analysis.

The crime at places literature has implications for social disorganization theory, routine activity theory, the geometric theory of crime, and rational choice theory. With regard to social disorganization theory it appears as though the neighborhood, or any other similar-sized spatial unit of analysis, is no longer appropriate for understanding the spatial patterns of crime. This is not to say that these spatial units of analysis are no longer of any use to research, but they should be used with caution and, along the lines of the discussion of the modifiable areal unit problem discussed in Chapter 9, when they are deemed to be the *natural* analysis unit rather than an arbitrarily aggregated spatial unit of convenience, such as census boundaries. Of course such a claim may not be particularly popular, particularly because of the long-standing use of the neighborhood and the census tract within spatial criminology, but we must remember that this is all part of the trajectory of spatial criminology. Recall that the work of Burgess (1916), Shaw et al. (1929), and Shaw and McKay (1931, 1942, 1969) all showed that the previous era of spatial criminology used spatial units of analysis that were too coarse for an appropriate understanding of the spatial distribution of crime—it was consistently found that there was a high degree of spatial heterogeneity within cities and counties. And similarly, the crime and places literature has consistently found that there is a high degree of spatial heterogeneity within neighborhoods such that dangerous neighborhoods are generally safe (Sherman et al., 1989). The theoretical implication of this result is that social disorganization theory can only continue to matter for crime at places if and only if socially disorganized neighborhoods (theoretically predicted to be high in crime) have more dangerous places than socially organized places. This, of course, is an empirical question, and is a direction for further research. The research of David Weisburd and colleagues published in their 2012 book does indicate that social disorganization still matters, but that does not necessarily mean that the neighborhood still matters.

In the context of routine activity theory, because it is easier to modify the routine activities of place, there is a need for more research along these lines (Felson, 1987; Sherman et al., 1989). Because of the high levels of stability and the high degree of criminal event concentrations at so few micro-places, an in-depth understanding of these places is in order. We need an in-depth understanding of these micro-places because, as discussed above, routine activity theory is about the convergence of motivated offenders and suitable targets in the absence of capable guardians at micro-places that leads to criminal events. The knowledge of why motivated offenders and suitable targets converge at this street segment and not that street segment needs to be incorporated into the further development of routine activity theory. Also, because temporal changes (across decades or just the day) are an integral component of routine activity theory, micro-temporal analyses of chronic street segments may prove to be invaluable for understanding crime patterns. As such, significant insight may be gathered by simultaneously considering the micro-place and the micro-time.

The geometric theory of crime was a highly developed theory when it first emerged over thirty years ago. However, because of the high degree of data requirements for the geometric theory of crime (detailed criminal event information as well as information on the awareness and activity spaces of many offenders), very few tests for the purpose of further understanding and refinement have been undertaken—see Chapter 4 for the few research studies that have tested components of the geometric theory of crime. Because of the importance of micro-places within activity nodes and along pathways, it will be important to gather the necessary data measured at the micro-place for any further developments within the geometric theory of crime.

And rational choice theory has always considered the importance of understanding rational choices that are specific to crime types because the decision process for committing a residential burglary is different from the decision process for committing an armed robbery of a liquor store. As outlined by Derek Cornish and Ronald Clarke in 1987, there are a number of choice-structuring properties for criminal events such as the accessibility of targets, risks of apprehension/detectability, and the time required to commit the crime. Because of the high degree of concentration of all crime types at particular micro-places (see Table 15.1), there are some micro-places that obviously make it easier to commit criminal events. Therefore, the micro-place must be considered one of the many rational choice-structuring properties for committing any given criminal event.

But, regardless of the theoretical perspective within spatial criminology, the importance of understanding the micro-place is critical for understanding criminal events. An understanding of these very few micro-places that generate the vast majority of criminal events across our landscapes reinforces that criminal events are indeed rare events. The convergences, activity patterns, and choices that lead to crime all occur in these discrete locations. This has led David Weisburd and his colleagues, in the 2012 book, to put forth the law of crime concentrations at places.

Review questions

1   Why is the street segment considered the "optimal" micro-spatial unit of analysis?

2   Considering the three primary theories in environmental criminology (routine activity theory, the geometric theory of crime, and the pattern theory of crime), why do we expect crime at micro-places?
3   What is the relationship between the crime drop of the 1990s and the street segment, according to the research in Seattle, Washington? What are the implications for policing?
4   What does it mean to have hot spots of crime within hot spots of crime?
5   What are the implications for crime prevention that emerge from the concentrations of crime at places?
6   Is the neighborhood "dead"? Explain. If so, should we mourn?
7   Why should the micro-place be considered one of the many choice-structuring properties in the rational choice theory framework?

References

Andresen, M. A. and Linning, S. J. (2012). The (in)appropriateness of aggregating across crime types. *Applied Geography*, 35(1/2), 275–82.
Andresen, M. A. and Malleson, N. (2011). Testing the stability of crime patterns: Implications for theory and policy. *Journal of Research in Crime and Delinquency*, 48(1), 58–82.
Barker, R. G. (1968). *Ecological psychology: Concepts and methods for studying the environment of human behavior.* Stanford, CA: Stanford University Press.
Brantingham, P. J., Dyreson, D. A., and Brantingham, P. L. (1976). Crime seen through a cone of resolution. *American Behavioral Scientist*, 20(2), 261–73.
Brantingham, P. J. and Brantingham, P. L. (1978). A theoretical model of crime site selection. In M. D. Krohn and R. L. Akers (eds.), *Crime, law and sanctions: Theoretical perspectives* (pp. 105–18). Beverly Hills, CA: Sage Publications.
Brantingham, P. L. and Brantingham, P. J. (1981b). Notes on the geometry of crime. In P. J. Brantingham and P. L. Brantingham (eds.), *Environmental criminology* (pp. 27–54). Prospect Heights IL, Waveland Press.
Burgess, E. W. (1916). Juvenile delinquency in a small city. *Journal of the American Institute of Criminal Law and Criminology*, 6(5), 724–8.
Chainey, S. and Ratcliffe, J. H. (2005). *GIS and crime mapping.* Chichester, UK: John Wiley & Sons.
Clarke, R. V. G. (1980). Situational crime prevention: Theory and practice. *British Journal of Criminology*, 20(2), 136–47.
Clarke, R. V. (1983). Situational crime prevention: Its theoretical basis and practical scope. *Crime and Justice: An Annual Review of Research*, 4, 225–56.
Cornish, D. B. and Clarke, R. V. G. (1987). Understanding crime displacement: An application of rational choice theory. *Criminology*, 25(4), 933–47.
Eck, J. E. and Weisburd, D. (eds.) (1995). *Crime prevention studies*, vol. 4, *Crime and place.* Monsey, NY: Criminal Justice Press.
Felson, M. (1987). Routine activities and crime prevention in the developing metropolis. *Criminology*, 25(4), 911–31.
Groff, E. R., Weisburd, D., and Morris, N. A. (2009). Where the action is at places: Examining spatio-temporal patterns of juvenile crime at places using trajectory analysis. In D. Weisburd, W. Bernasco, and G. J. N. Bruinsma (eds.), *Putting crime in its place: Units of analysis in geographic criminology* (pp. 61–86). New York, NY: Springer.

262 The practice of environmental criminology

Groff, E. R., Weisburd, D., and Yang, S.-M. (2010). Is it important to examine crime trends at a local "micro" level? A longitudinal analysis of street to street variability in crime trajectories. *Journal of Quantitative Criminology*, 26(1), 7–32.

Jeffery, C. R. (1969). Crime prevention and control through environmental engineering. *Criminologica*, 7(3), 35–58.

Jeffery, C. R. (1971). *Crime prevention through environmental design*. Beverly Hills, CA: Sage Publications.

Jeffery, C. R. (1976). Criminal behaviour and the physical environment. *American Behavioral Scientist*, 20(2), 149–74.

Jeffery, C. R. (1977). *Crime prevention through environmental design*, 2nd edition. Beverly Hills, CA: Sage Publications.

Rengert, G. F. and Wasilchick, J. (1985). *Suburban burglary: A time and place for everything*. Springfield, IL: Charles C. Thomas.

Rengert, G. F. and Wasilchick, J. (2000). *Suburban burglary: A tale of two suburbs* (2nd edition). Springfield, IL: Charles C. Thomas.

Robinson, W. S. (1950). Ecological correlations and the behavior of individuals. *American Sociological Review*, 15(3), 351–7.

Shaw, C. R., Zorbaugh, F., McKay, H. D., and Cottrell, L. S. (1929). *Delinquency areas: A study of the geographic distribution of school truants, juvenile delinquents, and adult offenders in Chicago*. Chicago, IL: University of Chicago Press.

Shaw, C. R. and McKay, H. D. (1931). *Social factors in juvenile delinquency*. Washington, DC: U.S. Government Printing Office.

Shaw, C. R. and McKay, H. D. (1942). *Juvenile delinquency and urban areas: A study of rates of delinquency in relation to differential characteristics of local communities in American cities*. Chicago, IL: University of Chicago Press.

Shaw, C. R. and McKay, H. D. (1969). *Juvenile delinquency and urban areas: A study of rates of delinquency in relation to differential characteristics of local communities in American cities*, revised edition. Chicago, IL: University of Chicago Press.

Sherman, L. W., Gartin, P., and Buerger, M. E. (1989). Hot spots of predatory crime: Routine activities and the criminology of place. *Criminology*, 27(1), 27–55.

Smith, W. R., Frazee, S. G., and Davidson, E. L. (2000). Furthering the integration of routine activity and social disorganization theories: Small units of analysis and the study of street robbery as a diffusion process. *Criminology*, 38(2), 489–524.

Taylor, R. B. (1997). Social order and disorder of street blocks and neighborhoods: Ecology, microecology, and the systemic model of social disorganization. *Journal of Research in Crime and Delinquency*, 34(1), 113–55.

Weisburd, D., Bushway, S., Lum, C., and Yang, S.-M. (2004). Trajectories of crime at places: A longitudinal study of street segments in the City of Seattle. *Criminology*, 42(2), 283–321.

Weisburd, D., Bruinsma, G. J. N., and Bernasco, W. (2009a). Units of analysis in geographic criminology: Historical development, critical issues, and open questions. In D. Weisburd, W. Bernasco, and G. J. N. Bruinsma (eds.), *Putting crime in its place: Units of analysis in geographic criminology* (pp. 3–31). New York, NY: Springer.

Weisburd, D., Morris, N. A., and Groff, E. R. (2009b). Hot spots of juvenile crime: A longitudinal study of street segments in Seattle, Washington. *Journal of Quantitative Criminology*, 25(4), 443–67.

Weisburd, D., Groff, E. R., and Yang, S.-M. (2012). *The criminology of place: Street segments and our understanding of the crime problem*. New York, NY: Oxford University Press.

Weisburd, D., Groff, E. R., and Yang, S.-M. (2013). Understanding and controlling hot spots of crime: The importance of formal and informal social controls. *Prevention Science*, in press.

Wolfgang, M. E., Figlio, R. M., and Sellin, T. (1972). *Delinquency in a birth cohort*. Chicago, IL: University of Chicago Press.

Index

Note: Page numbers in **bold** type refer to **figures**
Page numbers in *italic* type refer to *tables*
Page numbers followed by 'n' refer to notes

Marxists 11–12; Post-Modern 11–12; Post-Structural 11–12; Structural 11–12
Massachusetts Institute of Technology (MIT) 143; SENSEable City Lab 143
Maxfield, M.G.: *et al* 136
Mayhew, P. 79; and Braun, G. 44
measurement *see* crime measurement
media 121; social 121; traditional 121
mental health patients: deinstitutionalization 214
Messner, S.F.: *et al* 158; and Rosenfeld, R. 207
metaphysics 9, 48–51, 87; concentric zone model 13–15; human ecology 36–8; rationality 68–72; routine activity theory 33, 36–8; social ecology 13–15
metatheory 92
metropolis: changing 108–10
microeconomics 71; course 72
middle-class suburb **75**; burglary **75**
Miethe, T.D.: *et al* 122
Miller, J.: *et al* 179–83
Miller, M.M.: *et al* 134
mobile phones: theft 42, 209–11
modifiable areal unit problem (MAUP) 150–3, 172–4
Monmonier, M. 129, 164
Moran's I 133, 157–9
Morgan, F. 239
Mosher, C.J.: *et al* 122
movie theaters 110
Mulligan, G.: and Cahill, M. 162
murder *see* homicide

National Aeronautics and Space Administration (NASA) 42, 128; Visible Earth Web 128
natural surveillance 105–7
near-repeat victimization 231–49; implications 236–9, 244–5; Khox test 240, *240*; near-repeat and repeat connection 246–7; repeat victimization 232–6, *233*; review questions 247
Netherlands 195, 207, 242–3
New Zealand 210, 242
Newman, O. 30–1, 98, 102–9; crime prevention through urban design (CPTUD) 102–8
nineteenth century 3, 22, 200
noncriminal activities 64, 71, 86; spatial patterns 48, 64

North America 205–10, 226; deinstitutionalization of mental health patients 214
North American Free Trade Agreement (1994) 207
Numb3rs (television programme) 219
nurture-based model of behavior 99

Oak Ridge National Laboratory (ORNL) 127–8, 143
offenders 48–9, **53–5**, 59–60, 76, 83, 111; buffer 218; description 220; directionality **59–60**, 60; hunting style/pattern 220; motivated 54–8, 77, 170–1, 192; potential 76, 81, 91, 93–108, 228; rational 112; rationally motivated 71; routine activities 90; serial 83, 218–23, 229; spatial distribution 48, 188
offending behavior data 60
Okabe, A.: *et al* 172
Openshaw, S. 149–53; pedagogical guide 150
Opportunity Makes the Thief (Felson and Clarke) 111
Osborn, D.: *et al* 234
Ouimet, M. 207–10

Pacific National Exhibition (Vancouver) 200
Pallone, N.J. 121
paranoid schizophrenia 111–12
Pareto principle 119, 231
Park, S. 200
Parker, N. 67–8, 76
parole 64
passive territoriality 106–8
pathways 49–50
pattern theory of crime 29, 40, 86–92; importance 91–2; review questions 92
Pavlov, I.: Pavlov's dog 99; and Skinner, B.F. 99
pawnshops 135
Pease, K. 236–9; and Barr, R. 134; *et al* 234–5; and Farrell, G. 238, 246
pedagogical guide (Openshaw) 150
Petrossian, G.: *et al* 136
Phillips, C.: *et al* 235
phone theft 42, 209–11
physical ailments 68
physical assault 122, *123*
physical boundary 50

CPSIA information can be obtained
at www.ICGtesting.com
Printed in the USA
LVOW04s2359151216

517531LV00005B/82/P

9 780415 856133